Managing Data Science

D1474512

Effective strategies to manage data science projects and build a sustainable team

Kirill Dubovikov

BIRMINGHAM - MUMBAI

Managing Data Science

Copyright © 2019 Packt Publishing

Commissioning Editor: Mrinmayee Kawalkar
Acquisition Editor: Reshma Raman
Content Development Editor: Nathanya Dias
Senior Editor: Ayaan Hoda
Technical Editor: Manikandan Kurup
Copy Editor: Safis Editing
Project Coordinator: Kirti Pisat, Aishwarya Mohan
Proofreader: Safis Editing
Indexer: Tejal Daruwale Soni
Production Designer: Arvindkumar Gupta

First published: November 2019

Production reference: 1111119

Published by Packt Publishing Ltd.
Livery Place
35 Livery Street
Birmingham
B3 2PB, UK.

ISBN 978-1-83882-632-1

www.packt.com

To my family, who believed in me and encouraged me to write this book. To my wife and children, who provided great support and care throughout the writing process. To my friends and fellow editors, who pushed me forward and helped to make the book better.

Without you, this book wouldn't exist.

Packt.com

Subscribe to our online digital library for full access to over 7,000 books and videos, as well as industry leading tools to help you plan your personal development and advance your career. For more information, please visit our website.

Why subscribe?

- Spend less time learning and more time coding with practical eBooks and Videos from over 4,000 industry professionals

- Improve your learning with Skill Plans built especially for you

- Get a free eBook or video every month

- Fully searchable for easy access to vital information

- Copy and paste, print, and bookmark content

Did you know that Packt offers eBook versions of every book published, with PDF and ePub files available? You can upgrade to the eBook version at www.packt.com and as a print book customer, you are entitled to a discount on the eBook copy. Get in touch with us at customercare@packtpub.com for more details.

At www.packt.com, you can also read a collection of free technical articles, sign up for a range of free newsletters, and receive exclusive discounts and offers on Packt books and eBooks.

Contributors

About the author

Kirill Dubovikov works as a CTO for Cinimex DataLab. He has more than 10 years of experience in architecting and developing complex software solutions for top Russian banks. Now, he leads the company's data science branch. His team delivers practical machine learning applications to businesses across the world. Their solutions cover an extensive list of topics, such as sales forecasting and warehouse planning, **natural language processing** (**NLP**) for IT support centers, algorithmic marketing, and predictive IT operations.

Kirill is a happy father of two boys. He loves learning all things new, reading books, and writing articles for top Medium publications.

About the reviewers

Phuong Vo. T.H is a data science manager at FPT Telecom in Vietnam. She graduated with an MSc degree in computer science at Soongsil University, Korea. She has experience in analyzing user behavior and building recommendation or prediction systems for business optimization. She loves to read machine learning and mathematics-related algorithm books, as well as data analysis articles.

Jean-Pierre Sleiman works for BNP Paribas as a project owner in charge of the AI strategy for the retail activities of the Group. His work ranges from delivering data & analytics use cases for the business to co-designing the Group's target operating model for AI. Jean-Pierre has been involved with data analytics & AI projects for more than 3 years, working on several initiatives, such as crafting data strategies and managing the implementation of data products & services within multidisciplinary teams. He was also a lecturer at HEC Paris and École Polytechnique for MSc Data Science for Business, where he co-created the content of the course and animated the *Data science project management and the Business case for data projects* lessons.

Packt is searching for authors like you

If you're interested in becoming an author for Packt, please visit `authors.packtpub.com` and apply today. We have worked with thousands of developers and tech professionals, just like you, to help them share their insight with the global tech community. You can make a general application, apply for a specific hot topic that we are recruiting an author for, or submit your own idea.

Table of Contents

Preface

Data science and machine learning can transform any organization and open new opportunities. Any data science project is a unique mix of research, software engineering, and business expertise. A substantial managerial effort is needed to guide the solution from prototype development to production. Traditional approaches often fail as they have different conditions and requirements in mind. This book presents a proven approach to data science project management, with tips and best practices to guide you along the way.

With the help of this book, you will learn about the practical applications of data science and AI and will be able to incorporate them into your solutions. You will go through the data science project life cycle, explore the common pitfalls encountered at each step, and learn how to avoid them. Any data science project requires a balanced skillful team, and this book will present helpful advice for hiring and growing a skillful data science team for your organization. The book also shows you how you can efficiently manage and improve your data science projects through the use of DevOps.

By the end of the book, readers will have the practical knowledge required to tackle the various challenges they deal with on a daily basis and will have an understanding of various data science solutions.

Who this book is for

The book is intended for data scientists, analysts, and program managers who want to bring more productivity to their organization and improve their business by incorporating data science workflows efficiently. Some understanding of basic data science concepts will be useful.

What this book covers

Chapter 1, *What You Can Do with Data Science*, explores the practical applications of AI, data science, machine learning, deep learning, and causal inference.

Chapter 2, *Testing Your Models*, explains how to distinguish good solutions from bad ones with the help of model testing. This chapter will also look at different types of metrics by using mathematical functions that evaluate the quality of predictions.

Chapter 3, *Understanding AI*, looks into the inner workings of data science. Some of the main concepts behind machine learning and deep learning will be explored as well. This chapter will also give a brief introduction to data science.

Chapter 4, *An Ideal Data Science Team*, explains how to build and sustain a data science team that is capable of delivering complex cross-functional projects. This chapter also gives us an understanding of the importance of software engineering and sourcing help from software development teams.

Chapter 5, *Conducting Data Science Interviews*, covers how to conduct an efficient data science interview. This chapter also looks into the importance of setting goals before starting the interview process.

Chapter 6, *Building Your Data Science Team*, develops guidelines for building data science teams. You will learn the three key aspects of building a successful team and the role of a leader in a data science team.

Chapter 7, *Managing Innovation*, explores innovations and how to manage them. We will find out how to identify projects and problems that have real value behind them.

Chapter 8, *Managing Data Science Projects*, explores the data science project life cycle that allows you to structure and plan tasks for your team. We will also look into what distinguishes analytical projects from software engineering projects.

Chapter 9, *Common Pitfalls of Data Science Projects*, looks closely at the common pitfalls of data science projects. This chapter explores the mistakes that increase the risks associated with your projects and mitigates the issues one by one, following the data science project life cycle.

Chapter 10, *Creating Products and Improving Reusability*, looks at how to grow data science products and improve your internal team performance by using reusable technology. We will also look at strategies for improving the reusability of your projects and explore the conditions that allow the building of standalone products from your experience.

Chapter 11, *Implementing ModelOps*, will explore how ModelOps is related to DevOps and the main steps involved in the ModelOps pipeline. This chapter also looks at the strategies for managing code, versioning data, and sharing project environments between team members.

Chapter 12, *Building Your Technology Stack*, looks at how to build and manage the data science technology stack. This chapter also discusses the differences between core and project-specific technology stacks and examines an analytical approach for comparing different technologies.

`Chapter 13`, *Conclusion*, provides a list of books that help you advance your knowledge in the domain of data science.

To get the most out of this book

This book aims to be self-contained and friendly for non-technical professionals. It does not assume knowledge in data science, machine learning, and programming. A basic understanding of statistics and mathematical optimization will be beneficial but is not necessary.

Expertise in the main concepts of software development, project management, and DevOps will be helpful for the reader since this text draws parallels with these approaches.

An ideal management method for data science projects is far from complete. In fact, it will never be. A silver bullet solution to all the problems of every business in each situation does not exist. Instead of creating a rigid and complex set of managerial processes, this book gives recipes and practical advice. I hope that it will serve you as a good guide that will make your journey to the world of data science as seamless as possible.

Download the color images

We also provide a PDF file that has color images of the screenshots/diagrams used in this book. You can download it here: `https://static.packt-cdn.com/downloads/9781838826321_ColorImages.pdf`.

Conventions used

There are a number of text conventions used throughout this book.

`CodeInText`: Indicates code words in text, database table names, folder names, filenames, file extensions, pathnames, dummy URLs, user input, and Twitter handles. Here is an example: "They have also used the `--gitlab` flag for the `pyscaffold` command so that they will have a ready-to-use GitLab CI/CD template when they need it."

A block of code is set as follows:

```
├── AUTHORS.rst <- List of developers and maintainers.
├── CHANGELOG.rst <- Changelog to keep track of new features and fixes.
├── LICENSE.txt <- License as chosen on the command-line.
├── README.md <- The top-level README for developers.
├── configs <- Directory for configurations of model & application.
├── data
```

Any command-line input or output is written as follows:

```
pip install -e .
```

Bold: Indicates a new term, an important word, or words that you see on screen. For example, words in menus or dialog boxes appear in the text like this. Here is an example: "A running instance of a Docker image is called a **Docker Container**."

 Warnings or important notes appear like this.

 Tips and tricks appear like this.

Get in touch

Feedback from our readers is always welcome.

General feedback: If you have questions about any aspect of this book, mention the book title in the subject of your message and email us at customercare@packtpub.com.

Errata: Although we have taken every care to ensure the accuracy of our content, mistakes do happen. If you have found a mistake in this book, we would be grateful if you would report this to us. Please visit www.packtpub.com/support/errata, selecting your book, clicking on the Errata Submission Form link, and entering the details.

Piracy: If you come across any illegal copies of our works in any form on the Internet, we would be grateful if you would provide us with the location address or website name. Please contact us at copyright@packt.com with a link to the material.

If you are interested in becoming an author: If there is a topic that you have expertise in and you are interested in either writing or contributing to a book, please visit authors.packtpub.com.

Reviews

Please leave a review. Once you have read and used this book, why not leave a review on the site that you purchased it from? Potential readers can then see and use your unbiased opinion to make purchase decisions, we at Packt can understand what you think about our products, and our authors can see your feedback on their book. Thank you!

For more information about Packt, please visit packt.com.

1
Section 1: What is Data Science?

Before diving into the management issues of building systems around machine learning algorithms, we need to explore the topic of data science itself. What are the main concepts behind data science and machine learning? How do you build and test a model? What are the common pitfalls in this process? What kinds of models are there? What tasks can we solve using machine learning?

This section contains the following chapters:

- Chapter 1, *What You Can Do with Data Science*
- Chapter 2, *Testing Your Models*
- Chapter 3, *Understanding AI*

1
What You Can Do with Data Science

I once told a friend who works as a software developer about one of the largest European data science conferences. He showed genuine interest and asked whether we could go together. Sure, I said. Let's broaden our knowledge together. It will be great to talk to you about machine learning. Several days later, we were sitting in the middle of a large conference hall. The first speaker had come on stage and told us about some technical tricks he used to win several data science competitions. When the next speaker talked about tensor algebra, I noticed a depleted look in the eyes of my friend.

— *What's up?* I asked.

— *I'm just wondering when they'll show us the robots.*

To avoid having incorrect expectations, we need to inform ourselves. Before building a house, you'd better know how a hammer works. Having basic knowledge of the domain you manage is vital for any kind of manager. A software development manager needs to understand computer programming. A factory manager needs to know the manufacturing processes. A data science manager is no exception. The first part of this book gives simple explanations of the main concepts behind data science. We will dissect and explore it bit by bit.

Data science has become popular, and many business people and technical professionals have an increasing interest in understanding data science and applying it to solve their problems. People often form their first opinions about data science from the information that they collect through the background: news sites, social networks, and so on. Unfortunately, most of those sources misguide, rather than give a realistic picture of data science and machine learning.

Instead of explaining, the media describes the ultimate magical tools that easily solve all our problems. The technological singularity is near. A universal income economy is around the corner. Well, only if machines learned and thought like humans. In fact, we are far from creating general-purpose, self-learning, and self-improving algorithms.

This chapter explores current possibilities and modern applications of the main tools of data science: **machine learning** and **deep learning**.

In this chapter, we will cover the following topics:

- Defining AI
- Introduction to machine learning
- Introduction to deep learning
- Deep learning use case
- Introduction to causal inference

Defining AI

Media and news use AI as a substitute buzzword for any technology related to data analysis. In fact, AI is a sub-field of computer science and mathematics. It all started in the 1950s, when several researchers started asking whether computers can learn, think, and reason. 70 years later, we still do not know the answer. However, we have made significant progress in a specific kind of AI that solves thoroughly specified narrow tasks: **weak AI**.

Science fiction novels tell about machines that can reason and think like humans. In scientific language, they are described as **strong AI**. Strong AI can think like a human, and its intellectual abilities may be much more advanced. The creation of strong AI remains the main long-term dream of the scientific community. However, practical applications are all about weak AI. While strong AI tries to solve the problem of general intelligence, weak AI is focused on solving one narrow cognition task, such as vision, speech, or listening. Examples of weak AI tasks are diverse: speech recognition, image classification, and customer churn prediction. Weak AI plays an important role in our lives, changing the way we work, think, and live. We can find successful applications of weak AI in every area of our lives. Medicine, robotics, marketing, logistics, art, and music all benefit from recent advances in weak AI.

Defining data science

How does AI relate to machine learning? What is deep learning? And how do we define data science? These popular questions are better answered graphically:

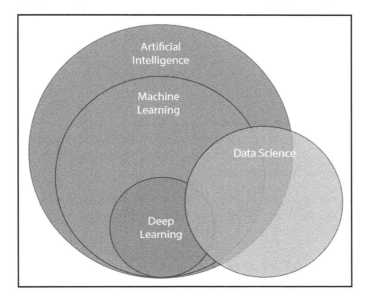

This diagram includes all the technical topics that will be discussed in this book:

- AI is a general scientific field that covers everything related to weak and strong AI. We won't focus much on AI, since most practical applications come from its subfields, which we define and discuss through the rest of *Section 1: What is Data Science?*
- Machine learning is a subfield of AI that studies algorithms that can adapt their behavior based on incoming data without explicit instructions from a programmer.
- Deep learning is a subfield of machine learning that studies a specific kind of machine learning model called deep neural networks.
- Data science is a multidisciplinary field that uses a set of tools to extract knowledge from data and support decision making. Machine learning and deep learning are among the main tools of data science.

The ultimate goal of data science is to solve problems by extracting knowledge from data and giving support for complex decisions. The first part of solving a problem is getting a good understanding of its domain. You need to understand the insurance business before using data science for risk analysis. You need to know the details of the goods manufacturing process before designing an automated quality assurance process. First, you understand the domain. Then, you find a problem. If you skip this part, you have a good chance of solving the wrong problem.

After coming up with a good problem definition, you seek a solution. Suppose that you have created a model that solves a task. A machine learning model in a vacuum is rarely interesting for anyone. So, it is not useful. To make it useful, we need to wrap our models into something that can be seen and acted upon. In other words, we need to create software around models. Data science always comes hand-in-hand with creating software systems. Any machine learning model needs software. Without software, models would just lie in computer memory, not helping anyone.

So, data science is never only about science. Business knowledge and software development are also important. Without them, no solution would be complete.

The influence of data science

Data science has huge potential. It already affects our daily lives. Healthcare companies are learning to diagnose and predict major health issues. Businesses use it to find new strategies for winning new customers and personalize their services. We use big data analysis in genetics and particle physics. Thanks to advances in data science, self-driving cars are now a reality.

Thanks to the internet and global computerization, we create vast amounts of data daily. Ever-increasing volumes of data allow us to automate human labor.

Sadly, for each use case that improves our lives, we can easily find two that make them worse. To give you a disturbing example, let's look at China. The Chinese government is experimenting with a new **social credit system**. It uses surveillance cameras to track the daily lives of its citizens on a grand scale. Computer vision systems can recognize and log every action that you make while commuting to work, waiting in lines at a government office, or going home after a party. A special social score is then calculated based on your monitored actions. This score affects the lives of real people. In particular, public transport fees can change depending on your score; low scores can prohibit you from interviewing for a range of government jobs.

On the other hand, this same technology can be used to help people. For example, it can be used to track criminals in large crowds. The way you apply this new technology can bring the world closer to George Orwell's *1984*, or make it a safer place. The general public must be more conscious of these choices, as they might have lasting effects on their lives.

Another example of some disturbing uses of machine learning is businesses that use hiring algorithms based on machine learning. Months later, they discovered that the algorithms introduced bias against women. It is becoming clear that we do not give the right amount of attention to the ethics of data science. While companies such as Google create internal ethics boards, there is still no governmental control over the unethical use of modern technology. Before such programs arrive, I strongly encourage you to consider the ethical implications of using data science. We all want a better world to live in. Our future, and the future of our children, depends on small decisions we make each day.

Limitations of data science

Like any set of tools, data science has its limitations. Before diving into a project with ambitious ideas, it is important to consider the current limits of possibility. A task that seems easily solvable may be unsolvable in practice.

Insufficient understanding of the technical side of data science can lead to serious problems in your projects. You can start a project only to discover that you cannot solve the task at all. Even worse, you can find out that nothing works as intended only after deployment. Depending on your use case, it can affect real people. Understanding the main principles behind data science will rid you of many technical risks that predetermine a project's fate before it has even started.

Introduction to machine learning

Machine learning is by far the most important tool of a data scientist. It allows us to create algorithms that discover patterns in data with thousands of variables. We will now explore different types and capabilities of machine learning algorithms.

Machine learning is a scientific field that studies algorithms that can learn to perform tasks without specific instructions, relying on patterns discovered in data. For example, we can use algorithms to predict the likelihood of having a disease or assess the risk of failure in complex manufacturing equipment. Every machine learning algorithm follows a simple formula. In the following diagram, you can see a high-level decision process that is based on a machine learning algorithm. Each machine learning model consumes data to produce information that can support human decisions or fully automate them:

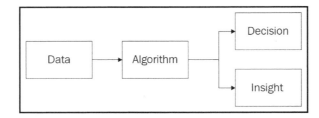

We will now explore the meaning of each block in more detail in the next section.

Decisions and insights provided by a machine learning model

When solving a task using machine learning, you generally want to automate a decision-making process or get insights to support your decision. For example, you may want an algorithm to output a list of possible diseases, given a patient's medical history and current condition. If machine learning solves your task completely, or end to end, this means that the algorithm's output can be used to make a final decision without further thinking; in our example, determining the disease the patient is suffering from and prescribing suitable medication automatically. The execution of this decision can be manual or automatic. We say that machine learning applications like these are end to end. They provide a complete solution to the task. Let's look at digital advertising as an example. An algorithm can predict whether you will click on an ad. If our goal is to maximize clicks, we can make automated and personalized decisions about which specific advertisement to show to each user, solving the click-through rate maximization problem end to end.

Another option is to create an algorithm that provides you with an insight. You can use this insight as part of a decision-making process. This way, the outputs of many machine learning algorithms can take part in complex decision making. To illustrate this, we'll look at a warehouse security surveillance system. It monitors all surveillance cameras and identifies employees from the video feed. If the system does not recognize a person as an employee, it raises an alert. This setup uses two machine learning models: face detection and face recognition. At first, the face detection model searches for faces in each frame of the video. Next, the face recognition model identifies a person as an employee by searching the face database. Each model does not solve the employee identification task alone. Yet each model provides an insight that is a part of the decision-making process.

Data for machine learning models

You may have noticed that algorithms in our examples work with different data types. In the digital advertising example, we have used structured customer data. The surveillance example used video feeds from cameras. In fact, machine learning algorithms can work with different data types.

We can divide the entire world's data into two categories: structured and unstructured. Most data is unstructured. Images, audio recordings, documents, books, and articles all represent unstructured data. Unstructured data is a natural byproduct of our lives nowadays. Smartphones and social networks facilitate the creation of endless data streams. Nowadays, you need little to snap a photo or make a video. Analyzing unstructured data is so difficult that we didn't come up with a practical solution until 2010.

Structured data is hard to gather and maintain, but it is the easiest to analyze. The reason is that we often collect it for this exact purpose. Structured data is typically stored inside computer databases and files. In digital advertising, ad networks apply huge effort to collect as much data as possible. Data is gold for advertising companies. They collect your browsing history, link clicks, time spent on site pages, and many other features for each user. Vast amounts of data allow the creation of accurate click probability models that can personalize your ad browsing experience. Personalization increases click probabilities, which increases advertisers' profits.

To increase their data supply, modern enterprises build their business processes in a way that generates as much structured data as possible. For example, banks record every financial transaction you make. This information is necessary to manage accounts, but they also use it as the main data source for credit scoring models. Those models use customers' financial profiles to estimate their credit default risk probability.

The difficulty of analyzing unstructured data comes from its high dimensionality. To explain this, let's take a data table with two columns of numbers: **x** and **y**. We can say that this data has two dimensions.

Each value in this dataset is displayed on the following plot:

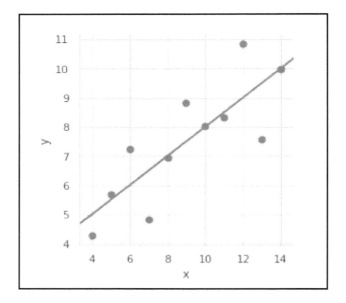

As you can see, we can have an accurate guess of what the value of **y** will be given a value of **x**. To do this, we can look at the corresponding point on the line. For example, for **x = 10**, **y** will be equal to **8**, which matches the real data points depicted as blue dots.

Now, let's shift to a photo made with an iPhone. This image will have a resolution of 4,032 x 3,024 pixels. Each pixel will have three color channels: red, green, and blue. If we represent pixels in this image as numbers, we will end up with over twelve million of them in each photo. In other words, our data has a dimensionality of 12 million.

In the following screenshot, you can see an image represented as a set of numbers:

Using machine learning algorithms on high-dimensional data can become problematic. Many machine learning algorithms suffer from a problem called the curse of dimensionality. To create a good model that recognizes objects in a photo, you need a model that's much more complex than a simple line. The complexity of the model increases the **data hunger** of the model, so models that work well on unstructured data usually require vast amounts of training data samples.

Origins of machine learning

Before the emergence of data science, machine learning, and deep learning, there was statistics. All fields related to data analysis have statistics at their core. From its very start, statistics was an alloy of many fields. The reason for this is that statistics was (and is) aimed at solving practical problems. In the 17th century, statisticians applied mathematics to data to make inferences and support decisions regarding economics and demographics. Doesn't this sound like data science? Here is an interesting fact: the first machine learning algorithm, linear regression, was invented over 200 years ago by Carl Friedrich Gauss. We still use it today, and its implementation is present in all major machine learning and statistical software packages.

The least squares algorithm invented by Gauss is the basic form of linear regression. The general form of the linear model was introduced much later.

Anatomy of machine learning

Let's look at the common use cases for machine learning. Arguably the most common one is prediction. Predictive algorithms tell us when something will happen, but not necessarily why it will happen. Some examples of prediction tasks are: *Will this user churn in the next month? Does this person have a high risk of developing Alzheimer's disease? Will there be a traffic jam in the next hour?* Often, we want to have explanations instead of predictions. Solving an inference task means to find supporting evidence for some claim in the data by asking *Why?* questions. *Why did this person win the election? Why does this medicine work and the other doesn't?* Statistical inference helps us to find an explanation or to prove the efficiency of our actions. When we do inference, we seek answers for the present or the past. When we try to look into the future, prediction comes into play.

Sometimes, we are not interested in predicting the future or finding evidence. We want machines to recognize complex patterns in data, such as objects in an image, or to analyze the sentiment of a text message. This group of tasks is called recognition.

Machine learning covers many types and flavors of models. But why do we need such variety of different algorithms? The reason lies in a theorem called the **no free lunch theorem**. It states that there is no best model that will consistently give you the best results on each task for every dataset. Each algorithm has its own benefits and pitfalls. It may work flawlessly on one task, but fail miserably at another. One of the most important goals of a data scientist is to find the best model to solve the problem at hand.

Main types of tasks you can solve with machine learning

The no free lunch theorem states that there is no best model that solves all tasks well. The consequence of this is that we have many algorithms that specialize in solving specific tasks.

For instance, let's look at fashion retail warehouse demand forecasting. A retailer sells a fixed set of clothes at their stores. Before an item makes it to the shelves, it must be bought from the manufacturer and transferred to a warehouse. Let's assume that their logistics cycle takes two weeks. How do we know the best quantity of each item to order? There is a good chance that we have item sales data for each store. We can use it to create a predictive model that estimates average customer demand for each item in the catalog of our warehouse over the next two weeks. That is, we forecast an average number of to-be-bought items over the next two weeks. The simplest model would be to take an average demand for each item from the last two weeks as an estimate of average future demand. Simple statistical models like this are frequently used at real retail stores, so we do not oversimplify. To be more general, let's call the thing we want to forecast the `target` variable. In the previous case, the `target` variable is the demand. To build a forecasting model, we will use two previous weeks of historical data to calculate arithmetic averages for each item. We then use those averages as estimates for the future values. In a way, historical data was used to teach our model about how it should predict the `target` variable. When the model learns to perform a given task using input/output examples, we call the process supervised learning. It would be an overstatement to name our average calculator as a supervised learning algorithm, but nothing stops us from doing this (at least technically).

Supervised learning is not limited to simple models. In general, the more complex your model is, the more data it requires to train. The more training data you have, the better your model will be. To illustrate, we will look into the world of information security. Our imaginary client is a large telecoms company. Over the years, they have experienced many security breaches in their network. Thankfully, specialists have recorded and thoroughly investigated all fraudulent activity on the network. Security experts labeled each fraudulent activity in network logs. Having lots of data with labeled training examples, we can train a supervised learning model to distinguish between normal and fraudulent activity. This model will recognize suspicious behavior from vast amounts of incoming data. However, this will only be the case if experts labeled the data correctly. Our model won't correct them if they didn't. This principle is called **garbage in, garbage out**. Your model can only be as good as your data.

Both the retail and security examples use supervised learning, but let's look at the `target` variables more closely. The forecasting algorithm used demand as the `target` variable. Demand is a continuous number ranging from 0 to infinity. On the other hand, the security model has a fixed number of outcomes.

Network activity is either normal or fraudulent. We call the first type of the `target` variable—continuous, and the second type—categorical. The `target` variable type strongly indicates which kind of task we can solve. Prediction tasks with continuous `target` variables are called regression problems. And when the total number of outcomes is limited, we say that we solve a classification problem. Classification models assign data points to categories, while regression models estimate quantities.

Here are some examples:

- House price estimation is a regression task.
- Predicting user ad clicks is a classification task.
- Predicting HDD utilization in a cloud storage service is a regression task.
- Identifying the risk of credit default is a classification task.

You can consider yourself lucky if you have found a good labeled dataset. You're even luckier if the dataset is large, contains no missing labels, and is a good match for an end-to-end solution to a problem. The labels we use for supervised learning are a scarce resource. A total absence of labels is a lot more common than fully labeled datasets. This means that often, we cannot use supervised learning. But the absence of labels does not mean that we are doomed. One solution is to label data by hand. You can assign this task to your employees if the data cannot be shared outside of the company. Otherwise, a much simpler and faster solution is to use crowdfunding services such as Amazon Mechanical Turk. There, you can outsource data labeling to a large number of people, paying a small fee for each data point.

While it's convenient, labeling data is not always affordable, and may be impossible. A learning process where the `target` variable is missing or can be derived from the data itself is called unsupervised learning. While supervised learning implies that the data was labeled, unsupervised learning removes this limitation, allowing an algorithm to learn from data without guidance.

For example, the marketing department may want to discover new segments of customers with similar buying habits. Those insights can be used to tailor marketing campaigns and increase revenue in each segment. One way to discover hidden structures in your dataset is to use a clustering algorithm. Many clustering algorithms can work with unlabeled data. This characteristic makes them particularly interesting.

Sometimes, labels hide inside the raw data. Look at the task of music creation. Suppose we want to create an algorithm that composes new music. We can use supervised learning without explicit labeling in this case. The next note in a sequence serves as a great label for this task. Starting with a single note, the model predicts the next note. Taking the previous two, it outputs the third. This way, we can add as many new notes as we need.

Now, let's see whether we can apply machine learning to games. If we take a single game, we may label some data and use supervised learning. But scaling this approach for all games is not possible in practice. On a typical gaming console, you use the same controller to play different games. Try to recall when you played for the first time in your life. I suppose it was Mario. It is likely that you were unsure of what to do. You might have tried pressing a few buttons and looked at a jumping character. Piece by piece, you must have figured out the rules of the game and started playing. I wouldn't be surprised if you felt confident playing and could finish the first levels after a few hours of experience.

Using the knowledge we have gained so far, can we design a machine learning algorithm that will learn how to play games? It might be tempting to use supervised learning, but think first. You had no training data when you took the controller for the first time in your life. But can we create algorithms that would figure out game rules by themselves?

It is easy to write a good bot for a specific computer game if we know the rules in advance. Almost all modern computer games have rule-based AIs or non-player characters that can interact with the player. Some games even have such advanced AI that all gameplay builds around this feature. If you are interested, look at *Alien: Isolation*, released in 2014. The biggest limitation of those algorithms is that they are game-specific. They cannot learn and act based on experience.

This was the case until 2015, when deep learning researchers discovered a way to train machine learning models to play Atari games as humans do: look at the screen and perform actions by using a game controller. The only difference was that the algorithm was not using physical eyes or hands to play the game. It received each frame of the game through RAM and acted via a virtual controller. Most importantly, the model received the current game score in each incoming frame. At the start, the model performed random actions. Some actions led to a score increase that was received as positive feedback. Over time, the model learned input/output or frame/action pairs that corresponded to higher scores. The results were stunning. After 75 hours of training, the model played *Breakout* at an amateur level. It wasn't provided with any prior knowledge of the game. All it saw were raw pixels. Sometime later, the algorithm had learned how to play *Breakout* better than humans. The exact same model can be trained to play different games. The learning framework that was used to train such models is called reinforcement learning. In reinforcement learning, an agent (player) learns a policy (a specific way of performing actions based on incoming inputs) that maximizes the reward (game score) in an unknown environment (a computer game).

Of course, there are limitations. Remember, there are no free lunches in the machine learning restaurant. While this algorithm performed well on a large set of games, it failed completely at others. In particular, a game called *Montezuma's Revenge* had stymied every model until 2018. The problem with this game is that you need to perform a specific series of actions over a long time before getting even a small reward signal.

To solve tasks in complex environments, reinforcement learning algorithms need extremely large amounts of data. You may have seen the news about the OpenAI Five model beating professional players in a complex multiplayer cybersports game called *Dota 2*. To give you an insight, the OpenAI team used a cluster of 256 GPUs and 128,000 CPU cores to train their agent. Each day, the model played 180 years' worth of games against itself. This process happened in parallel on a large computing cluster, so it took much less time in reality.

Another large victory for reinforcement learning was, of course, the game of *Go*. The total number of actions in *Go* is larger than the total number of atoms in our universe, making this game very hard to tackle using computers. Computer scientists defeated the best humans at chess in 1997. For *Go*, it took them another 18 years. If you are interested, Google filmed a documentary about AlphaGo, an algorithm that won at *Go* against world champions.

Reinforcement learning works well when you can completely simulate your environment, that is, you know the rules of the game in advance. This chicken and egg problem makes applying reinforcement learning tricky. Still, reinforcement learning can be used to solve real-world problems. A team of scientists used reinforcement learning to find the optimal parameters for a rocket engine. This was possible thanks to complete physical models of the inner workings of the engine. They used these models to create a simulation where a reinforcement learning algorithm changed the parameters and design of the engine to find the optimal setup.

Introduction to deep learning

Before writing this section, I was thinking about the many ways we can draw a line between machine learning and deep learning. Each of them was contradictory in some way. In truth, you can't separate deep learning from machine learning because deep learning is a subfield of machine learning. Deep learning studies a specific set of models called neural networks. The first mentions of the mathematical foundations of neural networks date back to the 1980s, and the theory behind modern neural networks originated in 1958. Still, they failed to show good results until the 2010s. Why?

The answer is simple: hardware. Training big neural networks uses a great amount of computation power. But not any computation power will suffice. It turns out that neural networks do a lot of matrix operations under the hood. Strangely, rendering computer graphics also involves many matrix operations, so many, in fact, that each computer has a dedicated circuit inside: a GPU. Nvidia knew of the scientific need for fast matrix operations, so they developed a special programming framework called **CUDA**. CUDA allows you to harness the power of your GPU not only for computer graphics, but for general computing tasks as well. GPUs can do insane amounts of parallel matrix operations. Modern graphics cards have thousands of cores, so you can perform thousands of operations in parallel. And all individual operations also work quickly. Modern GPUs can execute thousands of parallel, floating-point computations. GPUs specialize in solving one specific task much faster than general-purpose CPUs.

All this meant that scientists could train larger neural networks. The art and science of training large neural networks is called deep learning. The origin of the word **deep** in the name comes from the specific structure of neural networks that allows them to be efficient and accurate in their predictions. We will look more into the internals of neural networks in `Chapter 2`, *Testing Your Models*.

Deep learning is fantastic at solving tasks with unstructured datasets. To illustrate this, let's look at a machine learning competition called **ImageNet**. It contains over 14 million images, classified into 22,000 distinct categories. To solve ImageNet, an algorithm should learn to identify an object in the photo. While human performance on this task is around 95% accuracy, the best neural network model surpassed this level in 2015.

Traditional machine learning algorithms are not very good at working with unstructured data. However, they are equally important because the gap in performance between traditional machine learning models and deep learning models is not so big in the domain of structured datasets. Most winners of data science competitions on structured datasets do not use deep neural networks. They use simpler models because they showed better results on structured datasets. Those models train faster, do not need specialized hardware, and use less computational power.

 Simpler models are not easier to apply. Deep learning can show good results on structured data, too. Still, it is likely that you will spend more time, money, and computing power in a real-world scenario. The simplicity refers to the internal model's structure and the number of changing parameters inside the model.

To differentiate other machine learning algorithms from deep learning, professionals often refer to deep learning as a field that studies neural networks, and machine learning is used for every other model. Drawing a line between machine learning and deep learning is incorrect, but for the lack of a better term, the community has agreed on ambiguous definitions.

Diving into natural language processing

We write every day, whether it is documents, tweets, electronic messages, books, or emails. The list can go on and on. Using algorithms to understand natural language is difficult because our language is ambiguous, complex, and contains many exceptions and corner cases. The first attempts at **natural language processing** (**NLP**) were about building rule-based systems. Linguists carefully designed hundreds and thousands of rules to perform seemingly simple tasks, such as part of speech tagging.

From this section's title, you can probably guess it all changed with deep learning. Deep learning models can perform many more text processing tasks without the need to explicitly state complex grammatical rules and parsers. Deep learning models took the NLP world by storm. They can perform a wide range of NLP tasks with much better quality than previous generation NLP models. Deep neural networks translate text to another language with near-human accuracy. They are also quite accurate at doing part-of-speech tagging.

Neural networks also do a good job of solving comprehension problems: question answering and text summarization. In question answering, the model gets a chunk of text and a question about its contents. For example, given the introduction to this section, *Introduction to deep learning*, a question-answering model could correctly answer the following queries:

- How many cores do modern desktop CPUs have? (less than 10)
- When did neural networks originate? (1980s)

Text summarization seeks to extract the main points from the source. If we feed the first few paragraphs of this section into a text summarization model, we will get the following results:

> Now it is time to draw a line between machine learning and deep learning. In truth, we can't do this, because deep learning is a sub-field of machine learning. Formally, deep learning studies a specific set of models called neural networks. The theory behind neural networks originated in the 1980s. You can try out a sample text summarization model online at http://textsummarization.net/.

Another intersecting NLP problem is text classification. By labeling many texts as emotionally positive or negative, we can create a sentiment analysis model. As you already know, we can train this kind of model using supervised learning. Sentiment analysis models can give powerful insights when used to measure reactions to news or the general mood around Twitter hashtags.

Text classification is also used to solve automated email and document tagging. We can use neural networks to process large chunks of emails and to assign appropriate tags to them.

The pinnacle of practical NLP is the creation of dialog systems, or chatbots. Chatbots can be used to automate common scenarios at IT support departments and call centers. However, creating a bot that can reliably and consistently solve its task is not an easy task. Clients tend to communicate with bots in rather unexpected ways, so you will have a lot of corner cases to cover. NLP research is not quite at the point of providing an end-to-end conversational model that can solve the task.

General chatbots use several models to understand user requests and prepare an answer:

- The intent classification model determines the user's request.
- The entity recognition model extracts all named entities from the user's message.
- The response generator model takes the input from the intent classification and entity recognition models and generates a response. The response generator can also use a knowledge database to look up extra information to enrich the response.
- Sometimes, the response generator creates several responses. Then, a separate response ranking model selects the most appropriate one.

NLP models can also generate texts of arbitrary length based on initial input. State-of-the-art models output results that are arguably indistinguishable from human-written texts.

 You can look at the model output samples in an OpenAI blog post about the GPT-2 model: https://openai.com/blog/better-language-models/#sample1.

While the results are very compelling, we are yet to find useful and practical applications for text generation models. While writers and content creators could potentially benefit from these models by using them to expand a list of key points into a coherent text, unfortunately, these models lack the means to control their output, making them difficult to use in practice.

Exploring computer vision

We have explored how deep learning can understand text. Now, let's explore how deep learning models can see. In 2010, the first ImageNet Large Scale Visual Recognition Challenge was held. The task was to create a classification model that solved the ambitious task of recognizing an object in an image. In total, there are around 22,000 categories to choose from. The dataset contains over 14 million labeled images. If someone sat and chose the top 5 objects for each image, they would have an error rate of around 5%.

In 2015, a deep neural network surpassed human performance on ImageNet. Since then, many computer vision algorithms have been rendered obsolete. Deep learning allows us not only to classify images, but also to do object detection and instance segmentation.

The following two pictures help to describe the difference between object detection and instance segmentation:

The preceding photo shows us that object detection models recognize objects and place bounding boxes around them.

In the following image, from `https://github.com/matterport/Mask_RCNN`, we can see that instance segmentation models find the exact outlines of objects:

Thus, the main practical uses of deep learning in computer vision are essentially the same tasks at different levels of resolution:

- **Image classification**: Determining the class of an image from a predetermined set of categories
- **Object detection**: Finding bounding boxes for objects inside an image and assigning a class probability for each bounding box
- **Instance segmentation**: Doing pixel-wise segmentation of an image, outlining every object from a predetermined class list

Computer vision algorithms have found applications in cancer screening, handwriting recognition, face recognition, robotics, self-driving cars, and many other areas.

Another interesting direction in computer vision is generative models. While the models we have already examined perform recognition tasks, generative models change images, or even create entirely new ones. Style transfer models can change the stylistic appearance of an image to look more like another image. This kind of model can be used to transform photos into paintings that look and feel like the work of an artist, as follows:

Another promising approach for training generative models is called **Generative Adversarial Networks** (**GANs**). You use two models to train GANs: generator and discriminator. The generator creates images. The discriminator tries to distinguish the real images from your dataset from the generated images. Over time, the generator learns to create more realistic images, while the discriminator learns to identify more subtle mistakes in the image generation process. The results of this approach speak for themselves. State-of-the-art models can generate realistic human faces, as you can see on page 3 of Nvidia's paper, https://arxiv.org/pdf/1812.04948.pdf. Take a look at the following images. These photos are not real. A deep neural network generated these images:

We can also use GANs to perform conditional image generation. The word *conditional* means that we can specify some parameters for the generator. In particular, we can specify a type of object or texture that is being generated. For example, Nvidia's landscape generator software can transform a simple color-coded image, where specific colors represent soil, sky, water, and other objects, to realistic-looking photos.

Deep learning use case

To show how deep learning may work in practical settings, we will explore product matching.

Up-to-date pricing is very important for large internet retailers. In situations where your competitor lowers the price of a popular product, late reaction leads to large profit losses. If you know the correct market price distributions for your product catalog, you can always remain a step ahead of your competitors. To create such a distribution for a single product, you first need to find this product description on a competitor's site. While automated collection of product descriptions is easy, product matching is the hard part.

Once we have a large volume of unstructured text, we need to extract product attributes from it. To do this, we first need to tell whether two descriptions refer to the same product. Suppose that we have collected a large dataset of similar product descriptions. If we shuffle all pairs in our data, we will get another dataset of non-similar product descriptions. Using lots of examples of similar and dissimilar product descriptions, we can train an NLP model that can identify similar product descriptions. We may also think about comparing photos on the retailer's sites to find similar products. To do this, we can apply computer vision models to do the matching. Even with those two models, the total matching accuracy will probably be insufficient for our requirements. Another way to boost it is to extract product attributes from textual descriptions. We may train word-tagging models or develop a set of matching rules to do this task. Matching accuracy will increase, along with the diversity and descriptiveness of the data sources we use.

Introduction to causal inference

Up to this point, we have talked about predictive models. The main purpose of a predictive model is to recognize and forecast. The explanation behind the model's reasoning is of lower priority. On the contrary, causal inference tries to explain relationships in the data rather than to make predictions about the future events. In causal inference, we check whether an outcome of some action was not caused by so-called confounding variables. Those variables can indirectly influence action through the outcome. Let's compare causal inference and predictive models through several questions that they can help to answer:

- Prediction models:
    - When will our sales double?
    - What is the probability of this client buying a certain product?
- Causal inference models:
    - Was this cancer treatment effective? Or is the effect apparent only because of the complex relationships between variables in the data?
    - Was the new version of our recommendation model better than the other? If it is, by what amount does it increase our sales compared to the old model?
    - What factors cause some books to be bestsellers?
    - What factors cause Alzheimer's disease?

There is a mantra amongst statisticians: correlation does not imply causation. If some variables change together or have similar values, does not mean that they are connected in some logical way. There are many great examples of non-sensible absurd correlations in real-world data at `http://www.tylervigen.com/spurious-correlations`.

Look at the examples in the following screenshots:

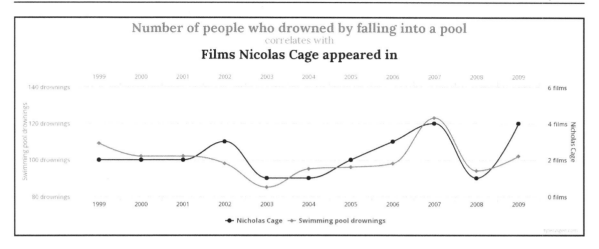

Some findings are as bewildering as they are humorous:

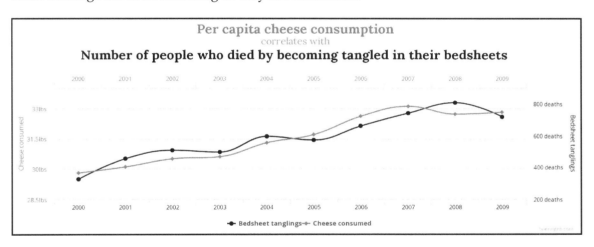

Seeking explanations and measuring effects is important when data-driven decisions affect people's lives. Specifically, when a new drug is invented, we need to check that it really works. To do this, we need to collect data and measure the statistical effect of using the new drug versus not using the new drug.

Causal inference poses this question in a rather ambitious way: the simplest way to measure the effect of some treatment is to split our universe into two parts. In the first part, we do not apply the treatment and act as if the drug was never discovered. In the second part, we apply the new treatment. Unfortunately, the creation of new universes is far beyond the capabilities of statisticians. But they have come up with a reasoning framework that allows you to design experiments and collect data as if it would come from two separate independent universes.

The simplest way to do this is to conduct a randomized experiment:

1. First, we will randomly sample a test group of people from the entire globe.
2. Then, each person will be assigned the new drug or a sugar pill (placebo) with 50% probability.
3. After a while, we can measure the treatment's effect in the two groups.

Studies like this can be very complex to execute. Imagine selecting a random sample of the entire world's population each time you need to test a new drug. Moreover, you cannot transport all individuals to a single place because a sudden change of environment or climate may affect treatment results. This experiment may also be considered unethical, especially if the treatment is associated with a risk of death. Causal inference allows you to design more complex experiment designs that will still be equivalent to a random experiment under certain conditions. This way, you can create an ethical and realistic study that has statistical rigor.

Another important feature of causal inference is a set of methods that work on observational data. It is not always feasible to conduct an experiment for a hypothesis check. Causal inference can be used to apply predictive models to measure effects on observational data that was not specifically collected for this sole purpose. For example, we can use customer data to measure and quantify the efficiency of marketing campaigns. Observational studies are convenient to execute as they require no experimental setup. However, they can only give you a strong educated guess about real causal relationships. It is always recommended to design and conduct a proper experiment before making data-driven decisions.

The framework of applying a treatment to a test group is very general. It is not limited to medical studies and can measure and explain the effects of any changes. The question—*is using a machine learning model better than not using it at all? If so, how much benefit does it give?* often occupies the minds of data scientists. Thanks to causal inference, we can find a solution. In this question, you can substitute a machine learning model for the treatment.

The only way to measure the real effect is to check both approaches on real users. While being difficult to conduct in a physical world, purely randomized experiments are easy on the internet. If you use machine learning models at a large internet company with a large number of customers, designing a randomized experiment can seem easy. You can randomly assign two different versions of your software to each user and wait until a sufficiently large sample of data has been collected.

However, you should be wary of many things that can distort results:

- Hidden biases in data are called confounders. Customer lifestyle, social factors, or environmental exposure can affect your seemingly random sample of users.
- A flaw in test group selection is called selection bias. For example, random selection of test participants from a single region could affect the study.
- Measurement errors: Erroneous or non-consistent data collection can lead to misleading results

Summary

In this chapter, we have explored the practical applications of AI, data science, machine learning, deep learning, and causal inference. We have defined machine learning as a field that studies algorithms that use data to support decisions and give insights without specific instructions. There are three main machine learning methodologies: supervised, unsupervised, and reinforcement learning. In practice, the most common types of task we solve using machine learning are regression and classification. Next, we described deep learning as a subset of machine learning devoted to studying neural network algorithms. The main application domains of deep learning are computer vision and NLP. We have also touched on the important topic of causal inference: the field that studies a set of methods for discovering causal relationships in data. You now know a lot about general data science capabilities. But can machine learning models successfully solve your specific set of problems?

In the next chapter, we will learn to distinguish good solutions from bad ones by performing model testing.

Testing Your Models 2

Coming up with a perfect machine learning model is not simple if you do not use a good testing methodology. This seemingly perfect model will fail the moment you deploy it. Testing the model's performance is not an easy task, but it is an essential part of every data science project. Without proper testing, you can't be sure whether your models will work as expected, and you can't choose the best approach to solve the task at hand.

This chapter will explore various approaches for model testing and look at different types of metrics, using mathematical functions that evaluate the quality of predictions. We will also go through a set of methods for testing classifier models.

In this chapter, we will cover the following topics:

- Offline model testing
- Online model testing

Offline model testing

Offline model testing encompasses all the model-evaluation processes that are performed before the model is deployed. Before discussing online testing in detail, we must first define model errors and ways to calculate them.

Understanding model errors

Every model can make mistakes because collected data, and the model itself, introduces implications about the nature of your problem. The best example of a good working model is inside your brain. You use modeling in real time—the brain renders everything you see by interpreting electromagnetic impulses recorded by your eyes. While this picture of the world is imperfect, it is useful as we receive over 90% of information through the visual channel. The last 10% comes from hearing, touch, and our other senses. Thus, each model, $\mathbf{M}$, tries to predict real value, $\mathbf{Y}$, by making a guess, $\hat{\mathbf{Y}}$.

The difference between the real value and model's approximation makes up the model error:

$$Error = Y - \hat{Y}$$

For regression problems, we can measure the error in quantities that the model predicts. For example, if we predict house prices using a machine learning model and get a prediction of $300,000 for a house with a real price of $350,000, we can say that the error is $350,000 - $300,000 = $50,000.

For classification problems in the simplest setting, we can measure the error as 0 for a guess, and 1 for a wrong answer. For example, for a cat/dog recognizer, we give an error of 1 if the model predicts that there is a cat in a dog photo, and 0 if it gives a correct answer.

Decomposing errors

You won't find a machine learning model that perfectly solves your problems without making even a single mistake, no matter how small. Since every model makes mistakes, it is critical to understand their nature. Suppose that our model makes a prediction and we know the real value. If this prediction is incorrect, then there is some difference between the prediction and the true value:

$$Error = real\ value - prediction$$

The other part of this error will come from imperfections in our data, and some from imperfections in our model. No matter how complex our model is, it can only reduce the modeling error. Irreducible error is out of our control, hence its name.

Let's look at it in the following formula:

$$Error = Error\_reducible + Error\_irreducible$$

Not all reducible errors are the same. We can decompose reducible errors further. For example, look at the following diagram:

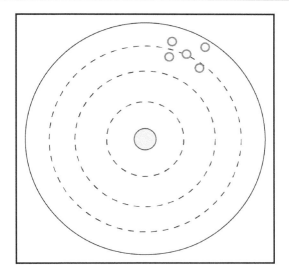

The red center of each target represents our goal (real value), and the blue shots represent the model predictions. In the target, the model's aim is off—all predictions are close together, but they are far away from the target. This kind of error is called **bias**. The simpler our model is, the more bias it will have. For a simple model, the bias component can become prevailing:

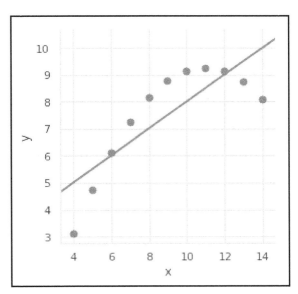

In the preceding plot, we try to model a complex relationship between variables with a simple line. This kind of model has a high bias.

The second component of the model error is **variance**:

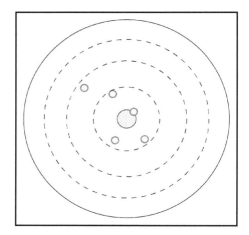

All predictions appear to be clustered around the true target, but the spread is too high. The source of this error comes from the model's sensitivity to fluctuations in data. If the model has high variance, randomness in measurements can lead to very different predictions.

So far, we have decomposed model error into the three following numbers:

$$\text{Error} = \text{bias} + \text{variance} + \text{irreducible error}$$

It is not a coincidence that bias and variance sit close together in the same formula. There is a relationship between them. Predictive models show a property called the **bias-variance tradeoff**—the more biased a model, the lower the variance component of the error. And in reverse, the more variance it has, the lower its bias will be. This important fact will be a game-changer for building ensemble models, which we will explore in `Chapter 3`, *Understanding AI*.

Typically, models that impose some kind of structure in the data have a high bias (they assume certain laws that the data conforms to). Biased models will work well, as long as the data does not contradict the underlying logic of the model. To give you an example of such a model, think of a simple line. For example, we will predict a housing price as a linear function of its size in square feet:

$$\text{housing price} = \$10000 \times \text{number of square feet}$$

Notice that if we change the square footage by a little, say 0.1, then the prediction won't change by much. Thus, this model has low variance. When the model is sensitive to changes in its input, its variance will outgrow the bias. The variance component will grow with your model increases in complexity and the total number of parameters grows. In the following plot, you can see how two different models fit the same dataset. The first simple model has low variance, and the second complex model has high variance:

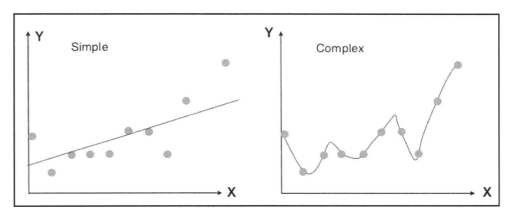

In the preceding plot, slight changes in **X** can lead to large fluctuations of **Y**. Models with high variance are robust and imply that the data is much less structured.

Understanding overfitting

The bias-variance trade-off goes hand in hand with a very important problem in machine learning called **overfitting**. If your model is too simple, it will cause large errors. If it is too complex, it will memorize the data too well. An overfitted model remembers data too well and acts like a database. Suppose that our housing dataset contains some lucky deals where previous houses had a low price because of circumstances not captured in the data. An overfit model will memorize those examples too closely and predict incorrect price values on unseen data.

Now, having understood the error decomposition, can we use it as a stepping stone to design a model-testing pipeline?

We need to determine how to measure model error in such a way that it will correspond to the real model performance on unseen data. The answer comes from the question itself. We will split all the available data into two sets: a training set and a test set, as shown in the following screenshot:

We will use data in the training set to train our model. The test set acts as unseen data and you should not use the test set in the training process. When the model's training is finished, you can feed the test data into your model. Now you can calculate errors for all predictions. The model did not use the test data during training, so the test set error represents the model error on unseen data. The drawback to this approach is that you take a significant amount of data, usually up to 30%, to use for testing. This means less training data and lower model quality. There is also a caveat – if you use your test set too much, error metrics will start to lie. For example, suppose that you did the following:

1. Trained a model
2. Measured the error on the test data
3. Changed your model to improve the metrics
4. Repeated steps 1-3 ten times
5. Deployed the model to production

It is likely that the quality of your model will be much lower than expected. Why did this happen? Let's look more closely *step 3*. You looked at a score, and changed your model or data processing code several consecutive times. In fact, you did several learning iterations by hand. By repeatedly improving the test score, you indirectly disclosed information about the test data to your model. When the metric values measured on a test set deviate from the metrics measured on the real data, we say that the test data has leaked into our model. Data leaks are notoriously hard to detect before they cause damage. To avoid them, you should always be mindful of the possibility of a leak, think critically, and follow best practices.

We can use a separate piece of data to fight test set leakage. Data scientists use validation sets to tune model parameters and compare different models before choosing the best one. Then, the test data is used only as a final check that informs you about model quality on unseen data. After you have measured the test metric scores, the only decision left is to make is whether the model will proceed to testing in a real-world scenario.

In the following screenshot, you can see an example of a train/validation/test split of the dataset:

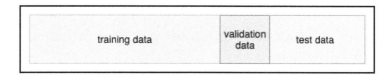

Unfortunately, the following two problems persist when we use this approach:

- The information about our test set might still leak into our solution after many iterations. Test-set leakage does not disappear completely when you use the validation set, it just becomes slower. To overcome this, change your test data from time to time. Ideally, make a new test set for every model-deployment cycle.
- You might overfit your validation data quickly, because of the train-measure-change feedback cycle for tuning your models.

To prevent overfitting, you can randomly select train and validation sets from your data for each experiment. Randomly shuffle all available data, then select random train and validation datasets by splitting the data into three parts according to proportions you have chosen.

There is no general rule for how much training, validation, and testing data you should use. Often, more training data means a more accurate model, but it means that you will have less data to assess the model's performance. The typical split for medium-sized datasets (up to 100,000 data points) is to use 60-80% of the data to train the model and use the rest for validation.

The situation changes for large datasets. If you have a dataset with 10,000,000 rows, using 30% for testing would comprise 3,000,000 rows. It is likely that this amount would be overkill. Increasing test and validation test sizes will yield diminishing returns. For some problems, you will get good results with 100,000 examples for testing, which would amount for a 1% test size. The more data you have, the lower the proportion you should use for testing.

Often, there is too little data. In those situations, taking from 30%-40% data for testing and validation might severely decrease the model's accuracy. You can apply a technique called cross-validation in data-scarce situations. With cross-validation, there's no need to create a separate validation or test set. Cross-validation proceeds in the following way:

1. You choose some fixed number of iterations—three, for example.
2. Split the dataset into three parts.
3. For each iteration, cross-validation uses 2/3 of the dataset as a training data and 1/3 as validation data.
4. Train model for each of the three train-validation set pairs.
5. Calculate the metric values using each validation set.
6. Aggregate the metrics into a single number by averaging all metric values.

The following screenshot explains cross-validation visually:

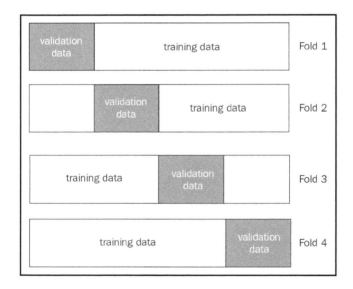

Cross-validation has one main drawback: it requires significantly more computational resources to assess model quality. In our example, to make a single assessment we needed to fit three models. With a regular train/test split, we would train only one model. In addition, cross-validation accuracy will grow with the number of iterations you use (also called folds). So cross-validation allows you to use more data for training, while requiring more computational resources. How do we choose between cross-validation and train-validation-test splits for projects?

In cross-validation, k is a variable parameter that is set up by a data scientist. The lowest possible value is 1, which is equivalent to a simple train/test split. The largest extreme is k equal to the number of data points in the dataset. This means that if we have N points in the dataset, the model will be trained and tested $N - 1$ times. This special case of cross-validation is called **leave-one-out cross-validation**. In theory, a larger number of folds means that the cross-validation will return more accurate metric values. While leave-one-out cross-validation is the most theoretically accurate method, it is seldom used in practice because of the large computational requirements. In practice, the values of k range from 3 to 15 folds, depending on the dataset size. Your project may need to use more, so take this as advice and not as a rule.

The following table sums up a general way of thinking:

	Model training requires low to moderate computational resources and time	Model training requires large computational resources and takes a long time
Small to medium dataset	Cross-validation	Either
Large dataset	Either	Train/validation/test split

Another important aspect related to model testing is how to split the data. A slight error in your splitting logic can mean all your testing efforts were in vain. Splitting is easy, if all observations in your dataset are independent. Then you can use random data splits. But what if we are solving the stock-price prediction problem? When our data rows are tied to time, we can't look at them as independent values. Today's stock prices depend on their past values. If this wasn't true, the prices would randomly jump from $0 to $1,000. In this situation, suppose we have two years' worth of stock data, from January 2017 to December 2018. If we use random splits, it is possible that our model will train in September 2018 and test on February 2017. This makes no sense. We must always think about causal relationships and dependencies between your observations and be sure to check whether your validation procedure is correct.

Next, we will learn about metrics, which are formulas we can use to summarize validation and test errors. Metrics will allow us to compare different models and choose the best candidates for production use.

Using technical metrics

Each model, no matter how complex and accurate, makes mistakes. It is natural to expect that some models will be better than others when solving a specific problem. Currently, we can measure errors by comparing individual model predictions with the ground truth. It would be useful to summarize them into a single number for measuring the model's performance. We can use a metric to do this. There are many kinds of metrics that are suitable for different machine learning problems.

In particular, for regression problems the most common metric is the **root mean square error**, or **RMSE**:

$$RMSE = \sqrt{\frac{\sum_{i=1}^{N}(predicted_i - actual_i)^2}{N}}$$

Let's examine the elements of this formula:

- N is the total number of data points.
- *predicted - actual* measures the error between ground truth and model prediction.
- The Sigma sign at the start of the formula means sum.

Another popular way to measure regression errors is **mean absolute error** (**MAE**):

$$MAE = \frac{1}{N}\sum_{i=1}^{N}|predicted_i - actual_i|$$

Note that MAE is very similar to RMSE. Compared to MAE, RMSE has a square root instead of absolute value and it squares errors. While MAE and RMSE may seem identical, there are some technical differences between them. Data scientists can choose best metrics for a problem, knowing their trade-offs and shortcomings. You don't need to learn them all, but I would like to highlight one difference to give you a general feel of the thought process. RMSE penalizes large errors more than MAE. This property comes from the fact that RMSE uses squared errors, while MAE uses absolute values. To illustrate, an error of 4 would be 4 in MAE, but in RMSE it will turn into 16 because of the square.

For classification problems, the metric-calculation process is more involved. Let's imagine that we are building a binary classifier that estimates the probability of a person having pneumonia. To calculate how accurate the model is, we may just divide the total of correct answers by the number of rows in the dataset:

$$Accuracy = \frac{n_{correct}}{N}$$

Here, $n_{correct}$ is the amount of correct predictions, and N is the total number of predictions. Accuracy is simple to understand and calculate, but it has a major flaw. Let's assume the average probability of having pneumonia is 0.001%. That is, one person out of 100,000 has the illness. If you had collected data on 200,000 people, it is feasible that your dataset would contain only two positive cases. Imagine you have asked a data scientist to build a machine learning model that estimates pneumonia probability based on a patient's data. You have said that you would only accept an accuracy of no less than 99.9%. Suppose that someone created a dummy algorithm that always outputs zeros.

This model has no real value, but its accuracy on our data will be high as it will make only two errors:

$$Accuracy = \frac{199998}{200000} = 99.999\%$$

The problem is that accuracy considers only global fraction of answers. When one class outnumbers the others, accuracy outputs misleading values.

Let's look at model predictions in more detail by constructing a confusion table:

	Model prediction: Has pneumonia	Model prediction: Does not have pneumonia
Real outcome: Has pneumonia	0	2
Real outcome: Does not have pneumonia	0	199,998

After looking at this table, we can see that the dummy model won't be helpful to anyone. It didn't identify two people with the condition as positive. We call those errors **False Negatives** (**FN**). The model also correctly identified all patients with no pneumonia, or **True Negatives** (**TN**), but it has failed to diagnose ill patients correctly.

Now, suppose that your team has built a real model and got the following results:

	Model prediction: Has pneumonia	Model prediction: Does not have pneumonia
Real outcome: Has pneumonia	2	0
Real outcome: Does not have pneumonia	30	199,968

This model correctly identified two cases, making two **True Positive** (TP) predictions. This is a clear improvement over the previous iteration. However, the model also identified 30 people as having pneumonia, while they were not ill in reality. We call such an error a **False Positive** (FP) prediction. Is having 30 false positives a significant disadvantage? That depends on how physicians will use the model. If all subjects will be automatically prescribed with heavy medication with side-effects, false positives can be critical.

It may be less severe if we consider a positive model only as a possibility of having a disease. If a positive model answer only signals that the patient must go through a specific set of diagnostic procedures, then we can see a benefit: to achieve the same level of pneumonia identification, therapists will diagnose only 32 patients, where previously they had to investigate 200,000 cases. If we had not used the confusion table, we might have missed dangerous model behavior that would negatively affect people's health.

Next, your team has done another experiment and created a new model:

	Model prediction: Has pneumonia	Model prediction: Does not have pneumonia
Real outcome: Has pneumonia	0	2
Real outcome: Does not have pneumonia	100,000	99,998

Does this model perform better? The model would have missed one patient that needed therapy and assigned 100,000 healthy people to a treatment group, making physicians do unnecessary work. In truth, you can make the final decision only after presenting results to the people who will use the model. They may have a different opinion on what is best. It would be best to define this at the first stages of the project by creating a model-testing methodology document by collaborating with experts in the field.

You will face binary classification problems everywhere, thus having a good understanding of terminology is important.

You can see all new concepts summed up in the following table:

	Model prediction: 1 (positive case)	Model prediction: 0 (negative case)
Real outcome: 1 (positive case)	TP	FN
Real outcome: 0 (negative case)	FP	TN

It is crucial to note that you can control the amount of false positive and false negative responses for a single model. Classifiers output a probability of a data point belonging to a class. That is, the model prediction is a number between 0 and 1. You can decide whether a prediction belongs to a positive or negative class by comparing it with a threshold. For example, if the threshold is 0.5, then any model prediction greater than 0.5 will belong to class 1 and to 0 otherwise.

By changing the threshold, you can change the proportions between the cells in the confusion table. By choosing a large threshold, like 0.9, the volume of false positive responses will decrease, but false negative responses will increase. Threshold selection is essential for binary classification problems. Some environments, such as digital advertising, will be more forgiving to false positives, while in others, such as healthcare or insurance, you may find them unacceptable.

Confusion tables provide deep insights into classification problems but require your attention and time. This can be limiting when you want to do numerous experiments and compare many models. To simplify the process, statisticians and data scientists have designed many metrics that sum up classifier performance without suffering from problems like accuracy metrics do. First, let's examine some ways to summarize confusion table rows and columns. From there, we will explore how to condense it into a single statistic.

In the following table, you can see two new metrics for summarizing different kinds of errors, precision and recall:

	Model prediction: 1 (positive case)	Model prediction: 0 (negative case)	Combined metric
Real outcome: 1 (positive case)	True Positive	False Negative	$precision = \dfrac{TP}{TP+FP}$
Real outcome: 0 (negative case)	False Positive	True Negative	

Combined metric	$recall = \dfrac{TP}{TP+FN}$, also called **True Positive Rate (TPR)**		

Precision measures a proportion of positive (relevant) cases that your model has identified. If your model predicted 10 positive cases and 2 positive predictions turned out to be negative in reality, then its precision would be 0.8. Recall represents a probability of correctly predicting a positive case. If out of 10 positive cases, the model had predicted all 10 correctly (10 true positives) and marked 5 negative cases as positive (5 false positives), then its recall would be 0.67. A recall of 0.67 means that if our model predicts a positive case, it will be correct 67 times out of 100.

For binary classification, precision and recall diminish the amount of metrics we must work with to two. This is better, but not ideal. We can sum up everything into a single number by using a metric called **F1-score**. You can calculate F1 using the following formula:

$$F1 = 2\,\frac{precision \times recall}{precision + recall}$$

F1 is 1 for a perfect classifier and 0 for the worst classifier. Because it considers both precision and recall, it does not suffer from the same problem as accuracy and is a better default metric for classification problems.

More about imbalanced classes

In the preceding examples, you might have noticed that many prediction problems suffer from a phenomenon where one class occurs much more frequently than the others. Identifying diseases such as cancer, estimating probabilities of credit default, or detecting fraud in financial transactions are all examples of imbalanced problems – positive cases are much less frequent than the negative ones. In such situations, estimating classifier performance becomes tricky. Metrics such as accuracy start to show an overly optimistic picture, so you need to resort to more advanced technical metrics. The F1 score gives much more realistic values in this setting. However, the F1 score is calculated from class assignments (0 or 1 in the case of binary classification) rather than class probabilities (0.2 and 0.95 in the case of binary classification).

Most machine learning models output a probability of an example belonging to a certain class, rather than direct class assignment. In particular, a cancer-detection model could output a 0.32 (32%) disease probability based on the incoming data. Then we must decide whether the patient will be labeled as having cancer or not. To do this, we can use a threshold: all values lower than or equal to this threshold will be labeled as 0 (does not have cancer), and all values greater than this threshold will be considered as 1 (has cancer). The threshold can greatly affect the resulting model's quality, especially for imbalanced datasets. For example, lower threshold values of will likely result in more 0 labels, however, the relationship is not linear.

To illustrate this, let's take a trained model and generate predictions for the test dataset. If we calculate class assignments by taking lots of different thresholds, and then calculate the precision, recall, and F1 score for each of those assignments, we could depict each precision and recall value in a single plot:

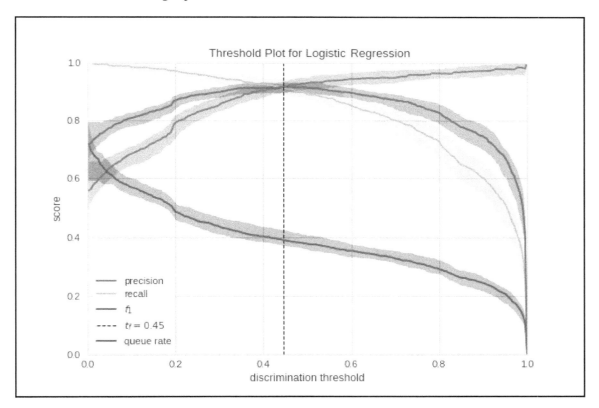

The preceding plot was made using the `yellowbrick` library, which contains many useful visualization tools for model selection and interpretation. You can see the capabilities of this library here: `https://www.scikit-yb.org/en/latest/index.html`.

In the preceding plot, you can see the precision (blue), recall (green), and F1 (red) values for each threshold between 0 and 1. Based on this plot, we can see that 0.5, which is the default in many machine learning libraries, might not be the best choice and that something like 0.45 would yield more optimal metric values.

Another useful concept shown in the plot is the queue rate (depicted in magenta), which shows the proportion of instances in the test dataset labeled as positive. For the 0.45 threshold (identified in the plot as a dashed line), you can see that the queue rate is 0.4. This means that approximately 40% of all cases will be labeled as fraudulent. Depending on the business process in which the model will be used, positive cases might need to be further investigated by humans. In some cases, manual checking takes a lot of time or resources, but it is OK to misclassify a few positive instances for a much lower queue rate. In such cases, you might want to choose models with lower queue rates even if their performance is lower.

All information about precision, recall, and thresholds can be further summarized into a single number called the **area under precision-recall curve** (**PR AUC**). This metric can be used to make quick judgments over a large number of different models without making manual evaluations of model quality on different thresholds. Another metric that is frequently used for binary classifier evaluations is called the **area under the receiver operating characteristic curve** (**ROC AUC**). In general, you will want to use PR AUC for imbalanced datasets and ROC AUC for balanced datasets.

The difference arises from the ways in which those metrics are calculated, but we will omit the technical details here for the sake of brevity. Calculating AUC metrics is a bit more involved than the other metrics presented in this chapter. For more information, check out `https://www.chioka.in/differences-between-roc-auc-and-pr-auc/` and `https://en.wikipedia.org/wiki/Receiver_operating_characteristic`.

There is no single rule for choosing the right balance for the precision, recall, F1, and queue rate. Those values should be thoughtfully investigated with respect to the business process. Relying solely on technical metrics for model selection can result in a disaster, as models that are the best for your customers are not always the most accurate models. In some cases, high precision might be more important than recall, while for others, the queue rate will be most important. At this point, we need to introduce another kind of metric that will act as a bridge between technical metrics and business requirements: business metrics.

Applying business metrics

While technical metrics may be essential in the model-development process, they do not speak the language of business. A bunch of confusion tables with the F1 score will rarely impress your customers or stakeholders. They are more concerned with the problem that the model will solve than with its internals. They won't be interested in the false positive rate, but they will listen when you will talk about the money that the model would save them in the next quarter. Therefore, designing a business metric is important. Your project will need a quality measure that is crystal clear for all key stakeholders, with or without experience in data science. If you are in the business environment, a good start would be to look at the **key performance indicators** (**KPI**) of business processes you are trying to improve using machine learning. It is likely that you will find a ready-to-use business metric.

At this point, we conclude an introduction to technical metrics. There are many more ways to test classification and regression models, all with pros and cons. Enumerating and describing them all would take a book in itself and would be unnecessary because we have already achieved our goal. Armed with new concepts from this chapter, you now understand the general flow of how to evaluate a machine learning model before testing it in real-world conditions. Now you can use offline model testing to check the model's quality before deploying the model. Next, we will explore online testing to complete your understanding of a model's quality assessment.

Online model testing

Even a great offline model testing pipeline won't guarantee that the model will perform exactly the same in production. There are always risks that can affect your model performance, such as the following:

- **Humans**: We can make mistakes and leave bugs in the code.
- **Data collection**: Selection bias and incorrect data-collection procedures may disrupt true metric values.
- **Changes**: Real-world data may change and deviate from your training dataset, leading to unexpected model behavior.

The only way to be certain about model performance in the near future is to perform a live test. Depending on the environment, such test may introduce big risks. For example, models that assess airplane engine quality or patient health would be unsuitable for real-world testing before we become confident in their performance.

When the time for a live test comes, you will want to minimize risks while making statistically valid conclusions. Thankfully, there is a statistical framework for that purpose known as hypothesis testing. When performing a hypothesis test, you check the validity of some idea (hypothesis) by collecting data and executing a statistical test. Imagine you need to check whether your new advertising model increases revenues from the ad service. To do this, you randomly split all your clients into two groups: one group uses the old advertising algorithm, while the others see ads recommended by a new algorithm. After you have collected a sufficient volume of data, you compare two groups and measure differences between them. Why do we need to bother with statistics, you may ask?

Because we can answer the following questions only with the help of stats:

- How should I sort (sample) individuals into each group? Can my sampling process distort results of the test?
- What is the minimum number of clients in each group? Can random fluctuations in the data affect my measurements?
- How long should I run the test for to get a confident answer?
- What formula should I use to compare results in each group?

The experiment setup for a hypothesis test splits test targets into two groups on purpose. We can try to use a single group instead. For instance, we can take one set of measurements with the old model. After the first part of the experiment is finished, we can deploy the new algorithm and measure its effect. Then, we compare two measurements made one after another. What could go wrong? In fact, the results we get wouldn't mean anything. Many things could have changed in between our measurements, such as the following:

- User preferences
- General user mood
- Popularity of our service
- Average user profile
- Any other attribute of users or businesses

All these hidden effects could affect our measurements in unpredictable ways, which is why we need two groups: test and control. We must select these groups in such a way that the only difference between them is our hypothesis. It should be present in the test group and missing from the control group. To illustrate, in medical trials, control groups are the ones who get the placebo. Suppose we want to test the positive effect of a new painkiller. Here are some examples of bad test setups:

- The control group consists only of women.
- The test and control groups are in different geographical locations.
- You use biased interviews to preselect people for an experiment.

The easiest way to create groups is random selection. Truly random selection may be hard to do in the real world, but is easy if you deal with internet services. There, you may just randomly decide which version of your algorithm to use for each active user. Be sure to always design experiment setups with an experienced statistician or data scientist, as correct tests are notoriously hard to execute, especially in offline settings.

Statistical tests check the validity of a null hypothesis, that is, that the results you got are by chance. The opposite result is called an alternative hypothesis. For instance, here is the hypothesis set for our ad model test:

- **Null hypothesis**: The new model does not affect the ad service revenue.
- **Alternative hypothesis**: The new model affects the ad service revenue.

Typically, a statistical test measures the probability of a null hypothesis being true. If the chances are low, then the alternative hypothesis is true. Otherwise, we accept the null hypothesis. If, according to a statistical test, the probability that the new model does not affect service revenue would be 5%, we would say that we accept the alternative hypothesis at a 95% confidence level. This means the model affects the ad service revenue with a 95% probability. The significance level for rejecting the null hypothesis depends on the level of risk you want to take. For an ad model, a 95% significance may be enough, while no less than a 99% significance is satisfactory for a model that tests patient health conditions.

The most typical hypothesis test is comparing two means. If we use this test in our ad model example, we would measure average revenues with and without the new ranking algorithm. We may accept or reject the null hypothesis using a test statistic when the experiment is finished.

The amount of data you need to collect for conducting a hypothesis test depends on several factors:

- **Confidence level**: The more statistical confidence you need, the more data is required to support the evidence.
- **Statistical power**: This measures the probability of detecting a significant difference, if one exists. The more statistical power your test has, the lower the chance of false negative responses.
- **Hypothesized difference and population variance**: If your data has large variance, you need to collect more data to detect a significant difference. If the difference between the two means is smaller than population variance, you would need even more data.

You can see how different test parameters determine their data hunger in the following table:

Confidence level	Statistical power	Hypothesized difference	Population variance	Recommended sample size
95%	90%	$10	$100	22 ad demonstrations to clients
99%	90%	$10	$100	30 ad demonstrations to clients
99%	90%	$1	$100	2,976 ad demonstrations to clients

While powerful, hypothesis tests have limitations: you need to wait until the experiment ends before you can apply its results. If your model is bad, you won't be able to reduce damage without compromising the test procedure. Another limitation is that you can test only one model at a time with a single hypothesis test.

In situations where you can trade off statistical rigor for speed and risk-aversion, there is an alternative approach called **Multi-Armed Bandits** (**MABs**). To understand how MABs work, imagine yourself inside a casino with lots of slot machines. You know that some of those machines yield better returns than others. Your task is to find the best slot machine with a minimal number of trials. Thus, you try different (multi) arms of slot machines (bandits) to maximize your reward. You can extend this situation to testing multiple ad models: for each user, you must find a model that is most likely to increase your ad revenue.

The most popular MAB algorithm is called an epsilon-greedy bandit. Despite the name, the inner workings of the method are simple:

1. Select a small number called **epsilon**. Suppose we have chosen 0.01.
2. Choose a random number between 0 and 1. This number will determine whether MAB will explore or exploit a possible set of choices.
3. If the number is lower or equal to epsilon, make a choice at random and record a reward after making an action tied to your choice. We call this process exploration – MAB tries different actions at random with a low probability to find out their mean reward.
4. If your number is greater than epsilon, make the best choice according to the data you have collected. We call this process exploitation – MAB exploits knowledge it has collected to execute an action that has the best expected reward. MAB selects the best action by averaging all recorded rewards for each choice and selecting a choice with the greatest reward expectation.

Frequently, we start with large values of epsilon and decrease it to smaller values. In this way, MAB explores lots of random choices at the start and exploits the most profitable actions toward the end. The exploration frequency is gradually diminishing, becoming closer to zero.

When you first launch MAB, it collects rewards from random actions. As time passes, you will see that average rewards for all choices converge to their true values. The major benefit of MABs is that they change their behavior in real time. While someone is waiting for a hypothesis test results, MAB gives you a changing picture while covering to the best choice. Bandits are one of the most basic reinforcement learning algorithms. Despite their simplicity, they can provide good results.

We now have two new testing approaches to use. How do we choose between them? Unfortunately, there is no simple answer. Hypothesis tests and MABs pose different constraints on data, sampling processes, and experiment conditions. It is better to consult an experienced statistician or a data scientist before deciding. Mathematical constraints are not the only things that affect the choice; the environment is also important. MABs are easy to apply in situations where you can test different choices on random individuals from the whole population. This may be very convenient when testing models for a large online retailer, but is impossible for clinical trials, where you are better to apply hypothesis testing. Let's see a rule of thumb for choosing between MABs and hypothesis tests:

- MABs are better suited to environments where you need to test many alternatives with a limited set of resources. You trade off statistical rigor for efficiency when using MABs. MABs can take a lot of time to converge, gradually improving over time.
- You should apply hypothesis tests if you have only one alternative, if your trial involves great risks, or if you need a statistically-rigorous answer. Hypothesis tests take a fixed amount of time and resources to complete, but impose larger risks than MABs.

While testing models in an online setting is extremely important for making sure that your offline test results stay true after the deployment stage, there is still a danger zone that we have not covered. Abrupt and unexpected changes in data can severely affect or even break the deployed model, so it is also important to monitor incoming data quality.

Online data testing

Even after performing successful online tests, you are not fully guarded against unexpected issues with model operation. Machine learning models are sensitive to incoming data. Good models have a certain degree of generalization, but significant changes in data or underlying processes that generate data can lead the model predictions astray. If online data significantly diverges from test data, you can't be certain about model performance before performing online tests. If the test data differs from the training data, then your model won't work as expected.

To overcome this, your system needs to monitor all incoming data and check its quality on the fly. Here are some typical checks:

- Missing values in mandatory data fields
- Minimum and maximum values
- Acceptable values of categorical data fields
- String data formats (dates, addresses)
- Target variable statistics (distribution checks, averages)

Summary

In this chapter, we answered a very important question: what does it mean for a model to work correctly? We explored the nature of errors and studied metrics that can quantify and measure model errors. We drew a line between offline and online model testing and defined testing procedures for both types. We can perform offline model testing using train/validation/test data splits and cross-validation. For online testing, we can choose between hypothesis tests and MABs.

In the next chapter, we will look into the inner workings of data science. We will dive into the main concepts behind machine learning and deep learning, giving an intuitive understanding of how machines learn.

Understanding AI 3

You now have a good understanding of what data science can do and how we can check whether it works. We have covered the main domains of data science, including machine learning and deep learning, but still, the inner workings of the algorithms are difficult to discern through the fog. In this chapter, we will look at algorithms. You will get an intuitive understanding of how the learning process is defined using mathematics and statistics. Deep neural networks won't be so mystical anymore, and common machine learning jargon will not scare you but provide understanding and ideas to complete the ever-growing list of potential projects.

You are not the only one who will benefit from reading this chapter. Your new knowledge will streamline communication with colleagues, making meetings short and purposeful and teamwork more efficient. We will start at the heart of every machine learning problem: defining the learning process. To do this, we will start with the two subjects that lie at the root of data science: mathematics and statistics.

In this chapter, we will be covering the following topics:

- Understanding mathematical optimization
- Thinking with statistics
- How do machines learn?
- Exploring machine learning
- Exploring deep learning

Understanding mathematical optimization

First, we will explore the concept of mathematical optimization. Optimization is the central component of machine learning problem. It turns out that the learning process is nothing more than a mere mathematical optimization problem. The trick is to define it properly. To come up with a good definition, we first need to understand how mathematical optimization works and which problems it can solve.

If you work in the business sector, I bet that you hear the word optimization several times a day. To optimize something means to make it more efficient, cut costs, increase revenues, and minimize risks. Optimization involves taking a number of actions, measuring results, and deciding whether you have ended up in a better place.

For example, to optimize your daily route to work, you can minimize the total time you spend driving from home to the office. Let's suppose that in your case the only thing that matters is time. Thus, optimization means minimization of the time. You may try different options such as using another road or going by public transport instead of driving your car. To choose the best, you will evaluate all routes using the same quantity, that is, the total time to make it from home to the office.

To get a better idea of defining optimization problems, let's consider another example. Our friend Jonathan was tired of his day-to-day job at a bank, so he has started a rabbit farm. It turns out that rabbits breed fast. To start, he bought four rabbits, and after a while he had 16. A month later, there were 256 of them. All of those new rabbits causing additional expense. Jonathan's rabbit sale rates fell lower than the rate at which the rabbits bred. Jonathan's smart farmer friend Aron was impressed with his rabbit production rates, so he proposed to buy all excess rabbits for a discounted price. Now, Jonathan needs to find out how many rabbits to sell to Aron so that he can keep within the following boundaries:

- He won't get in a situation where he can't sell a rabbit to someone who desperately wants one. The rabbit breeding rate should not fall below the rabbit selling forecasts.
- His total expenses for rabbit care stay within the budget.

As you can see, we have defined another optimization problem, and the rabbit farm started to remind the bank job that Jonathan left before. This optimization task is quite different though, it looks harder. In the first problem, we tried to minimize commuting time. In this problem, we need to seek the minimum amount of rabbits to sell so it does not violate other conditions. We call problems like these **constrained optimization**. Additional constraints allow us to model more realistic scenarios in complex environments. To name a few, constrained optimization can solve planning, budgeting, and routing problems. In the end, Jonathan was disappointed with his rabbit farm and sold it to Aron. He then continued his path of finding a perfect occupation that wouldn't end up similar to his banking job.

There is one place where profits and losses cease making you mad; that is the mathematics department at a technical university. To get a position there, they ask you to pass an exam. The first task is to find a minimum of a function, $f(x) = x^2$.

The following is the plot of this function:

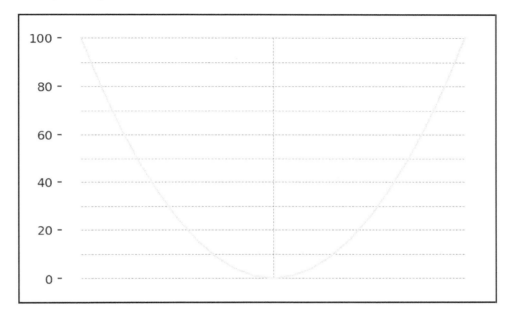

While examining the plot, you notice that this function takes values no less than 0, so the answer is obviously 0. The next question looks like the previous one but with a twist—*Find a minimum of the function* $f(x) = a + x^2$, *where* a *is an arbitrary number*. To solve it, you draw a bunch of plots and find out that the minimum value is always a.

The last question takes it to the extreme. It says that you won't be given a formula for $f(x)$, but you can go to your teacher and ask for values of f for some x as many times as you want. It is impossible to draw a plot. In other plots, the minimum was always the lowest point. How can we find that point without looking at the plot? To tackle this problem, we will first imagine that we have a plot of this function.

First, we will draw a line between two arbitrary points of the function, as seen in the following plot:

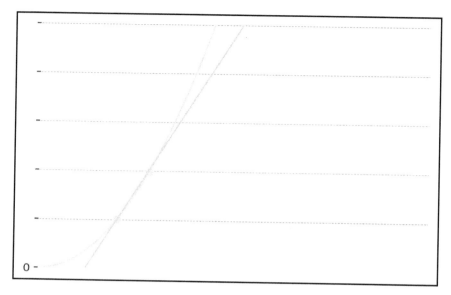

We will call the distance between those points ϵ. If we make ϵ smaller and smaller, two points will be so close that they will visually converge to a single point:

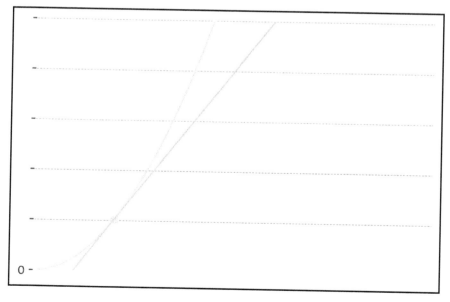

The line in the preceding plot is called a tangent. It has a very convenient property, and the slope of this line can help us find the minimum or maximum of a function. If the line is flat, then we have found either the minimum or maximum of a function. If all nearby points are higher, then it should be a maximum. If all nearby points are lower, then this is the minimum.

The following plot shows a function (drawn in blue) and its maximum, along with the tangent (drawn in orange):

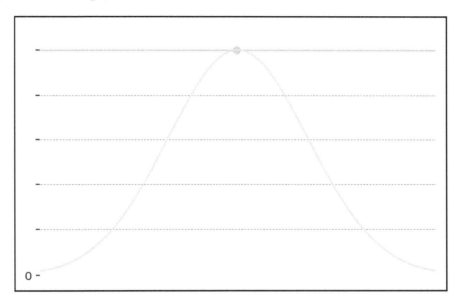

Drawing a bunch of lines and points becomes mundane after a while. Thankfully, there is a simple way to compute a slope of this line between $f(x)$ and $f(x + \epsilon)$. If you recall the Pythagorean theorem, you will quickly find an answer: $\frac{f(x + \epsilon) - f(x)}{\epsilon}$. We can easily find the slope using this formula.

Congratulations, we have just invented our first mathematical optimization algorithm, a gradient descent. As always, the name is scary, but the intuition is simple. To have a good understanding of function optimization, imagine that you are standing on a large hill. You need to descend from it with your eyes closed. You will probably test the area around you by moving your feet around. When you feel a descending direction, you will take a step there and repeat. In mathematical terminology, the hill would be a function, $f(x)$. Each time you evaluate a slope, you calculate the gradient of the function, $\Delta f(x)$. You can follow this gradient to find the minimum or maximum of a function. That's why it is called gradient descent.

You can solve the final task by using gradient descent. You can choose a starting point, x_0, ask for the value of $f(x_0)$, and calculate the slope using the small number, ϵ. By looking at the slope, you can decide whether your next pick, x_1, should be greater or less than x_0. When the slope becomes zero, you can test whether your current value of $f(x)$ is the minimum or maximum by looking at several nearby values. If every value is less than $f(x)$, then x is the maximum. Otherwise, it is a minimum.

As always, there is a caveat. Let's examine this function:

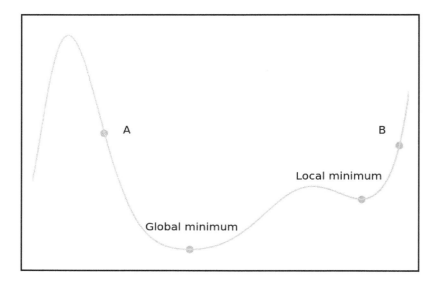

If we start gradient descent at point **A**, we will end up with a real minimum. But if we start at point **B**, we will be stuck at the local minimum. When you use gradient descent, you can never actually know whether you are in a local or global minimum. One way to check is to repeat the descent from various points that are far away from each other. The other way to avoid local minima is to increase the step size, ϵ. But be careful; if ϵ is too large, you will just jump over the minima again and again, never reaching your true goal, the global minimum.

Like in machine learning, there are many mathematical optimization algorithms with different trade-offs. Gradient descent is one of the simplest and easiest to get started with. Despite being simple, gradient descent is commonly used to train machine learning models.

Let's review a few key points before moving on:

- Mathematical optimization is the central component of machine learning.
- There are two kinds of optimization problems: constrained and unconstrained.
- Gradient descent is a simple and widely applied optimization algorithm. To understand the intuition behind gradient descent, recall the hill descent analogy.

Now you have a good grip on the main principles of mathematical optimization in your tool belt, we can research the field of statistics—the grandfather of machine learning.

Thinking with statistics

Statistics deal with all things about data, namely, collection, analysis, interpretation, inference, and presentation. It is a vast field, incorporating many methods for analyzing data. Covering it all is out of the scope of this book, but we will look into one concept that lies at the heart of machine learning, that is, **maximum likelihood estimation** (**MLE**). As always, do not fear the terminology, as the underlying concepts are simple and intuitive. To understand MLE, we will need to dive into probability theory, the cornerstone of statistics.

To start, let's look at why we need probabilities when we already are equipped with such great mathematical tooling. We use calculus to work with functions on an infinitesimal scale and to measure how they change. We developed algebra to solve equations, and we have dozens of other areas of mathematics that help us to tackle almost any kind of hard problem we can think of. We even came up with category theory that provides a universal language for all mathematics that almost no one can understand (Haskell programmers included).

The difficult part is that we all live in a chaotic universe where things can't be measured exactly. When we study real-world processes we want to learn about many random events that distort our experiments. Uncertainty is everywhere, and we must tame and use it for our needs. That is when probability theory and statistics come into play. Probabilities allow us to quantify and measure uncertain events so we can make sound decisions. Daniel Kahneman showed in his widely known book *Thinking, Fast and Slow*, that our intuition is notoriously bad in solving statistical problems. Probabilistic thinking helps us to avoid biases and act rationally.

Frequentist probabilities

Imagine that a stranger suggested you play a game: he gives you a coin. You toss it. If it comes up heads, you get $100. If it is tails, you lose $75. Before playing a game, you will surely want to check whether or not it is fair. If the coin is biased toward tails, you can lose money pretty quickly. How can we approach this? Let's conduct an experiment, wherein we will record 1 if heads come up and 0 if we see tails. The fun part is that we will need to make 1,000 tosses to be sure that our calculations are right. Imagine we got the following results: 600 heads (1s) and 400 tails (0s). If we then count how frequent heads or tails came up in the past, we will get 60% and 40%, respectively. We can interpret those frequencies as probabilities of a coin coming up heads or tails. We call this a frequentist view on the probabilities. It turns out that our coin is actually biased toward heads. The expected value of this game can be calculated by multiplying probabilities with their values and summing everything up (the value in the following formula is negative because $40 is a potential loss, not gain):

$$0.6 \times 100 - 0.4 \times 0.75 = \$30$$

The more you play, the more you get. Even after having several consecutive unlucky throws in a row, you can be sure that the returns will average out soon. Thus, a frequentist probability measures a proportion of some event to all other possible events.

Conditional probabilities

It is handy to know the probability of an event given some other event has occurred. We write the conditional probability of an event A given event B as $P(A|B)$. Take rain, for example:

- What is the probability of rain given we hear thunder?
- What is the probability of rain given it is sunny?

In the following diagram, you can see the probabilities of different events occurring together:

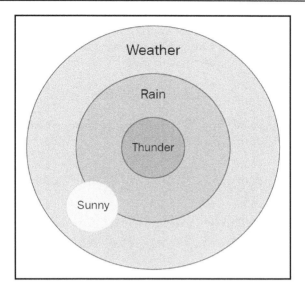

From this Euler diagram, we can see that $P(Rain|Thunder) = 1$, meaning that there is always rain when we hear thunder (yes, it is not exactly true, but we'll take this as true for the sake of simplicity).

What about $P(Rain|Sunny)$? Visually, this probability is small, but how can we formulate this mathematically to do the exact calculations? Conditional probability is defined as follows:

$$P(Rain|Sunny) = \frac{P(Sunny, Rain)}{P(Sunny)}$$

In words, we divide the joint probability of both *Rain* and *Sunny* by the probability of sunny weather.

Dependent and independent events

We call a pair of events independent, if the probability of one event does not influence the other. For example, take the probability of rolling a die and getting a 2 twice in a row. Those events are independent. We can state this as follows:

$$P(roll2) = P(roll2_{1st\ time})P(roll2_{2nd\ time})$$

But why does this formula work? First, let's rename events for the first and second tosses as A and B to remove notational clutter and then rewrite the probability of a roll explicitly as a joint probability of both rolls we have seen so far:

$$P(A, B) = P(A)P(B)$$

And now multiply and divide $P(A)$ by $P(B)$ (nothing changes, it can be canceled out), and recall the definition of conditional probability:

$$P(A) = \frac{P(A)P(B)}{P(B)} = \frac{P(A, B)}{P(B)} = P(A|B)$$

If we read the previous expression from right to left, we find that $P(A|B) = P(A)$. Basically, this means that A is independent of B! The same argument goes for $P(B)$.

Bayesian view on probability

Before this point, we always measured probabilities as frequencies. The frequentist approach is not the only way to define probabilities. While frequentists think about probabilities as proportions, the Bayesian approach takes prior information into account. Bayes' theory is centered around a simple theorem that allows us to compute conditional probabilities based on prior knowledge:

$$P(Sunny|Rain) = \frac{P(Sunny)P(Rain|Sunny)}{P(Rain)}$$

In this example, the prior value is $P(Rain|Sunny)$. If we do not know the real prior value, we can substitute an estimate that is based on our experience to make an approximate calculation. This is the beauty of Bayes' theorem. You can calculate complex conditional probabilities with simple components.

Bayes' theorem has immense value and a vast area of application. The Bayesian theory even has its own branch of statistics and inference methods. Many people think that the Bayesian view is a lot closer to how we humans understand uncertainties, in particular, how prior experience affects decisions we make.

Distributions

Probabilities work with sets of outcomes or events. Many problems we describe with probabilities share common properties. In the following plot, you can see the bell curve:

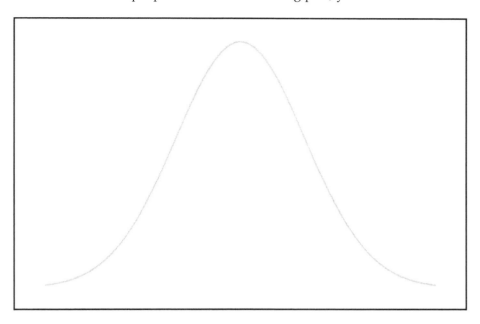

The bell curve, or Gaussian distribution, is centered around the most probable set of outcomes, and the tails on both ends represent the least likely outcomes. Because of its mathematical properties, the bell curve appears everywhere in our world. Measure the height of lots of random people, and you will see a bell curve; look at the height of all grass blades in your lawn, and you will see it again. Calculate the probability of people in your city having a certain income, and here it is again.

The Gaussian distribution is one of the most common distributions, but there are many more. A probability distribution is a mathematical law that tells us the probabilities of different possible outcomes of events formulated as a mathematical function.

When we measured relative frequencies of a coin-toss event, we calculated the so-called empirical probability distribution. Coin tosses also can be formulated as a Bernoulli distribution. And if we wanted to calculate the probability of heads after n trials, we may use a binomial distribution.

It is convenient to introduce a concept analogous to a variable that may be used in probabilistic environments—a random variable. Random variables are the basic building blocks of statistics. Each random variable has a distribution assigned to it. Random variables are written in uppercase by convention, and we use the ~ symbol to specify a distribution assigned to a variable:

$$X \sim Bernoulli(0.6)$$

This means that the random variable X is distributed according to a Bernoulli law with the probability of success (heads) equal to 0.6.

Calculating statistics from data samples

Suppose you are doing research on human height and are eager to publish a mind-blowing scientific paper. To complete your research, you need to measure the average person's height in your area. You can do this in two ways:

- Collect the heights of every person in your city and calculate average
- Apply statistics

Statistics allows us to reason about different properties of the population without collecting a full dataset for each person in the population. The process of selecting a random subset of data from the true population is called sampling. A statistic is any function that is used to summarize the data using values from the sample. The ubiquitous statistic that is used by almost everyone on a daily basis is the sample mean or arithmetic average:

$$\bar{x} = \frac{1}{n} \sum_{i=1}^{n} x_i$$

We have collected a random sample of 16 people to calculate an average height. In the following table, we can see the heights over the course of four days:

Day	Heights	Average
Monday	162 cm, 155 cm, 160 cm, 171 cm	162.00 cm
Tuesday	180 cm, 200 cm, 210 cm, 179 cm	192.25 cm
Wednesday	160 cm, 170 cm, 158 cm, 176 cm	166.00 cm
Thursday	178 cm, 169 cm, 157 cm, 165 cm	167.25 cm
Total		171.88 cm

We collected a sample of four heights for each day, a total of 16 heights. Your statistician friend Fred told you on Friday that he had already collected a sample of 2,000 people and the average height in the area was about 170 cm.

To investigate, we can look at how your sample average changed with each new data point:

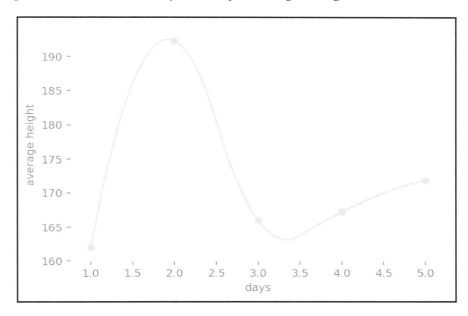

Notice, that on day 2, the average value was unexpectedly high. It may just have happened that we had stumbled upon four tall people. The random fluctuations in the data are called variance.

We can measure sample variance using the following formula:

$$s^2 = \frac{1}{n-1} \sum_{i=1}^{n} (x_i - \bar{x})^2$$

Sample variance summarizes our data, so we can consider it as another statistic. The larger the variance is, the more sample size you need to collect before calculating the accurate average value, which will be close to the real one. This phenomenon has a name—the law of large numbers. The more measurements you make, the better your estimate will be.

Statistical modeling

Statistics is more than simply calculating summary numbers. One of the most interesting aspects of statistics is modeling. Statistical modeling studies mathematical models that make a set of statistical assumptions about data. To be more clear, let's return to our weather example. We have collected a dataset with random variables that describe the current weather:

- Average speed of the wind
- Air humidity
- Air temperature
- Total number of birds seen in the sky in a local area
- Statistician's mood

Using this data, we want to infer which variables are related to rain. To do this, we will build a statistical model. Besides the previous data, we have recorded a binary rain variable that takes the value 1 if it rained, and 0 otherwise.

Now, we pose a set of assumptions in relation to the data:

- Rain probability has a Bernoulli distribution.
- Rain probability depends on data we have collected. In other words, there is a relationship between the data and rain probability.

You may find it strange thinking about rain in terms of probability. What does it mean to say that last Wednesday, the probability of rain was 45%? Last Wednesday is a past date, so we can examine the data and check whether there was rain. The trick is to understand that in our dataset, there are many days similar to Wednesday. Let's suppose that we have collected the following values:

Day of week	Speed of wind	Humidity	Temperature	Outcome
Monday	5 m/s	50%	30 C	no rain
Tuesday	10 m/s	80%	25 C	rain
Wednesday	5 m/s	52%	28 C	rain
Thursday	3 m/s	30%	23 C	no rain
Friday	8 m/s	35%	27 C	no rain

In this example, Monday and Wednesday are very similar, but their rain outcomes are different. In a sufficiently large dataset, we could find two rows that match exactly but have different outcomes. Why is this happening? First, our dataset does not include all the possible variables that can describe rain. It is impossible to collect such a dataset, so we make an assumption that our data is related to rain, but does not describe it fully. Measurement errors, the randomness of events, and incomplete data make rain probabilistic. You may wonder if rain is probabilistic in nature? Or is every period of rain predetermined? To check whether rain events are deterministic, we must collect a daily snapshot of the complete state of the universe, which is impossible. Statistics and probability theory help us to understand our world even if we have imperfect information. For example, imagine that we have 10 days similar to last Wednesday in our dataset. By similar, I mean that all variables we have collected differ only by a small amount. Out of those 10 days, 8 were rainy and 2 were sunny. We may say that on a day typical to last Wednesday there is an 80% probability of rain. That is the most accurate answer we can give using this data.

Having assumptions about data in place, we can proceed to modeling. We can make another assumption that there exists some mathematical model M, that uses data to estimate rain probability. That is, model M uses data d to learn the relationship between the data and rain probability. The model will infer this relationship by assigning rain probabilities that are closest to real outcomes in our dataset.

The main goal of model M is not to make accurate predictions, but to find and explain relationships. This is where we can draw a line between statistics and machine learning. Machine learning seeks to find accurate predictive models, while statistics uses models to find explanations and interpretations. Goals differ, but the underlying concepts that allow models to learn from data are the same. Now, we can finally uncover how this model M can learn from data. We will disentangle the magic, leaving a straightforward understanding of the mathematics behind machine learning.

How do machines learn?

How do algorithms learn? How can we define learning? As humans, we learn a lot throughout our lives. It is a natural task for us. In the first few years of our lives, we learn how to control our body, walk, speak, and recognize different objects. We constantly get new experiences, and these experiences change the way we think, behave, and act. Can a piece of computer code learn like we do? To approach machine learning, we first need to come up with a way to transmit experience directly to the algorithm.

In practical cases, we are interested in teaching algorithms to perform all kinds of specific tasks faster, better, and more reliably that we can do ourselves. For now, we will focus on prediction and recognition tasks. Thus, we want to build algorithms that are able to recognize patterns and predict future outcomes. The following table shows some examples of recognition and prediction tasks:

Recognition tasks	Is this a high-paying customer? How much does this house cost in the current market? What are those objects in an image?
Prediction tasks	Is this customer likely to return his debt in the next 6 months? How much will we sell in the next quarter? How risky is this investment?

The first idea may be to approach learning as humans do, and provide explanations and examples through speech, images, and sets of examples. Unfortunately, while learning in this way, we perform many complex cognitive tasks, such as listening, writing, and speaking. A computer algorithm by itself cannot collect new experiences the way we do. What if, instead, we take a simplified model of our world in the form of digital data? For example, predicting customer churn for Acme Co could be done only using data about customer purchases and product ratings. The more complete and full the dataset is, the more accurate the model of customer churn is likely to be.

Let's look at another example. We will build a machine learning project cost estimator. This model will use the attributes of a project to calculate the cost estimate. Suppose that we have collected the following data attributes for each project in our company:

Attribute name	Attribute type	Attribute description	Possible values
Number of attributes	Integer	Number of data attributes in the project dataset	0 to ∞
Number of data scientists	Integer	Number of data scientists requested by the customer for project implementation	0 to ∞
Integration	Integer	Integration with customer's software systems requested by the customer	0 for no integration in project scope 1 for integration in project scope

Is a large company	Integer	Indicates if the customer has a large number of employees	0 = customer's company employee number greater than 100 1 = customer's company employee number less or equal to 100
Total project cost	Integer	Total cost in USD	0 to ∞

The example dataset containing these attributes is provided in the following table:

Number of attributes	Number of data scientists	Integration	Is a large company	Total project cost
10	1	1	0	135,000
20	1	0	1	140,000
5	2	1	0	173,200
100	3	1	1	300,000

The simplest model we can imagine is a so-called linear model. It sums data attributes multiplied by variable coefficients to calculate the project cost estimate:

$$Total\ project\ cost = \ base\ cost + \ cost\ per\ data\ attribute \times number\ of\ attributes + \\ cost\ per\ data\ scientist \times number\ of\ data\ scientists + \ integration\ cost \times integration + \\ customer\ relation\ complexity\ cost \times is\ a\ large\ company$$

In this simplified scenario, we do not know the real values of cost variables. However, we can use statistical methods and estimate them from data. Let's start with a random set of parameters:

- Base cost = 50,000
- Cost per data attribute = 115
- Cost per data scientist = 40,000
- Integration cost = 50,000
- Customer relation complexity cost = 5,000

If we use the parameters for every project we have in our dataset, we will get the following results:

Total project 1 cost = 50,000 + 115 x 10 + 40,000 x 1 + 50,000 x 1 + 50,000 x 0 = 141,150

Total project 2 cost = 50,000 + 115 x 20 + 40,000 x 1 + 50,000 x 0 + 50,000 x 1 = 142,300

Total project 3 cost = 50,000 + 115 x 5 + 40,000 x 2 + 50,000 x 1 + 50,000 x 0 = 180,575

Total project 4 cost = 50,000 + 115 x 100 + 40,000 x 3 + 50,000 x 1 + 50,000 x 1 = 281,500

You have probably noticed that the values differ from the real project costs in our dataset. This means that if we use this model on any real project our estimates will be erroneous. We can measure this error in multiple ways, but let's stick with one of the most popular choices:

$$Error = \sqrt{(estimated\ project\ cost - real\ project\ cost)^2}$$

There are many ways to quantify prediction errors. All of them introduce different trade-offs and limitations. Error measure selection is one of the most important technical aspects of building a machine learning model.

For the overall error, let's take an arithmetic average of individual errors of all projects. The number that we calculated is called the **root mean squared error** (**RMSE**).

The exact mathematical form of this measure is not a consequence. RMSE has straightforward logic behind it. While we can derive the RMSE formula using several technical constraints posed on a linear model, mathematical proofs are out of the scope of this book.

It turns out that we can use optimization algorithms to tweak our cost parameters so that RMSE will be minimized. In other words, we can find the best fit for cost parameters that minimize the error for all rows in the dataset. We call this procedure MLE.

MLE gives a way to estimate the parameters of a statistical model given data. It seeks to maximize the probability of parameters given data. It may sound difficult, but the concept becomes very intuitive if we rephrase the definition as a question: what parameters should we set so the results we get will be closest to the data? MLE helps us to find the answer to this question.

Let's focus on another example to get a more general approach. Imagine that we have started a coffee subscription service. A customer chooses her favorite flavors of coffee in our mobile app and fills in an address and payment information. After that, our courier delivers a hot cup of coffee every morning. There is a feedback system built in the app. We promote seasonal offerings and discounts to clients via push notifications. There was a big growth in subscribers last year: almost 2,000 people are already using the service and 100 more are subscribing each month. However, our customer churn percentage is growing disturbingly fast. Marketing offers do not seem to make a big difference. To solve this problem, we have decided to build a machine learning model that predicts customer churn in advance. Knowing that a customer will churn, we can tailor an individual offer that will turn them into active user again.

This time, we will be more rigorous and abstract in our definitions. We will define a model **M** that takes customer data **X** and historical churn outcomes **Y**. We will call **Y** the target variable.

The following table describes the attributes of our dataset:

Attribute name	Attribute type	Attribute description	Possible values
Months subscribed	Integer	The number of months a user has been subscribed to our service	0 to ∞
Special offerings activated	Integer	The number of special offers the user activated last month	0 to ∞
Number of cups on weekdays	Float	The average number of cups the user orders on weekdays, last month	1.0 to 5.0
Number of cups on the weekend	Float	The average number of cups the user orders on weekends, last month	1.0 to 2.0

This kind of table is called a data dictionary. We can use it to understand the data coming in and out of the model, without looking into the code or databases. Every data science project must have an up-to-date data dictionary. More complete examples of data dictionaries will be shown later in this book.

Our target variable, **Y**, can be described in the following way:

Target variable name	Target variable type	Target variable description	Target variable possible values
Churn	Integer	Indicates whether the user stopped using our service last month	0 or 1

Given the customer description, x, the model outputs churn probability, $\hat{y}$. A hat over y means that $\hat{y}$ is not a real churn probability, but only an estimate that can contain errors. This value will not be strictly zero or one. Instead, the model will output a probability between 0% and 100%. For example, for some customer x, we got a $\hat{y}$ of 76%. We may interpret this value like this: based on historical data, the expectancy of this customer to churn is 76%. Or, out of 100 customers like customer x, 76 will churn.

A machine learning model must have some variable parameters that can change to better match churn outcomes. Now that we have used formulas, we can't go on without introducing at least one Greek letter. All the parameters of our model will be represented by θ.

Now, we have everything in place:

- Historical customer data X and churn outcomes Y, which we will call the training dataset X_{train}
- Machine learning algorithm M that accepts customer description x and outputs churn probability $\hat{y}$
- Model parameters θ that can be tuned using MLE

We will estimate the parameters $\hat{\theta}$ for our model M using MLE on the training dataset X_{train}. I have placed a hat on top of θ to indicate that in theory there may be the best parameter set θ, but in reality we have limited data. Thus, the best parameter set we can get is only an estimate of true that may contain errors.

Now, we can finally use our model to make predictions about customer churn probability $\hat{y}$:

$$M(x, \theta) = \hat{y}$$

The exact interpretation of probability depends heavily on the model **M** we used to estimate this probability. Some models can be used to give probabilistic interpretations, while others do not have such qualities.

Note that we had not explicitly defined the kind of machine learning model **M** we use. We have defined an abstract framework for learning from data that does not depend on the specific data or concrete algorithms it uses. This is the beauty of mathematics that opens up limitless practical applications. With this abstract framework, we can come up with many models **M** that have different trade-offs and capabilities. This is how machines learn.

How to choose a model

There are many different types of machine learning models and many estimation methods. Linear regression and MLE are among the simplest examples that show the underlying principles that lie beneath many machine learning models. A theorem called the **no free lunch theorem** says that there is no model that will give you the best results for each task for every dataset. Our machine learning framework is abstract, but this does not mean it can yield a perfect algorithm. Some models are best for one task, but are terrible for another. One model may classify images better than humans do, but it will fail at credit scoring. The process of choosing the best model for a given task requires deep knowledge of several disciplines, such as machine learning, statistics, and software engineering. It depends on many factors, such as statistical data properties, the type of task we are trying to solve, business constraints, and risks. That is why only a professional data scientist can handle the selection and training machine of learning models. This process has many intricacies and explaining all of them is beyond the scope of this book. An interested reader may refer to the book list at the end of this book. There you can find free books that explain the technical side of machine learning in great depth.

Exploring machine learning

Now that you understand the general flow of thought on how to define learning processes using mathematics and statistics, we can explore the inner workings of machine learning. Machine learning studies algorithms and statistical models that are able to learn and perform specific tasks without explicit instruction. As every software development manager should have some expertise in computer programming, the data science project manager should understand machine learning. Grasping the underlying concepts between any machine learning algorithm will allow you to understand better the limitations and requirements for your project. It will ease communication and improve understanding between you and the data scientists on your team. Knowledge of basic machine learning terminology will make you speak in the language of data science.

We will now dive into the main intuitions behind popular machine learning algorithms, leaving out technical details for the sake of seeing the wood for the trees.

Defining goals of machine learning

When we speak about machine learning we speak about accurate predictions and recognition. Statisticians often use simple but interpretable models with a rigorous mathematical base to explain data and prove points. Machine learning specialists build more complex models that are harder to interpret and often work like black boxes. Thus, many machine learning algorithms are more suited to prediction quality than model interpretability. Trends change slowly, and while more researchers look into topics of model interpretation and prediction explanation, the prime goal of machine learning continues to be the creation of faster and more accurate models.

Using a life cycle to build machine learning models

When creating machine learning models, we typically follow a fixed set of stages:

- **Exploratory data analysts**: In this stage, a data scientist uses a set of statistical and visualization techniques to have a better understanding of data.
- **Data preparation**: In this part, a data scientist transforms data into a format suitable for applying a machine learning algorithm.
- **Data preprocessing**: Here, we clean prepared data and transform it so that a machine learning algorithm can properly use every part of the data.
- **Modeling**: In this part, a data scientist trains machine learning models.
- **Testing**: In this stage, we evaluate the model using a set of metrics that measure its performance.

This process repeats many times before we achieve sufficiently good results. You can apply the life cycle to train many kinds of machine learning models, which we will explore next.

Linear models

The most basic type of machine learning models is a linear model. We have already seen a detailed example of a linear model in the previous section. Predictions of a linear model can be interpreted by looking at coefficients of a model. The greater the coefficient, the more its contribution to the final prediction. While simple, those models are often not the most accurate. Linear models are fast and computationally efficient, which makes them valuable in settings with lots of data and limited computational resources.

Linear models are fast, efficient, simple, and interpretable. They can solve both classification and regression problems.

Classification and regression trees

Classification and regression tree (**CART**) take a very intuitive approach for making predictions. CART build a decision tree based on the training data. If we use CART for a credit default risk task, we may see a model like this:

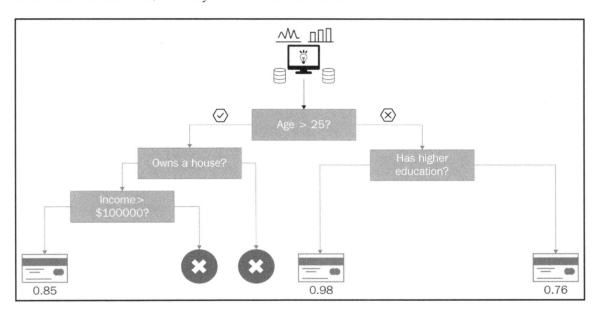

To make a prediction, an algorithm starts from the top of the tree and makes consecutive choices based on values in the data. For binary classification, at the bottom of the tree you will get a proportion of positive cases for similar customers.

While simple, CART models suffer from two disadvantages:

- Low prediction accuracy.
- There are many possible trees for a single dataset. One tree may have significantly better prediction accuracy than the other.

But how does CART choose columns and values for splits? We will explore the general logic of CART on binary classification:

1. At first, it takes a single column and divides the data into two parts for each value of this column.
2. Then it computes a proportion of positive cases for each split.
3. *Step 1* and *step 2* are repeated for each column in the data.
4. We rank each split by how well it divides the data. If the split divides the dataset perfectly, then positive cases would be for all values, lower than a threshold and negative cases would be on the other side. To illustrate, if **Age > 25** is a perfect split, then all customers younger than 25 will have credit defaults and all customers older than 25 will have a perfect credit history.
5. According to *step 4*, the best split is chosen for the current level of the tree. The dataset is divided into two parts according to the split value.
6. *Steps 1* to *5* are repeated for each new dataset part.
7. The procedure continues before the algorithm meets a stopping criterion. For example, we can stop building a tree by looking at the depth of the decision tree or the minimum number of data points available for the next split.

We can also apply CART to regression problems, although the algorithm would be slightly more complicated. CART is simple and interpretable, but it produces very weak models that are rarely applied in the practice. However, the properties of the algorithm and implementation tricks allow us to use their weakest point as their main strength. We will learn how to exploit these properties in the following section.

Ensemble models

Suppose that you own a retail store franchise. Business is growing and you are ready to build a new store. The question is, where should you build it? Selection of a building location is extremely important as it is permanent and it defines the local customer base that will go into your shop.

You have several options to make this decision:

1. Decide yourself.
2. Ask for the advice of the most competent employee.
3. Ask the opinion of many slightly less experienced employees.

Options 1 and *2* encompass one and two persons that make a decision. *Option 3* encompasses opinions of several of experts. Statistically, *option 3* is likely to yield a better decision. Even world-class experts can make a mistake. Several professionals, sharing information between each other, are much more likely to succeed. That is the reason why living in big communities and working in large organizations leads to great results.

In machine learning, this principle works too. Many models can contribute to making a single decision in an ensemble. Model ensembles tend to be more accurate than single models, including the most advanced ones. Be wary, though; you need to build many models to create an ensemble. A large number of models increase computational resource requirements quite rapidly, making a tradeoff between prediction accuracy and speed.

Tree-based ensembles

A particularly useful model for ensembles is a decision tree. There is an entire class of machine learning models devoted to different ways of creating tree ensembles. This type of model is the most frequent winner of Kaggle competitions on structured data, so it is important to understand how it works.

Trees are good candidates to build ensembles because they have high variance. Because of the randomness in a tree-building algorithm, every decision tree differs from the previous one, even if the dataset does not change. Each time we build a decision tree, we may come up with something that's different from before. Thus, each tree will make different errors. Recall the following diagram:

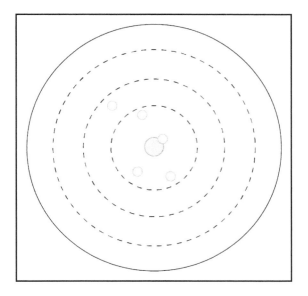

It turns out that decision trees have extremely low bias and high variance. Imagine that many different trees make hundreds of predictions for each individual, creating an ensemble. What would happen if we average all predictions? We will be a lot closer to the real answer. When used in an ensemble, decision trees can handle complex datasets with high prediction accuracy.

In the following diagram, you can see how multiple trees can create an ensemble:

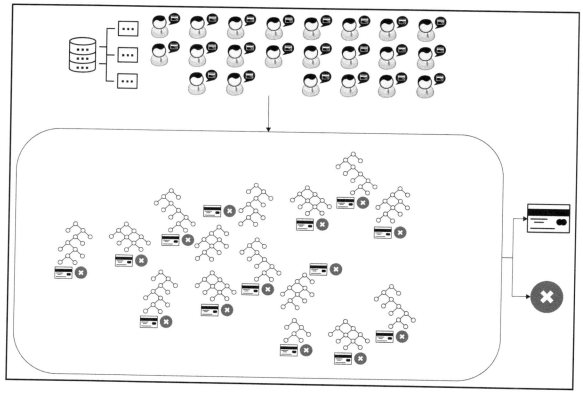

If you are working with structured data, be sure to try decision tree ensembles before jumping into other areas of machine learning, including deep learning. Nine times out of ten, the results will satisfy both you and your customer. Media often overlooks the value of this algorithm. Praise for ensemble models is rare to find, yet it is arguably the most commonly used algorithm family for solving practical applied machine learning problems. Be sure to give tree ensembles a chance.

Clustering models

Another useful application of machine learning is clustering. In contrast to other machine learning problems we have studied in this section, clustering is an unsupervised learning problem. This means that clustering algorithms can work with unlabeled data. To illustrate, let's look at a task that's central to marketing departments—customer segmentation. Coming up with marketing offers for each individual client may be impossible. For example, if you own a large retail store network, you want to apply different discounts at stores depending on customer interests to boost sales. To do this, marketing departments create customer segments and tailor marketing companies to each specific segment.

In the following diagram, you can see six customers assigned to two different segments:

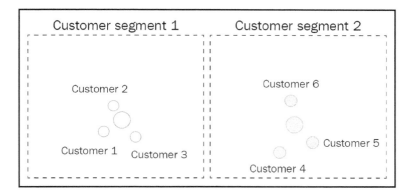

We may automate customer segmentation by taking all purchase histories for all customers and applying a clustering algorithm to group similar customers together. The algorithm will assign each customer to a single segment, allowing you to further analyze those segments. While exploring data inside each segment, you may find interesting patterns that will give insights for new marketing offers targeted at this specific segment of customers.

We can apply clustering algorithms to data in an ad hoc manner because they don't require prior labeling. However, the situation can get complicated, as many of the algorithms suffer from the curse of dimensionality and can't work with many columns in the data.

The most popular clustering algorithm is K-means. In its simplest form, the algorithm has only one parameter: the number of clusters to find in the data. K-means approaches clustering from a geometrical standpoint. Imagine each data row as a point in space. For us, this idea is easy for datasets with two or three points, but it works well beyond three dimensions. Having laid out our dataset in a geometric space, we can now see that some points will be closer to each other. K-means finds center points around which other points cluster.

It does this iteratively, as follows:

1. It takes the current cluster centers (for the first iteration, it takes random points).
2. It goes through all data rows and assigns them to the closest cluster's center point.
3. It updates cluster centers by averaging the locations of all points from *step 2*.

The algorithm is explained in the following diagram:

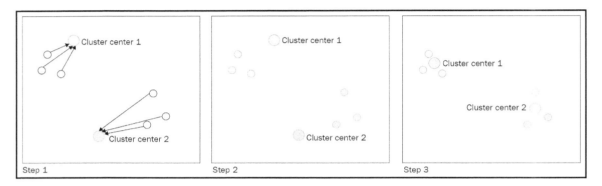

At this point, we conclude the introduction to machine learning. While there are many more machine learning algorithms to study, describing them is beyond the scope of this book. I am sure you will find that knowledge about regression, decision trees, ensemble models, and clustering covers a surprisingly large portion of practical applications and will serve you well. Now we are ready to move on to deep learning.

Exploring deep learning

Deep neural networks that classify images and play Go better than we do create an impression of extremely complex models whose internals are inspired by our own brain's structure. In fact, the central ideas behind neural networks are easy to grasp. While first neural networks were indeed inspired by the physical structure of our brain, the analogy no longer holds and the relation to physical processes inside the human brain is mostly historical.

To demystify neural networks, we will start with the basic building blocks: artificial neurons. An artificial neuron is nothing more than two mathematical functions. The first takes a bunch of numbers as input and combines them by using its internal state—weights. The second, an activation function, takes the output of the first and applies special transformations. The activation function tells us how active this neuron is to a particular input combination. In the following diagram, you can see how an artificial neuron converts the input to output:

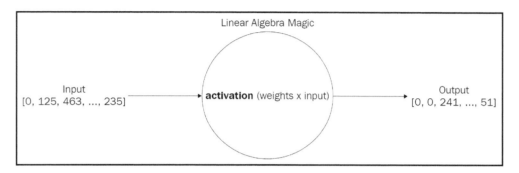

In the following diagram, we can see the plot of the most popular activation function:

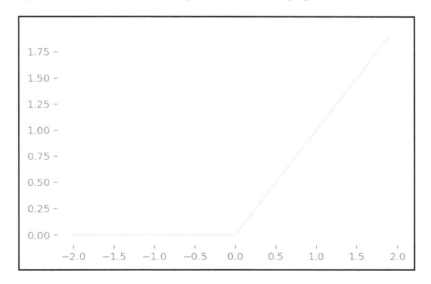

If the output is less than 0, the function will output 0. If it is greater, it will echo its input. Simple, isn't it? Try to come up with the name for this function. I know, naming is hard. Names should be simple, while conveying deep insights about the core concept of the thing you are naming. Of course, mathematicians knew this and, as we have witnessed many times before, came up with a perfect and crystal-clear name—**rectified linear unit** (**ReLU**). An interesting fact is that ReLU does not conform to basic requirements for an activation function, but still gives better results than other alternatives. Other activation functions may be better in specific situations, but none of them beat ReLU in being a sensible default.

Another important activation function you need to know about is sigmoid. You can see it in the following screenshot:

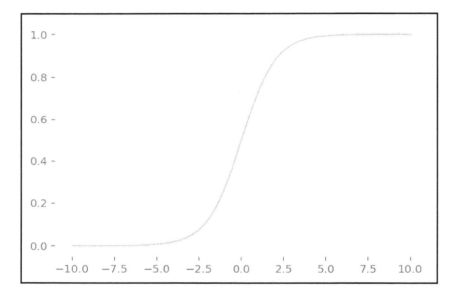

Before ReLU came to the throne, sigmoid was a popular choice as an activation function. While its value as an activation function has faded, the sigmoid is still important for another reason. It often comes up in binary classification problems. If you look at the plot closely, you will find it can map any number to a range between 0 and 1. This property makes sigmoid useful when modeling binary classification problems.

Note that we use sigmoid in binary classification problems not because it conveniently maps any number to something between 0 and 1. The reason behind this useful property is that sigmoid, also called the logistic function, is tightly related to the Bernoulli probability distribution. This distribution describes events that can happen with probability *p* between 0 and 1. For example, a Bernoulli distribution can describe a coin toss with *p = 0.5* or 50%. As you can see, any binary classification problem can be naturally described by the Bernoulli distribution. To see how, look at the following questions: *What is the probability of a client clicking on an ad? What is the probability of a client stating a default while being in debt?* We can model these cases as Bernoulli distributions.

Now, we know the main components of an artificial neuron: weights and activation function. To make a neuron work, we need to take its input and combine it with neuron weights. To do this, we can recall linear regression. Linear regression models combine data attributes by multiplying each attribute to a weight and then summing them up. Then, apply an activation function, and you will get an artificial neuron. If our data row had two columns named *a* and *b*, the neuron would have two weights, w_1 and w_2. A formula for a neuron with ReLU activation is shown as follows:

$$Neuron\ outpt = RELU(w_0 + w_1a + w_2b)$$

Note that w_0 is a special weight called a bias that is not tied to any input.

So, an artificial neuron is just a bunch of multiplications and additions:

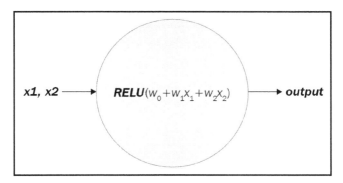

Or, to give you a more concrete example of an actual calculation, take a look at the following:

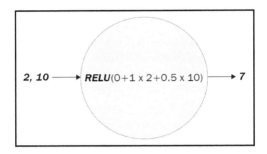

The operation of combining numbers by multiplying each term by a constant and adding the results is omnipresent in machine learning and statistics. It is called a linear combination of two vectors. You can think of a vector as a fixed set of numbers. In our example, the first vector would be a data row and the second vector would contain the weights for each data attribute.

Building neural networks

We are ready to build our first neural network. Let's start with an example: our company is struggling with customer retention. We know a lot about our customers, and we can create an offer that would make them want to stay. The problem is, we cannot identify which customers will churn. So, our boss, Jane, asks us to build a churn prediction model. This model will take customer data and predict the probability of churning in the next month. With this probability estimate, Jane can decide if she needs to create a personalized marketing offer for this client.

We have decided to use a neural network to solve this churn prediction problem. Our network will comprise multiple layers of neurons. Neurons in each layer will be connected to neurons in the next layer:

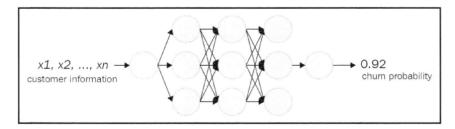

That is a lot of arrows, isn't it? A connection between two neurons means that a neuron will pass its output to the next neuron. If a neuron receives multiple inputs, they are all summed up. This type of network is called a **fully connected neural network** (**FCNN**).

We see how we can make predictions using neural networks, but how can we learn what predictions to make? If you look closer, a neural network is nothing more than a large function with lots of weights. The model prediction is determined by using weights and information incoming through the neuron inputs. Thus, to have an accurate neural network, you must set the right weights. We already know that we can use mathematical optimization and statistics to minimize prediction error by changing the parameters of a function. A neural network is nothing more than a large and complex mathematical function with variable weights. Therefore, we can use MLE and gradient descent to do the optimization. I will give the formal names of each stage in bold, followed by intuitive explanations of each stage:

1. **Network initialization**: At first, we can initialize our weights with random values.
2. **Forward pass**: We can take an example from our training dataset and make a prediction using our current set of weights.
3. **Loss function calculation**: We measure the difference between our prediction and ground truth. We want to make this difference as closely to 0 as possible. That is, we want to minimize the loss function.
4. **Backward pass**: We can use an optimization algorithm to adjust the weights so that the prediction will be more accurate. A special algorithm called backpropagation can calculate updates to each layer of neurons, going from the last layer to the first.
5. *Steps 1* to *4* are repeated until the desired accuracy level is achieved, or until the network stops learning:

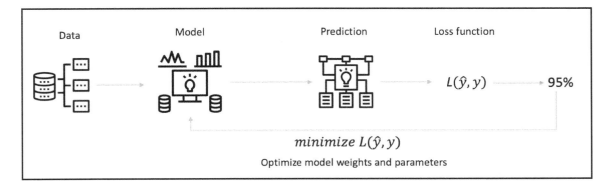

Backpropagation is the most widely used learning algorithm for training neural networks. It takes a prediction error and calculates how much we should change each weight in the network to make predictions closer to the ground truth. The name backpropagation comes from the specific way of how the algorithm updates the weights: it starts from the last layer, propagating changes to every neuron until it reaches the network input. When inputs go through the network to calculate an output prediction, we call it a forward pass. When we change the weights by propagating the error, we call it a backward pass.

Nowadays, there are many different types of building blocks that you can use to compose a neural network. Some specific neuron types work better with image data, while others can utilize the sequential nature of text. Many specialized layers were invented to improve the speed of training and fight overfitting. A specific composition of layers in a neural network devoted to solving a specific task is called a neural network architecture. All neural network architectures, no matter how complex and deep, still conform to basic laws of backpropagation. Next, we will explore the domain-specific applications of deep learning.

Introduction to computer vision

First, we will look at computer vision. Let's start with an example. Our client, Joe, likes animals. He is the happy owner of six cats and three dogs. Being a happy owner, he also likes to take pictures of his pets. Large photo archives have accumulated on his computer over the years. Joe has decided that he needs to bring order into his dreaded photo folder, containing 50,000 pet photos. To help Joe, we have decided to create a neural network that takes an image and decides whether a cat or dog is present on the photo. The following diagram shows how a neural network classifier works with a cat photo:

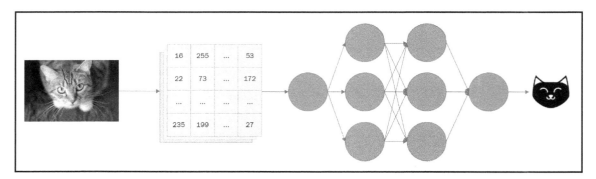

At first, we transform an image into three tables of numbers, one each for the red, green and blue channel of every pixel. If we try to use a plain FCNN as before, we will see unimpressive results. Deep neural networks shine at computer vision tasks because of a specific neuron type called a convolutional filter or a convolution. **Convolutional neural networks** (**CNNs**) were invented by a French machine learning researcher Yann LeCun. In CNNs, a single neuron can look at a small patch of an image, say, 16x16 pixels, instead of taking the entire set of pixels as an input. This neuron can go through each 16x16 region of an image, detecting some feature of an image it had learned through backpropagation. Then, this neuron can pass information to further layers. In the following illustration, you can see a single convolutional neuron going through small image patches and trying to detect a fur-like pattern:

The remarkable achievement of CNNs is that a single neuron can reuse a small number of weights and still cover the entire image. This feature makes CNNs a lot faster and lighter than regular neural networks. The idea found implementation only in the 2010s, when a CNN surpassed all other computer vision methods in an ImageNet competition, where an algorithm had to learn to classify photos between 21,000 possible categories. The development of CNNs took so long because we lacked the computational capabilities to train deep neural networks with a large number of parameters on big datasets. To achieve good accuracy, CNNs require significant amounts of data. For example, the ImageNet competition includes 1,200,000 training images.

At first layers, CNNs tend to detect simple patterns, such as edges and contours in an image. As the layer depth progresses, convolutional filters become more complex, detecting features such as eyes, noses, and so on.

In the following visualizations, you can see an example visualization of convolutional filters at different layers of the neural network:

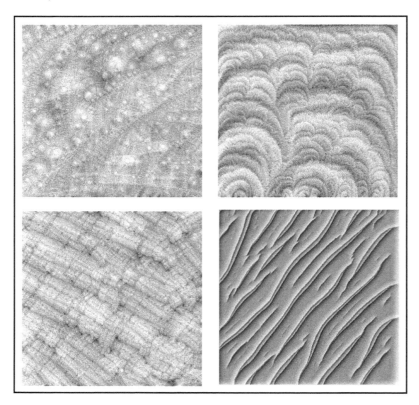

Many neurons learn to recognize simple patterns that are useful for any computer vision task. This observation leads us to a very important idea: a neural network that was trained to perform one task well can be retrained to perform another task. Moreover, you will need much less training data for the second task, as the network has already learned many useful features from the previous training dataset. In particular, if you want to train a CNN classifier for two classes from scratch, you will need to label tens of thousands of images to reach a good performance level. However, if you use a network that was pretrained on ImageNet, you will probably get good results with only 1,000 to 2,000 images. This approach is called transfer learning. Transfer learning is not limited to computer vision tasks. In recent years, researchers made significant progress in using it for other domains: natural language processing, reinforcement learning, and sound processing.

Now that you have an understanding of how deep CNNs work, we will proceed to the language domain, where deep learning has changed everything.

Introduction to natural language processing

Before the deep learning revolution, **natural language processing** (**NLP**) systems were almost fully rule based. Linguists created intricate parsing rules and tried to define our language's grammar to automate tasks such as part of speech tagging or named entity recognition. Human-level translation between different languages and free-form question answering were in the domain of science fiction. NLP systems were hard to maintain and took a long time to develop.

As with computer vision, deep learning took the NLP world by storm. Deep-learning-based NLP algorithms successfully perform near-human-level translation between different languages, can measure the emotional sentiment of a text, can learn to retrieve information from a text, and can generate answers on free-form questions. Another great benefit of deep learning is a unified approach. A single part-of-speech tagging model architecture will work for French, English, Russian, German, and other languages. You will need training data for all those languages, but the underlying model will be the same. With deep learning, we need not try to hardcode the rules of our ambiguous language. While many tasks, such as long-form writing and human-level dialogue, are yet unconquerable for deep learning, NLP algorithms are a great help in business and daily life.

For NLP deep learning, everything began with an idea: the meaning of a word is defined by its neighbors. That is, to learn a language and the meaning of words, all you need is to understand the context for each word in the text. This idea may seem to be too simple to be true. To check its validity, we can create a neural network that will predict a word by receiving surrounding words as an input. To create a training dataset, we may use any text in any language.

If we take a context window of two words, then we can generate the following training samples for this sentence:

If, we, take, a → will

We, can, following, training → generate

Following, training, for, this → samples

And so on...

Next, we need to come up with a way to convert all words to numbers, because neural networks only understand numbers. One approach would be to take all unique words in a text and assign them to a number:

Following → 0

Training → 1

Samples → 2

For → 3

This → 4

...

Then, we represent each word by a set of weights inside a neural network. In particular, we start with two random numbers between 0 and 1 for each word.

We place all the numbers into a table as follows:

Word identifier	Word vector
0	0.63, 0.26
1	0.52, 0.51
2	0.72, 0.16
3	0.28, 0.93
4	0.27, 0.71
...	...
N	0.37, 0.34

Now we have a way to convert every word in the text into a pair of numbers. We will take all numbers that we have generated as weights for our neural network. It will get four words as input, convert them into eight numbers, and use them to predict the identifier for the word in the middle.

For example, for the training sample **Following, Training, For, This → Samples**:

Input:

Following → 0 → 0.63, 0.26

Training → 1 → 0.52, 0.51

For → 3 → 0.28, 0.93

This → 4 → 0.27, 0.71

Output:

2 → Samples

We call each pair of numbers associated with a word, a word vector. Our neural network will output a vector of probabilities from zero to one. The length of this vector will match the total number of unique words in our dataset. Then, the number with the largest probability will represent the word that is the most likely completion of our input according to the model.

In this setup, we can apply the backpropagation algorithm to adjust word vectors until the model matches right words to their contexts. In our example, you can imagine each word lives on a coordinate grid. The elements of the word vector could represent X and Y coordinates. If you think about words in this geometric fashion, you may conclude that you can add or subtract word vectors to get another word vector. In the real world, such vectors contain not two but 100 to 300 elements, but the intuition remains the same. After many training iterations, you will see remarkable results.

Try to calculate the following using word vectors:

King - Man + Woman = ?

You will get a vector for the word Queen. By learning to put words into their surrounding contexts, the model learns how different words relate to each other.

The model we have built is called Word2Vec. We can train Word2Vec models in two ways:

- Predict a word by using its surrounding context. This setup is called a **continuous bag of words** (**CBOW**).
- Predict the surrounding context by word. This setup is called **Skipgram**.

The two approaches do not differ in anything, except model input and output specifications.

Word vectors are also referred to as word embeddings. Embeddings contain much more information about words than simple numeric identifiers, and NLP models can use them to achieve better accuracy. For example, you can train a sentiments classification model by following these steps:

1. Create a training dataset that contains user reviews and their sentiment, labeled 0 as negative and 1 as positive.
2. Embed the user reviews into sets of word vectors.
3. Train deep learning classifier using this dataset.

Current state-of-the-art models rarely use word embeddings created by training a separate model. Newer architectures allow learning task-specific word embeddings on the fly, without the need to use Word2Vec. Nonetheless, we have covered word embeddings in this chapter as they give us an idea of how computers can understand the meaning of a text. While modern models are more complex and robust, this idea remains intact.

The concept of embeddings originated in NLP, but now it has found applications in recommended systems, face recognition, classification problems with lots of categorical data, and many other domains.

To train a classifier that uses word embeddings, you can use a CNN. In a CNN, each neuron progressively scans the input text in windows of words. Convolutional neurons learn weights that combine word vectors of nearby words into more compact representations that are used by the output layer to estimate sentence sentiment.

You can see how a single convolutional neuron works on a single sentence in the following screenshot:

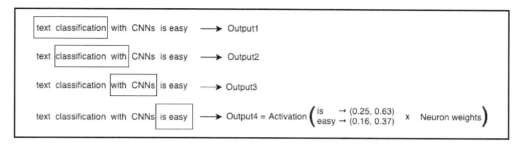

CNNs process text in a fixed window, which is an oversimplification. In reality, a word at the beginning of the sentence can affect its ending, and vice versa. Another architecture called **recurrent neural networks** (**RNNs**) can process sequences of any length, passing information from start to end. This is possible because all recurrent neurons are connected to themselves:

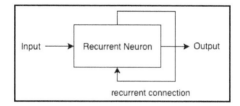

Self-connection allows a neuron to cycle through its input, pulling its internal state through each iteration:

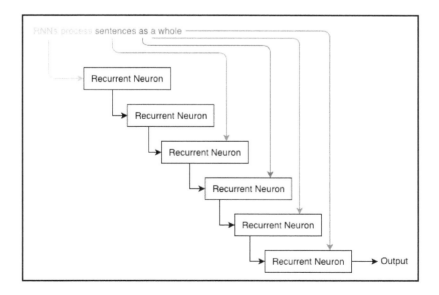

The preceding screenshot depicts a single recurrent neuron as it unfolds. With each new word, a recurrent neuron changes its previous state. When the final word is processed, it returns its internal state as the output. This is the most basic recurrent architecture. Neural networks that are used in practice have a more complex internal structure, but the idea of recurrent connections holds. When speaking about recurrent networks, you will probably hear about **long short-term memory networks** (**LSTMs**). While they differ in the details, the flow of thought is the same for both RNNs and LSTMs.

Summary

In this chapter, we uncovered the inner workings of machine learning and deep learning. We learned the main concepts of mathematical optimization and statistics. We connected them to machine learning and, finally, learned how machines learn and how we can use optimization algorithms to define learning. Lastly, we covered popular machine learning and deep learning algorithms, including linear regression, tree ensembles, CNNs, word embeddings, and recurrent neural networks. This chapter concludes our introduction to data science.

In the next chapter, we will learn how to build and sustain a data science team capable of delivering complex cross-functional projects.

Section 2: Building and Sustaining a Team

2

Data science is an innovation for most organizations. However, every innovation requires deep and careful thinking – not all ideas are equally good, and not all of them have the necessary resources for implementation. This chapter helps you to identify the best ideas and strip them down to the minimum valuable product.

Another important consideration is how successfully you can sell your idea to all stakeholders who might benefit from it.

Merging a knowledge of modern data analysis algorithms and business domain expertise is a necessary step for every project. This chapter outlines the importance of using a scientific approach in business. It helps you to answer the following questions: how can you find an efficient data science application for your business? What are business metrics and technical metrics and how should we define them? How can we introduce project goals that align well with our business?

This section contains the following chapters:

- Chapter 4, *An Ideal Data Science Team*
- Chapter 5, *Conducting Data Science Interviews*
- Chapter 6, *Building Your Data Science Team*

An Ideal Data Science Team 4

Since you are reading this book, it's likely you already understand the importance of teamwork. You can complete a complex project with a team more efficiently than in isolation. Of course, one person can build a house alone, but by working with others, they will finish the house faster, and the result will be better.

When you work with a team, everyone can specialize in performing several closely-related types of work. To explore different specialties, let's look at an example of how houses are built. Building a roof requires one set of skills, while setting up electricity is completely different. As a manager, you need to have a basic understanding of all specialties, so as to understand all components necessary for completing a task. In the *What is Data Science?* section, you were introduced to the central concepts of data science. Then, we will use this knowledge to derive roles and specialties in a data science team. In this chapter, we will define, explore, and understand different team roles as well as each role's key skills and responsibilities. We will also look at two case studies.

In this chapter, we will cover the following topics:

- Defining data science team roles
- Exploring data science team roles and their responsibilities

Defining data science team roles

Data science teams need to deliver complex projects where system analysis, software engineering, data engineering, and data science are used to deliver the final solution. In this section, we will explore the main data science project roles. The project role depicts a set of related activities that can be performed by an expert. Role-expert is not strictly a one-to-one correspondence, as many experts have the expertise to handle multiple roles at once.

An average data science team will include a business analyst, a system analyst, a data scientist, a data engineer, and a data science team manager. More complex projects may also benefit from the participation of a software architect and backend/frontend development teams.

Here are the core responsibilities of each team role:

- **Project stakeholders**: Represent people who are interested in the project; in other words, your customers. They generate and prioritize high-level requirements and goals for the project.
- **Project users**: People who will use the solution you are building. They should be involved in the requirements-specification process to present a practical view on the system's usability.

Let's look at the core responsibilities in the analysis team:

- **Business analysts**: The main business expert of the team. They help to shape business requirements and help data scientists to understand the details about the problem domain. They define business requirements in the form of a **business requirements document** (**BRD**), or stories, and may act as a product owner in agile teams.
- **System analysts**: They define, shape, and maintain software and integration requirements. They create a **software requirements document** (**SRD**). In simple projects or **Proof of Concepts** (**PoC**), this role can be handled by other team members.
- **Data analysts**: Analysis in data science projects often requires building complex database queries and visualizing data. Data analysts can support other team members by creating datamarts and interactive dashboards and derive insights from data.

Let's look at the core responsibilities in the data team:

- **Data scientists**: They create models, perform statistical analysis, and handle other tasks related to data science. For most projects, it will be sufficient to select and apply existing algorithms. An expert who specializes in applying existing algorithms to solve practical problems is called a **machine** or **deep learning engineer**. However, some projects may ask for research and the creation of new state-of-the-art models. For these tasks, a machine or deep learning researcher will be a better fit. For those readers with computer science backgrounds, we can loosely describe the difference between a machine learning engineer and research scientist as the difference between a software engineer and a computer scientist.

- **Data engineers**: They handle all data preparation and data processing. In simple projects, data scientists with data engineering skills can handle this role. However, do not underestimate the importance of data engineers in projects with serious data processing requirements. Big data technology stacks are very complicated to set up and work with on a large scale, and there is no one better to handle this task than data engineers.
- **Data science team manager**: They coordinate all tasks for the data team, plan activities, and control deadlines.

Let's look at the core responsibilities in the software team:

- **Software teams** should handle all additional requirements for building mobile, web, and desktop applications. Depending on the ramifications, the software development can be handled by a single developer, a single team, or even several teams.
- In large projects that comprise multiple systems, you may need the help of a **software architect**.

Let's now see the general flow of how roles can work together to build the final solution:

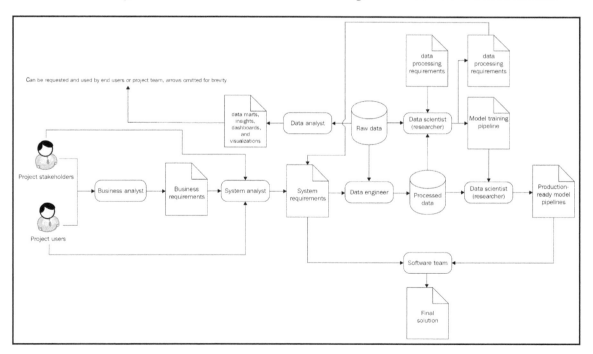

Let's look at the flow and delivery artifacts of each step:

1. The **business analyst** documents business requirements based on querying project stakeholders and users.

2. The **system analyst** documents system (technical) requirements based on business requirements and querying project stakeholders and users.

3. The **data analyst** supports the team by creating requested datamarts and dashboards. They can be used by everyone on the team in the development process, as well as in production. If the data analyst uses a Business Intelligence tool, they can build dashboards directly for end users.

4. The **data scientist (researcher)** uses documented requirements and raw data to build a model training pipeline and document data processing requirements that should be used to prepare training, validation, and testing datasets.

5. The **data engineer** builds a production-ready data pipeline based on the prototype made in *Step 3*.

6. The **data scientist (engineer)** uses processed data to build a production-ready model for training and prediction pipelines and all necessary integrations, including model APIs.

7. The **software team** uses the complete model training and prediction pipelines to build the final solution.

Please note that this process can be simplified or more granular depending on project complexity. For example, large projects may require splitting analysis experts into two groups: data and software analysis. Then, the software team will have separate requirements documentation. Simpler projects might fuse some steps or roles together, or omit them.

In the next section, we will look at how to assemble teams and assign project roles to experts depending on project complexity.

Exploring data science team roles and their responsibilities

To complete a data science project, you will need a data scientist. Can a single expert lead a project? To answer this question, we can break down data science projects into stages and tasks that are, to some extent, present in all projects.

Before starting a project, you need an idea that will allow your client to achieve their goals and simplify their life. In business, you will look to improve key business processes within a company. Sometimes, the idea is already worked out, and you may start directly from implementation, but more often, your team will be the driver of the process. So, our ideal expert must be able to come up with an idea of a data science project that will provide value for the client.

Next, we will study two project examples to look at how simple projects can be handled with small teams or even one cross-functional expert, while larger projects need more diverse teams, where each team member handles one or two specific roles.

Case study 1 – Applying machine learning to prevent fraud in banks

To explore what data science projects can be like, we will look at a case study. Mary is working as a data scientist in a bank where the fraud analysis department became interested in **machine learning** (**ML**). She is experienced in creating machine learning models and integrating them into existing systems by building APIs. Mary also has experience in presenting the results of her work to the customer.

One of the main activities of this department is to detect and prevent credit card fraud. They do this by using a rule-based, fraud detection system. This system looks over all credit card transactions happening in the bank and checks whether any series of transactions should be considered fraudulent. Each check is hardcoded and predetermined. They have heard that ML brings benefits over traditional, rule-based, fraud detection systems. So, they have asked Mary to implement a fraud detection model as a plugin for their existing system. Mary has inquired about the datasets and operators of the current fraud detection system, and the department confirmed that they will provide all necessary data from the system itself. The only thing they need is a working model, and a simple software integration. The staff were already familiar with common classification metrics, so they were advised to use F1-score with k-fold cross-validation.

In this project setup, project stakeholders have already finished the business analysis stage. They have an idea and a success criterion. Mary has clean and easy access to the data source from a single system, and stakeholders can define a task in terms of a classification problem. They have also defined a clear way to test the results. The software integration requirements are also simple. Thus, the role flow of the project is simplified to just a few steps, which are all performed by a single data scientist role:

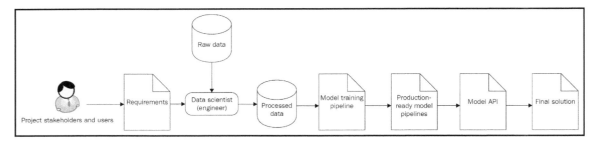

As a result, Mary has laid out the following steps to complete the tasks:

1. Create a machine learning model.
2. Test it.
3. Create a model training pipeline.
4. Create a simple integration API.
5. Document and communicate the results to the customer.

This project looks simple and well-defined. Based on this description, we can believe that Mary can handle it by herself, with little supervision.

Case study 2 – Finding a home for machine learning in a retail company

Now, let's look into another case. The retail company where our friend Jonathan works asked him to generate ideas of how they can apply data science and analytics to improve their business. Jonathan worked in retail for many years, so he knows the business side pretty well. He has also read some books and attended several data science events, so he understands the practical capabilities of data science. With knowledge of both business and data science, Jonathan can see how data science can change his environment. After writing out a list of ideas, he will evaluate them from the business viewpoint. Projects with the lowest complexity and highest value will become candidates for implementation.

The retail company has over 10,000 stores across the country, and ensuring the proper level of service quality for all stores is becoming difficult. Each store has a fixed number of staff members working full-time. However, each store has a different number of visitors. This number depends on the geographical location of the store, holidays, and possibly many more unknown factors. As a result, some stores are overcrowded and some experience a low number of visits. Jonathan's idea is to change the staff employment strategy so that customer satisfaction will rise, and the employee burden will even out.

Instead of hiring a fixed store team, he suggests making it elastic. He wants to create a special mobile application that will allow stores to adjust their staff list with great speed. In this application, a store manager can create a task for a worker. The task can be as short as one hour or as long as one year. A pool of workers will see all vacant slots in nearby stores. If a worker with the necessary skills sees a task that interests them, they can accept it and go to the store. An algorithm will prepare task suggestions for the store manager, who will issue work items to the pool. This algorithm will use multiple machine learning models to recommend tasks. One model would forecast the expected customer demand for each store. The second model, a computer vision algorithm, will measure the length of the lines in the store. This way, each store will use the right amount of workforce, changing it based on demand levels. With the new app, store employees will be able to plan vacations and ask for a temporary replacement. Calculations show that this model will keep 50,000 workers with an average load of 40 hours per week for each worker, and a pool of 10,000 part-time workers with an average load of 15 hours per week. Management considered this model to be more economically viable and agreed to perform a test of the system in one store. If the test is successful, they will continue expanding the new policy.

The next thing they ask Jonathan is to come up with an implementation plan. He now needs to decompose the project into a series of tasks that are necessary to deploy the system in one store. Jonathan prepared the following decomposition:

1. Collect and document initial requirements for the mobile app, forecasting, and computer vision models.
2. Collect and document non-functional requirements and Service Level Agreements for the system.
3. Decide on necessary hardware resources for development, testing, and production.
4. Find data sources with training data.
5. Create data adapters for exporting data from source systems.
6. Create a software system architecture. Choose the technology stack.
7. Create development, test, and production environments.
8. Develop a forecasting model (full ML project life cycle).
9. Develop a line-length recognition model (full ML project life cycle).

10. Develop a mobile app.
11. Integrate the mobile app with the models.
12. Deploy the system to the test environment and perform an end-to-end system test.
13. Deploy the system to the production environment.
14. Start the system test in one store.

Each point in this plan could be broken down further into 10-20 additional tasks. A full task decomposition for this project could easily include 200 points, but we will stop at this level, as it is sufficient for discussion purposes.

In reality, plans constantly change, so Jonathan has also decided to use a software development project management framework, such as SCRUM, to manage deadlines, requirement changes, and stakeholder expectations.

Let's now see what areas of expertise Jonathan needs to be proficient in order to complete this project. He needs to be adept in the following areas:

- Retail business
- Software project management
- Requirements-collection
- Software and hardware architecture
- Data engineering
- Data science
- Machine learning
- Deep learning and computer vision
- Mobile application development
- Backend software development
- Software integration
- Software testing
- Development operations

Can Jonathan possess all those skills on a level necessary to deliver a working software system? We can be sure that there are a few people who can do this, but it is far more likely to meet an expert who knows several closely related domains. In particular, a data engineer is likely to be good with databases, database administration, and software integration. Many data scientists are also good with backend software development. Some are proficient in creating data visualization dashboards. In terms of the role flow of the project, the full diagram can be used for this project.

In an average data science project, expect to fill in the following team roles:

- Data scientist
    - Machine or deep learning engineer
    - Machine or deep learning researcher
- Data engineer
- Data analyst
- Systems analyst
- Business analyst
- Backend software developer
- Frontend software developer
- Technical team leader
- Project manager

Depending on the project's complexity, you can merge some of these roles. The bigger your project scale, the more diverse and large your team will be. Next, we will look at the key skills and responsibilities of data science team roles.

Key skills of a data scientist

A data scientist is a relatively new profession, and vague definitions of their responsibilities are common. This uncertainty leads to many problems. Generic position descriptions on job boards are unappealing to good candidates. Professionals looking for a job won't be able to figure out what's required from them to get this position if you don't crystallize this definition in your head first. If someone goes to a job without knowing what is expected of them, it becomes even worse. Without a clear goal, or at least a clear definition, of the next milestone, your team will get lost. Defining clear responsibilities for team roles is the basis that will allow your team to function coherently.

An ideal data scientist is often described as a mix of the following three things:

- **Domain expertise**: This includes knowledge of an environment data scientists are working in, such as healthcare, retail, insurance, or finance.
- **Software engineering**: Even the most advanced model won't make a difference if it can only present pure mathematical abstractions. Data scientists need to know how to shape their ideas into a usable form.
- **Data science**: Data scientists need to be proficient in mathematics, statistics, and one or more key areas of data science, such as machine learning, deep learning, or time series analysis.

It is important to understand why each area of expertise is present in this list. We will start with the domain expertise. You are very unlikely to find a world-class business expert who can also train state-of-the-art deep learning models. The good thing is that you don't need to search for unicorns. A data scientist needs domain expertise mainly to understand data. It is also handy when working with requirements and stakeholder expectations. A basic to medium understanding of insurance business can help data scientists throughout the process of building a model.

For example, let's look at how business expertise can help to build models for an insurance company:

- Speaking with insurance experts in the same language can help to discover their pain and desires, so the data scientist can adjust their goals to achieve better results.
- Insurance expertise will help in exploring and understanding the raw data from the company's databases.
- Insurance expertise can help in data preprocessing. It aids data scientists in assembling datasets for machine learning models.

Thus, domain expertise is not the prime skill for a data scientist, but a basic to medium level of understanding can improve results by a large margin.

The next component, software engineering expertise, is often overlooked. Algorithms are often tied to the most critical processes of an organization, hence, the availability and stability requirements for these algorithms are high. Data scientists never create an abstract model. Even in research organizations, data scientists write code. And the closer you are to real-world applications, the more good code matters. Good programming skills allow data scientists to write well-architected, well-documented, and reusable code other team members can understand. Software engineering expertise enables them to build systems that do not fail under high loads and can scale from simple proof-of-concept tests to organization-wide deployments.

And last, but not least, are the data science skills. They are key tools without which no one can build a working model. However, data science is a very wide field. Be sure to understand what algorithms you will need to use, and understand what kind of expert you need. A computer vision expert won't be the best fit for a movie recommender project. If you hire a data scientist, it does not automatically mean that they are proficient in all areas of machine learning and mathematical statistics.

Key skills of a data engineer

As a project becomes more complex, managing data becomes difficult. Your system may consume data from many sources, some of them being real-time data streams, while others may be static databases. Volumes of data that your system will need to process can also be large. All this leads to the creation of a data processing subsystem that manages and orchestrates all data streams. Managing large volumes of data and creating systems that can process large volumes of data quickly requires the usage of highly specialized software stacks suited to this task.

Hence, a separate role of a data engineer emerges. The key areas of knowledge for data engineers are as follows:

- **Software engineering**
- **Big data engineering**: This includes distributed data processing frameworks, data streaming technologies, and various orchestration frameworks. Data engineers also need to be proficient with the main software architecture patterns related to data processing.
- **Database management and data warehousing**: Relational, NoSQL, and in-memory databases.

Software engineering skills are very important for data engineers. Data transformation code frequently suffers from bad design choices. Following the best practices of software design will ensure that all data processing jobs will be modular, reusable, and easily readable.

Working with big data involves creating highly parallel code, so a knowledge of distributed processing systems is also essential. Major software platforms, such as the Hadoop ecosystem, Apache Spark, and Apache Kafka, all require a good understanding of their internals to write performant and stable code.

Understanding classical relational database systems and data warehousing methodologies is also an important skill for a data engineer. Relational databases are a very frequent choice for data storage in large corporations. SQL is so widespread that we can consider it the *lingua franca* of data. So you can expect **Relational Database Management Systems (RDBMS)** to be a frequent data source in your projects. Relational databases are very good at storing and querying structured data, so there is a good chance that your project will also use them if the data volumes are moderate. Experience with popular NoSQL databases is also convenient.

Key skills of a data science manager

In this section, we will look at a few of the skills a data science manager needs to have, namely:

- **Management**: A data science team manager should have a good understanding of the main software management methodologies, such as SCRUM and Kanban. They should also know approaches and specific strategies for managing data science projects.
- **Domain expertise**: They should know the business domain well. Without it, task decomposition and prioritization becomes impossible, and the project will inevitably go astray.
- **Data science**: A good understanding of the basic concepts behind data science and machine learning is essential. Without it, you will be building a house without knowing what a house is. It will streamline communication and help to create good task decompositions and stories.
- **Software engineering**: Knowledge of basic software engineering will ensure that the manager can keep an eye on crucial aspects of a project, such as software architecture and technical debt. Good software project managers have development experience. This experience taught them to write automated tests, refactoring, and building a good architecture. Unfortunately, many data science projects suffer from bad software design choices. Taking shortcuts is only good in the short term; in the long term, they will come back to bite you. Projects tend to scale with time; as the team increases, a number of integrations grow, and new requirements arrive. Bad software design paralyzes the project, leaving you with only one option—a complete rewrite of the system.

Getting help from the development team

Creating data products is tied to creating new software systems. Large-scale projects may have many software requirements, including building a UI, developer APIs, and creating role-based workflows in your system. Be sure to get help from a software development team with software engineers, analysts, and architects when you feel that the data science team cannot handle everything by themselves. You may be good to go with a data science team if the only thing you need to build besides a machine learning model is a couple of REST services, data integration jobs, and a simple admin UI. But be sure to expand your team if you need to handle something more complex than that.

Summary

In this chapter, we first covered what a data scientist is. Then, we looked at two examples that showed us whether a data scientist can work in isolation or needs a team. Next, we looked at the various skills and qualities that a data scientist, a data engineer, and a data science manager need to have. We also briefly explored when we need to ask for help from the development team.

Finally, we defined the key domains of a data science team, which are analysis, data, and software. In those domains, we defined project roles that will allow you to create a balanced and powerful team. We may solve simple projects with small teams where team members share responsibilities for different roles. But when the project's complexity grows, your organizational structure will need to scale with it. We also noted the importance of following the best practices of software engineering and sourcing help from software development teams.

Knowing that defining responsibilities and expectations is critical for delivering complex data science projects, we will use those ideas in the next chapter, where we will explore how to create effective hiring procedures for data science teams.

5
Conducting Data Science Interviews

In this chapter, you will learn how to conduct an efficient data science interview. We will explore how a hiring process can be tied to real working experience so that the candidates you seek will clearly understand what kind of job they will need to do. The advice in this chapter will help you to get rid of unnecessary interviewing rituals and make the hiring process more efficient.

How long has it been since you went through a technical interview? Was it a pleasant experience? And if you got through it, can you judge the relevance of your interview questions to your day-to-day work? I bet that the experience was awful. The common complaints are that all interviews are stressful, and the questions are not relevant. Technical interviews are deeply flawed. We imagine that we are using a rational way of thought to pass candidates through a sieve, selecting only the stellar experts who will do the job. In fact, interviews are biased. There is almost no correlation between success in an interview and success at the actual job. I would not be surprised if random candidate selection showed better results than the hiring processes of many companies.

In this chapter, we will cover the following topics:

- Common flaws of technical interviews
- Introducing values and ethics into the interview
- Designing good interviews

Common flaws of technical interviews

If you have a software engineering background, how often have interviewers asked you to reverse a binary tree on a whiteboard, or to find a maximum subarray sum? If you come from a data science background, how many central limit theorem proofs did you lay out on a piece of paper or a whiteboard? If you are a team leader, have you asked such questions yourself? I am not implying that those questions are bad, but quite the opposite. Knowledge of core computer science algorithms and the ability to derive proofs may be important for some jobs. But for what purpose do we ask those questions? What do we want to know about the person on the other side of the table? For most companies, the ability to give answers to those questions is not relevant at all. What is the reason for asking them? Well, because stereotypical programmers must know algorithms, and data scientists must know their mathematics and statistics; this way of thinking is logical and straightforward. When we think in this way, we imagine a general collective image of a rockstar programmer and a data science wizard. Reversing binary trees may be relevant for some projects in some company, but why is it relevant for yours?

I ask you to be open-minded, critical, and honest with yourself while reading this chapter. This text will not give you secret knowledge that will improve your interviews. It will give you tools. If you invest in them, you'll get back more straightforward, simple, and enjoyable interviews that will find the right people for the right job.

Searching for candidates you don't need

Most companies are looking for rockstar developers, stellar data scientists, and consist purely of the best people in the entire world. Let's look at a data scientist job description from a real job board.

The primary focus for a candidate will be on applying different techniques (data mining/statistical analysis/build prediction systems/recommendation systems) using large company datasets. Apply machine learning models and test the effectiveness of different actions. The candidate must have strong technical expertise and be able to use a wide set of tools for data mining/data analysis methods. The candidate must be able to build and implement mathematical models, algorithms, and simulations. We seek candidates with the following skillset:

- Work with business cases: seek opportunities and leverage company data to create business solutions.
- Mine and analyze data from company databases to drive optimization and improvement of product development and sales techniques.

- Assess the effectiveness and accuracy of new data sources and data gathering.
- Extending the company's data with third-party sources of information when needed.
- Use predictive modeling to increase revenue generation, ad targeting, and other business outcomes.
- Analyze business cases and identify data sources (internal/external) and data mining/analysis methods to use.
- Develop a normalization engine to execute cleansing/deduplication for a raw data through **extract transform load** (**ETL**) process for data sources.
- Create, train, and test predictive models to solve defined business cases.
- Develop algorithms to apply to data sets.
- Design data structure models for collected data.
- Facilitate the build of a solution from **proof of concept** (**POC**) to production.
- Work with business owners to gather additional information about business cases.
- Work with data that generated by core business.
- Be ready to work in agile style (daily, sprint planning, sprint review, retrospective).
- Work in an environment that adapts quickly to creative change using agile principles.
- Actively works with different development groups inside of organization.
- Be ready to adapt a new tool/library/technology/platform.
- Excellent understanding of machine learning techniques and algorithms, such as **k-nearest neighbors** (**kNNs**), Naive Bayes, **support vector machines** (**SVM**), decision tree, clustering, artificial neural networks.
- Strong understanding of math statistics (such as distributions, statistical testing, regression, and so on).
- Experience creating and using advanced machine learning algorithms and statistical methods such as regression, simulation, scenario analysis, modeling, clustering, decision trees, neural networks, and so on.
- Proficiency in using query languages such as SQL.
- Experience working with and creating data architectures, data models, data warehouses/data lakes.
- Ability to work with minimal supervision.
- Strong data analytical skills.

- Creative and analytical thinker with strong problem-solving capabilities.
- Background in technology or professional services preferably in one or more domains of AWS, Azure, Security, or AI/ML.
- Strong understanding of consulting business.
- Strong structural work methods, multitasking, and time management skills.
- Self-driven independent work ethic that drives internal and external accountability.
- Experience with common data science toolkits and libraries, such as pandas, Keras, SciPy, scikit-learn, TensorFlow, NumPy, MatLab, and other popular data mining technologies.
- Experience using statistical computer languages (R, Python, and so on) to manipulate and draw insights from large data sets.
- Knowledge and experience using SQL language.
- Experience using Azure/AWS services.
- Experience with C++/C# as a plus.
- Based on this description, the candidate must know 4 to 5 programming languages to a level that allows them to start a POC and finish with a production-ready system. More so, machine learning, deep learning, ETL, and business analysis skills are also a must. The candidate should be able to learn any new technology not present in the list. And he/she should be self-driven and independent.

If you think about it, this is an ideal candidate. A one-man army, a unicorn. Do such people exist? Yes, but they are extremely rare. Does every company need people like this to complete their projects and achieve their goals? I will answer with a bold no. Instead of seeking the best fit for their goals, they seek the best fit for all possible goals. Being general and all-encompassing, this job search will be long, tiresome, and stressful. After reading this long list of requirements, the candidate won't be able to figure out what their job will be like. All descriptions are vague and hard to understand. This description does not give a hint about what this job will be like. The job description should give a clear listing of the following aspects:

- The future responsibilities of the candidate
- Requirements for handling these responsibilities

When the job description is vague and convoluted, testing all required skills will surely require several interview sessions, which will make the process even more tiring. Adequate assessment of multiple candidates based on this list is close to impossible. After a long search, the company will just hire someone randomly. After this, the troubles won't end. The greatest problem of this job description is a lack of direction. The employer is not sure about the candidate's functions and responsibilities. This problem is deeper than it seems to be; the job description is actually only a symptom, not the illness itself. For the new employee, the obscurity and vagueness will not end on the first day on the new job. If the employer did not fully figure out what the new employee should do, the workflow itself will become an undetermined mess. Most of the interviews and hiring processes are a rationalization of a suboptimal, stressful, and biased candidate selection process. The good thing is that we can fix these problems. The only things you will need are honesty, a clear definition of your goals, and a bit of preparation.

Discovering the purpose of the interview process

First, you should figure out why you need to do interviews. Let's do a quick exercise. Ask yourself why and write out answers until there is nothing left to say. After that, recall the last interview that you did. Was it well aligned with your goals? The results should give you an instant vector for improvement.

From the employer's side, the sole purpose of the interview is to fill the position with a capable candidate. From the side of the employee, the purpose of the interview is to find a good team, an interesting project, a reliable company to work with, and satisfactory compensation. We often forget that the interview is a dialogue, not a mere test of skill.

Unfortunately, there is no clear and ubiquitous definition of the main interview goal. That is because each goal is unique for each position. You should define this goal based on the detailed understanding of the job you are interviewing for. If you are looking for a data scientist, define rigorously what you expect them to do. What tasks will the new team member solve? Think deeply about what the first working day in this position will look like. What are the core responsibilities? What skills are useful but not mandatory? Based on that, you can start drafting a set of desired skills for the candidates. Be specific. If you demand knowledge of SQL, then be sure to have a definite reason for this requirement.

If your interview goal is to find an ideal, top 0.1 percentile, world-class expert, then think again. The primary goal is to find an able person who can do the job. It might be that this person must be the best expert in the world. If so, this requirement should be explained and justified. To create this understanding, you need to describe what the job will be like. After you decide that the description is finished, rewrite it with the candidate in mind. It should be short, easy to read, and give a complete idea of that the job will be like and what the expectations are. The ambiguity of job descriptions often comes from a lack of this understanding. *We just need someone*, their job description says. Yours should say *We know exactly what we need, and you can rely on us*. If you can't, do you really need to post a new job?

Concrete understanding of your goals will be helpful in several ways:

- You will understand what kind of expert you should search for.
- Candidates looking at your job description will know exactly what you expect of them. It will be easier to judge whether their experience is relevant or not.
- Clear goal definitions will allow you to design purposeful and insightful interview questions.

If your requirements list looks too long, try to simplify it. Maybe you were overzealous and some skills you have listed are not vital. Or perhaps you could consider hiring two people with different backgrounds? If you are posting a job description with a wide cross-functional set of requirements, be sure to have a reason behind it.

If your job description is complex, then you will find the following is true:

- The candidate search will take longer since you are demanding more skills and experience.
- The candidates will expect a higher salary.
- The interview process will be long and could extend to several sessions.
- You will have fewer options to choose from.

All those restrictions should have good supporting arguments. If you have none, consider simplifying.

Having a good goal is not all you need, the execution matters too. We will now look at the interview process from the candidate's standpoint to discuss the topics of bias and empathy.

Introducing values and ethics into the interview

We often look at interviews from a one-sided perspective. We want to find a reliable team member who can do the job well. It is easy to forget that bad interviews can scare good candidates. More so, a constant flow of potential candidates make judgments about your company through the interviews. Bad interviews lead to bad publicity. The key to effective and smooth interviews is to think about the candidate experience.

If you have successfully defined honest requirements for the candidate, the next step is to think about the interview experience as a whole. To see a new teammate in the best light, the interview should look like a real working process, not like a graduate examination.

Consider how most technical interviews are conducted:

- You go through a resume filter. The best people have PhDs and at least 5 years of (questionable) experience in major tech companies.
- You finish some kind of online test for your technical skills.
- You submit your GitHub repositories and portfolio projects for review.
- Then, you go through an online screening interview. You answer a series of technical questions related to a multitude of technologies and scientific areas that might be useful in your future work.
- Next, you find yourself in a room with a whiteboard, where you answer a set of complicated and very specific problems on software development, software architecture, machine learning, combinatorial optimization, category theory, and other important topics that are used to select the best from the best.
- Multiple people, each an expert in their field, will test you for different skills. It is likely that the interviewers will test you with tricky problems from their experience, each of which took them days to tackle.
- Finally, a company executive will see if you are a good cultural fit and go along with the company values and goals.

The only things left to add are a handful of DNA tests, IQ score filtering, a test on a lie detector, along with two checks for artistic and chess-playing abilities.

 You may find it funny, but in certain Russian companies, software developers really do need to pass a lie detector test to get on board.

If you have clearly defined the position requirements, you will already see that most of those steps are unnecessary. More so, they can bias your interview process toward people who will be a bad fit for your job.

This process is nothing like your real working experience, where the following is true:

- Interviews are intensely stressful, which significantly affects your performance.
- You are being tested on topics unrelated to the tasks you will solve in the position.
- Interview questions and home assignments are not related to tasks you will do at work.

If you could design an interview that is as close to real working experience as possible, all futile parts of the interview can go away, including prior work experience and education filters.

The interview process must respect the candidate's emotional condition and treat them as a human. It should be humanistic. The moment you start doing this, the potential candidate lists will grow and the interviews will be shorter and more effective.

 Be open-minded and clear yourself of prejudices. Some of the most talented and successful software engineers, software architects, and data scientists I have worked with had unrelated job experiences or a lack of formal education. I am not stating that those things do not matter. They do, but they are not determining factors. Correlation does not mean causation. By rejecting candidates using unnecessary pre-screening filters, you miss opportunities to meet talented people who will stay with you for many years. Of course, some organizations need pre-screening filters. For example, you would not hire a surgeon without a diploma. In some fields, such as medicine, education gives essential experience that you can't get by yourself. But the situation changes drastically with fields such as software engineering and data science, where the knowledge and experience is accessible with a few keystrokes.

At last, remember to be human. Be nice to people you are talking with. Create a pleasant experience and you will get much better results. This can be hard if you are interviewing people for the whole day, so it is better to limit yourself to one or two interviews per day at the most.

You may think such interviews will take an unreasonable amount of your time and looking at every candidate is impossible. In fact, it is the opposite. The key to designing humanistic interviews is to shift the focus from your organization to the candidate, and we will explore ways to do this in the next section.

Designing good interviews

How can we make interviews more relevant and time-intensive? An ideal interview would be testing in a real working environment for a couple of months. While there are several companies that can afford to operate without interviews, using paid probation periods instead, this is a very costly hiring strategy that not every business can afford. A good interview should serve as a substitute for real working experience. It should not be a test of a person's skill, but a test for a person's ability to perform a specific job well. If an ideal test for a candidate is a probation period, then the worst kind is a whiteboard interview (unless you are interviewing a computer science lecturer). To design a great interview, bring it as close as possible to your working process and to the issues you solve on a daily basis.

Designing test assignments

Of course, there might have been a couple of times when you or your colleagues in the same position needed to prove a theorem or implement a complex algorithm from scratch, but is it enough to include this problem in your interviewing process? If your team has encountered this problem only a few times, it deserves to be a supplementary question at most. Create most of the interview questions from the most frequent problems that your team solves daily. By no means search the web for interview questions. Your interview should be as specific as possible and generic questions will make it dull and unrelated to what you are searching for.

A frequent source of questions is the interviewer's own knowledge resources. You may have read many intricate and interesting books and blog posts. If the knowledge you gained from those materials, no matter how intellectually valuable, is unrelated to the candidate's job, please keep it out of the interview. Imagine a machine learning engineer interview where the candidate gets a question about mathematical details of the reparametrization trick in variational autoencoders when his job will be about delivering pretrained classifiers to production as scalable services.

The previous case might seem unrealistic to you, but it has happened to one of the software developers that I know. He was interviewing for a distributed system developer position. After some initial technical questions, the interviewer started asking about the subtleties of native code integration in Java applications:

Developer: *Do you integrate native code into your applications?*
Interviewer: *No.*
Developer: *That's good. Because I do not really know much about this topic.*
Interviewer: *I'd like to ask about it anyway.*

Developer: *But I know little about native code integration. And, as you said, this is not relevant. Could we move on?*

Interviewer asks the question.

This question was bad, no matter how you look at it:

- It was irrelevant to the skill requirements in this position.
- It was irrelevant to the company.
- The interviewer already knew that the candidate could not provide an answer.
- It increased the stress factor of the interview, possibly affecting the answers to the more relevant questions that followed.
- It diminished the value of this company for the candidate.

On the contrary, a good interview question should be the following:

- Related to the problems that the candidate will solve in his/her job
- As hard or as simple as the candidate's daily working experience

The largest problem of any interview question is its time span. We expect a typical interview problem to be solved in less than 10 minutes. The real working environment does not have such time constraints. To narrow the gap, you can create a test assignment. Ideally, this assignment should be implementable in 2 to 4 hours.

To create a test assignment, do the following:

1. Take a core task that is performed by similar roles (or directly by teammates with the same title) in your company.
2. Then, describe this task in one paragraph. You want your task description to be **SMART** (which stands for **specific, measurable, achievable, relevant, and time-bound**).
3. Try to estimate how long it will take to implement. Since you are basing it on a real working experience, it could take days or weeks to finish the task. Only very dedicated candidates will be ready to take on an assignment with such a time span. You can shorten its length by decomposing it into several tasks and taking only the most important ones as a part of the assignment. You can transform all additional tasks into questions that you will ask while examining the test assignment results.
4. If you have the necessary skills, complete the assignment yourself, or ask for the help of your teammates. Note that if you cannot do the assignment yourself, you will need the help of your teammates during the interview.

While doing the assignment, check everything about it:

- Is it relevant?
- Can you finish it within the expected time frame?
- Does it test all the necessary skills for the position you are interviewing for?
- Can you create additional questions about the assignment to structure the interview around it?

It may take you a few iterations before you create a good test assignment. When you are done, you will need to decide where the candidates will implement the assignment. Depending on your requirements, the candidate may implement it remotely or you may ask them to sit in your office. If the assignment takes a significant amount of time to implement and you can't strip it down further, consider paying candidates for their time. Remember: hiring candidates who are not fit for the job will cost you a lot more.

For example, we can create a test assignment for a junior data scientist. Imagine that our company provides predictive analytics services for remote education platforms. Those companies need to estimate the propensity of successfully finishing a course for each of their students. Each client collects different data about their students. Although the model building process is fairly standardized, custom data preprocessing and feature engineering are required to create classifiers with satisfiable quality for each client. Our company promises that each client will get a model with an F1 score of at least 0.85.

Junior data scientists follow a standard procedure to create and deploy a classification model. The process is well documented and explained. It comprises several stages, such as the following:

1. Get a training dataset provided by a data engineering team from the company's data portal web app.
2. Create a web-based data analysis and modeling environment using the company's self-service portal.
3. Upload data into the environment and create a holdout test set with at least 10% of the dataset.
4. Perform **exploratory data analysis** (**EDA**) and create a baseline classifier using the **gradient boosting algorithm**. Use 10-fold cross-validation for measuring the baseline F1 score.
5. Create new features from customer data and tune model parameters to improve the F1 score.
6. If you can reach an F1 validation score of no less than 0.85, measure the test score.

7. Report the results to your manager by generating a link to your environment.
8. Create a REST API using the company's guidelines if the results are approved.
9. Report the results to your manager.

The most essential skills we want to test for this position are the following:

- Ability to work with frameworks and tools our company uses for building classifiers
- Ability to build binary classifiers
- Ability to perform EDA and feature engineering on datasets similar to those we face in our daily work
- Ability to follow the process and report results
- Understanding of the reasoning behind the company's classifier building process

To create a test assignment for a junior data scientist, we may create a dataset similar to ones from our customers. The candidate's model could achieve the necessary F1 score if the candidate creates several useful features from the raw data. The ideal environment for the candidate would be our company's office, but the remote option is also acceptable. We have offered both options to each candidate.

Our junior data scientists solve similar tasks in 2 to 3 hours. They spend most of the time on *step 5*. We have decided to artificially simplify the task so it will be solvable in under 1.5 hours. Learning how to use all the company's internal tooling, including a self-service portal, generally takes up to 4 hours, so we have also decided to use widely known open source tools for the test assignment. Most of the candidates will be already familiar with this option, and all of our internal systems are compatible with open source alternatives, so this would be a viable simplification.

We have created the following test assignment description:

We give you a CSV file with customers data. We ask you to build a binary classifier for student's propensity to finish a course. The description of each column in the data file is below: [… the description is missing for breviry]. You can use the following steps to build your model:

1. Perform EDA and create a baseline classifier using the gradient boosting algorithm. Use 10-fold cross-validation for measuring the baseline F1 score.
2. Create new features from customer data and tune model parameters to improve F1 score.
3. If you can reach F1 validation score no less than 0.85, measure the test score.
4. Report results to us.

The expected time frame for this task is 1.5 hours, but you may ask for extensions. Please use the following tools to create the solution: [...].

We have also created several additional questions to check the candidate's understanding of our process:

- How does cross-validation work?
- What are the alternatives to cross-validation?
- Why did you use a **gradient boosting machine** (**GBM**) to solve this problem?
- Could you explain the general idea behind GBM? What implementations of GBM have you used previously? Could you tell us about their features?
- What is an F1 score?
- How does an F1 score differ from an accuracy score? In what situations do you prefer to use accuracy? And when does F1 work better?
- Why do we need a separate test set?

Remember that a technical assessment is not the only thing you want to check in the interview. Tell the candidate about your workflow and what your team does. Try to figure out whether the things you do will interest them enough. Highly motivated candidates who will flawlessly integrate into your workflow are often the best option even if their technical skills are inferior to those of other candidates.

To conclude, I will leave a simple rule for creating interview questions: ask questions about activities that are relevant for the daily working experience of the position you are searching for. A question should be highly abstract, theoretical, or complex only if the candidate should be able to solve such problems alone, on a daily basis (if this is so, provide an explanation why). Make interviews realistic and relevant. Ask for what you are looking for, no more and no less.

Interviewing for different data science roles

Interviewing should be a highly personal experience for each company, so providing interview templates or question sets would defeat the purpose of this chapter. However, a general checklist about what competencies and daily problems are relevant for each role of a data science project may serve you as a good first step in creating a personal and purposeful interview process.

General guidance

No matter what position you are interviewing for, you should always check for the following abilities of a candidate:

- **Information search or Google skills**: This might seem funny, but the ability to search for information is an extremely valuable skill for any technical expert. You never know what kind of algorithms, frameworks, or bugs you will encounter during a project. The ability to quickly find existing solutions and reuse the experience of the global data science community can save you spectacular amounts of time. If the candidate struggles to answer a technical question but can look up the solution and understand it, consider marking this answer as at least partially correct.

- **Communication skills**: When emulating a real workflow, take notice of the candidate's communication ability. Take notice of how he understands the task definition, asks for additional clarifications, and reports status. It is a good idea to tell the candidate that you will also be testing this set of skills beforehand and to provide a minor set of instructions. For example, you can allow and encourage intermediate communication during a take-home assignment. Many take-homes are finished in an isolated environment that is nowhere near to how we really collaborate on projects. Encouraging communication will allow you to have a glance at a real working experience with the candidate, make it an integral part of the test task.

- **Software engineering skills**: Every data science project role except the project manager needs coding skills. The better software the candidate can build, the less work will be required to integrate their piece into the whole system.

- If the candidate does not know something, it's OK. People get nervous, forget details, or lack relevant experience. Look at the interview as a two-sided process, where you are trying to work through the questions together with the candidate. Real work does not look like an examination, does it? Plus, in most cases, the person who is able to quickly work through the problem together with the team even if they don't know the solution will be valuable.

- Do not be a victim of the *curse of knowledge*. The curse of knowledge is a cognitive bias that is often seen when a person with certain knowledge assumes that others have all the necessary background to understand them well, or at least overestimates this background. Do not expect the candidate to fully understand and easily solve the problem that your team solved a few days ago. Deep knowledge of specifics of the datasets you work with and subtleties of the problems that your team solves on a daily basis are simply inaccessible to the candidate. Be conscientious about the curse of knowledge and simplify your questions to match the candidate's background.

Interviewing data scientists

When interviewing data scientists, keeping your eye on the following qualities might help you to make a better choice:

- What kind of data scientist are you looking for? A research data scientist will be able to implement state-of-the-art models and push the boundaries of the discipline, but a machine learning engineer will be more proficient in quick application of existing best practices while maintaining good software design. Many companies need the second type of data scientist but are trying to hire the first one. Do not make this mistake and be honest about your needs as a company.

- Ask about the overall workflow of building a model, and specifically about delivering the model into production. Pay attention to the offline and online testing strategies that the candidate chooses to evaluate the model. Many experts have a good understanding of the inner workings of the algorithms but lack a coherent end-to-end approach for testing and delivering a model.

- Ask about common problems in the datasets you are working with. If your team constantly faces the problem of imbalanced data, be sure to check whether the candidate has an instinct for solving problems of this kind.

- If you work in a specific business domain, do not forget to ask about domain expertise.

Interviewing data engineers

Don't forget to look for the following qualities when searching for data engineers:

- Start from the specific technologies the data engineer will work with. There is a multitude of different databases and data processing technologies, so you should have a good understanding of what technology stack you are looking for because nobody knows everything. A big data engineer will back you up on taming the big data zoo of technologies and writing complex Apache Spark jobs. A backend developer with extensive experience in relational databases and data integration will help you to process datasets from traditional data warehouses and will easily integrate your solution with other systems.

- If the data engineering work at your company is related to distributed data processing systems (Apache Spark, for example), then do not forget to touch on this topic in the interview. Distributed systems suffer from the problem of leaky abstractions: when problems in code start to arise, the developer should have a good instinct about how the system works internally to solve the issue. This does not mean that every data engineer should be an expert in distributed algorithms and know everything about quorums, but they should be able to have enough knowledge to make reasonable choices when designing distributed data processing flows.

Summary

In this chapter, we have looked at the importance of setting goals before starting the interview process. We have explained why asking complex theoretical questions without a clear purpose is harmful not only to the candidate but also to the interviewer's company. We have explored the flaws of modern interviews and gained tools for making them purposeful and meaningful. We have seen what separates a good job description from a bad one. Also, we have defined a framework for creating interview questions from real tasks that you and your teammates solve on a daily basis.

In the next chapter, we will develop guidelines for building data science teams.

6
Building Your Data Science Team

In this chapter, we will learn about the three key aspects of building a successful team and explain the role of a leader in a data science team. We will learn how to build and sustain a balanced team that's capable of delivering end-to-end solutions. Then, we will set out a plan that we will improve and add several useful management skills to our arsenal: leadership by example, active listening, empathy and emotional quotient, trust, and delegation. We will also consider how advocating a growth mindset can be a major part of the team development process.

In this chapter, we will cover the following topics:

- Achieving team Zen
- Leadership and people management
- Facilitating a growth mindset

Achieving team Zen

A balanced team solves all incoming tasks efficiently and effortlessly. Each team member complements others and helps others to find a solution with their unique capabilities. However, balanced teams do not just magically come into existence when a skillful leader assembles their elite squad. Finding team Zen is not a momentary achievement; you need to work to find it. It may seem that some teams are stellar performers while others are underwhelming. It is crucial to realize that team performance is not a constant state. The best teams can become the worst, and vice versa. Each team should work to improve. Some teams may need less work, while others will be harder to change, but no team is hopeless.

But what makes a balanced team? Each team member is unique in their soft and hard skill sets. Some people are a universal jack of all trades, while others are highly specialized in a single area of expertise. Also, we all have vast emotional differences. In a balanced team, everyone complements and augments each other. Each team member knows at what point they can participate to yield the best results. Balanced teams are self-organizing. They can efficiently plan and act without direct interventions from the team leader. The leader unites the team and makes it coherent, but the actual work process of a balanced team looks highly decentralized. The leader frequently takes part in teamwork and helps everyone reach a common goal. The team members have good relationships and want to advance themselves to new heights. Another feature of balanced teams is that they do not have a single point of failure. If someone is ill or has decided to move on, it is not a big deal regarding how the core team functions.

Unbalanced teams can be hard to distinguish at first glance. An unbalanced team can function properly and even be a top performer, but unbalanced teams can be very efficient but fragile. People do not stick around long in an unbalanced team because it is hard to do so. Unbalanced teams have many forms, so they are hard to define. Here are two examples of an unbalanced team:

- In the first case, the team leader is the best expert in the team. They do most of the important work, while other team members work on the simplest delegated tasks. The team leader decomposes the task into many simple subtasks and assigns them to their team. No one sees the whole picture but them. The unwillingness to share important parts of the work and to involve the team in the task's decomposition process creates a strong imbalance. The team is very fragile and will not function properly without its leader. Employees in this team burn out quickly because they do not see the result of their work. Most of the tasks are boring and repetitive, so they seek challenges in another team, project, or company. This is a case of expertise imbalance in a team.
- In the second case, the team is building a very large project. The development has been going on for 3 years. The team leader and several data scientists who were working on the project from the start developed strong relationships and a team culture. However, not all of the team members stayed with them for the whole 3 years, so the team leader found several new experts eager to take on the project. However, these new team members found it hard to assimilate into the team. The **core team** unwillingly communicates with the **new team**. They find it hard to do so because of the cultural gap. It is a lot easier to interact with familiar people than with the **new team**. Thus, cultural imbalance has emerged.

Imbalance in teams is very hard to fight once it has sprung its roots. Each specific case needs careful examination and a plan to bring the team to a more balanced state. The best way to fight imbalance is to avoid it in the first place.

Just like when you're hiring staff to build a balanced team, you should look toward your goal. Without a goal, there is no reason for action, no balance, and no imbalance. For example, your goal could be *delivering solutions for problems using data science with a short time to market*. From this goal, the main characteristics of your team will arise. To successfully apply data science, you will need experts in the field. To do this with a short time to market, you will need good internal processes so that everyone works smoothly and reliably. The team will need to improve over time, and it will need to grow and last; this is the need for balance.

State your goals clearly and ensure all team members understand them so that everyone is on the same page about the definition of success. It would be impossible to train machine learning algorithms with no metrics and loss functions. Without feedback, humans stop developing too. When there is no notion of good and bad, we stagnate, and goals help us define these contrasts.

Another important component of each team is its roles. Roles define sets of activities that team members can perform. You may think you do not need roles because your team is agile and cross-functional, so everyone can and should be able to do everything. This may be crucial for small teams to survive while being adroit at what they do. But being cross-functional does not contradict having clearly defined roles. In fact, cross-functionality and size are different dimensions of a team, with the latter affecting the former through the number of roles each team member is performing.

For example, our data science team should handle everything from the definition of business requirements to the delivery of the final solution. We have loosely defined the project delivery process and assigned each stage to a role:

- **Defining business requirements**: Business analyst
- **Defining functional requirements**: System analyst
- **Defining nonfunctional requirements**: System analyst
- **Discovering and documenting incoming data sources, creating data marts, and reports**: Data analyst
- **Exploratory data analysis and modeling**: Data scientist
- **Building software around the model**: Software engineer
- **Creating documentation for the final product**: Software engineer and systems analyst
- **Delivery and deployment**: DevOps engineer and software engineer
- **Management and team leadership**: Team leader

Suppose that this team is limited to only three members, including the team leader. We can combine several roles into one to fulfill the team size constraint, while simultaneously creating goals for individual team members. Recall that forming goals for each position is the foundation of a good hiring process, and creating a team goal, defining roles, and mapping them to positions is a prerequisite for that.

For our example, there are many options, but the most realistic would be the following:

- **Defining business, functional, and nonfunctional requirements**: Analyst
- **Delivering software and models**: Machine learning engineer
- **Project management, team leadership, and the acceptance of final and intermediate results**: Team leader

Creating individual goals that are aligned with team goals can be done through the following set of transformations:

$$\text{Team goal} \rightarrow \text{Team roles} \rightarrow \text{Positions} \rightarrow \text{Individual goals}$$

The more roles your team has, and the smaller its size, the vaguer the boundaries between the team members will be, and the harder it will be to find teammates to fill in those roles. Defining roles helps you to be realistic regarding the amount of work and the budget it will take you to create a good team, so never leave this step out. Mapping roles to positions is equally helpful if your team is large and the responsibilities of every employee are clearly isolated or if your team is small and responsibilities are less segregated.

By following this process, you can create a feedback system that will optimize not only global team goals but also individual goals, providing everyone with an understanding of what their part in the big picture is. When designing deep neural networks, you need to create a loss function and make sure that the gradient passes through each layer. When building teams, you need to make sure that feedback passes through each part of your team, starting from yourself.

Understanding roles, goals, and size constraints will also help you grow and develop your team. Over time, your team will grow, but if you maintain the core goal-role-position framework, adding new responsibilities and team members will be straightforward with growth, and you will assign positions to fewer roles. Goal-position-role maintenance and revision is also necessary to keep your team balanced. Changes in organizational structure or in the main goals of a team always bring a risk of creating an imbalance, so be careful when introducing changes and plan ahead.

The concepts of team balance and a feedback system are simple but powerful tools that will help you build a balanced team and scale it in the right way.

Leadership and people management

In the *Achieving the team Zen* section, we concluded that a team leader should not be at the core of the team because this situation leads to severe organizational imbalance. Nonetheless, a team leader should be everywhere and nowhere at the same time. A team leader should facilitate team functioning, help every team member take part in the process, and mitigate any risks that threaten to disrupt the team functions before they become real issues. A good team leader can substitute and provide support for all or most of the roles in their team. They should have good expertise regarding the core roles of the team so that they can be helpful in as many of the team activities as possible.

The team leader should make sure that information propagates through the team effortlessly, and that all communication takes place as needed. If we take the internet as an analogy, the team leader should provide a fast and reliable communication network for all the servers.

Another important activity for a team leader is expanding the team constantly and in a balanced manner. All team members should have sufficient motivation, be challenged, and have a clear understanding of how they can grow according to their individual goals.

Most importantly, a team leader should set goals and achieve those goals together with their team. The team leader should unify everyone's efforts into a single focal point and make sure that focal point is the right one.

But how can we keep everyone focused on their efforts? If you were to ask me about the one most important aspect of leadership, I would say it is leadership by example. The modern idea of a successful leader can rarely be allowed in the real world. Many imagine that all leaders are highly skilled communicators and negotiators who can persuade anyone to do anything with the power of words. Of course, communication skills are important, but not those of a manipulative kind. Skilled manipulators could have an edge in some situations, but each action has consequences—and manipulation is always destructive in the long run.

Leading by example

The most simple and effective leadership advice was likely given to you in childhood: if you want to have good relationships with others, take the first step. Want people to trust you? Build incrementally by trusting other people. Want your team to be motivated? Be involved in the workflow and give everyone a helping hand; show them progress. Management literature calls this principle leadership by example. Walk your talk, and everyone will follow the example.

This kind of leadership is very effective for team building:

- It does not require you to learn and apply complex theoretical methodologies
- It builds relationships and trust in your team
- It ensures that the team leader is involved in the workflow of every role in the team
- It helps everyone grow professionally, including yourself

The only downside of leadership by example is that it can be hard. It requires you to be deeply involved in your team—emotionally and intellectually—and this can be debilitating. It is important to avoid exhaustion because your team will feel it instantly. If you burn out, so will everyone on your team. Thankfully, there is a simple way to avoid leadership burnout. Make sure that you have time during your workday that allows you to take a rest from team leadership activities. Maybe it is a small research project that will help your team members or maybe it is a prototype you can handle yourself.

Another caveat is that leadership by example can be hard to let go of. Many aspiring team leaders take too much work on themselves. The leader is often the most experienced professional on the team, and delegating work may be emotionally hard, especially when you know that you can do it yourself. A team cannot function without task delegation, so such teams fall apart quickly. Imbalance appears when the team leader cannot delegate tasks properly, and from thereon it builds upon itself.

Using situational leadership

Thankfully, in most cases, problems regarding task delegation are mostly emotional. To delegate without fear, you should build trust. And to build trust, you need to take the first step. If you find it hard to delegate, just force yourself to try it. It may seem like a leap of faith, but jump and see what your team is capable of. At first, you may be scared, but I assure you, they will surprise you. The tricky part of delegation is the task description step. Delegation will cause failure if you cannot describe what needs to be done correctly and without over-complicating the matter. To delegate effectively, you can make use of situational leadership. At its core, it is a very simple concept: you must measure your teammate's competence and commitment levels. Then, you need to choose your leadership style according to those levels.

The following diagram represents a simple and useful tool for choosing a leadership style for task delegation:

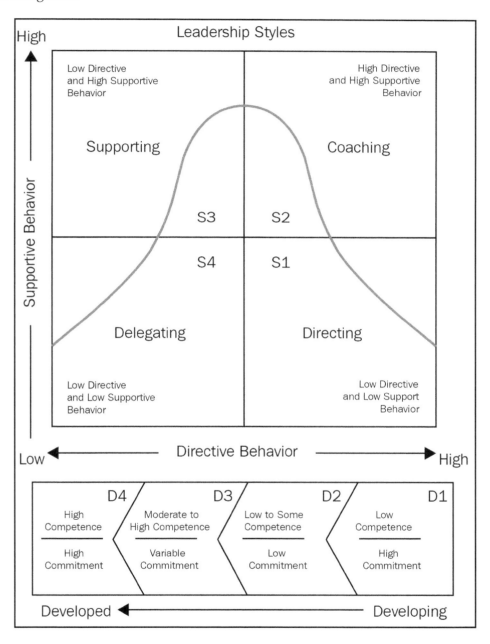

The preceding diagram measures employees' readiness by two variables: commitment and competence levels. Commitment stands for the employee's level of motivation. People with high commitment levels find their work interesting and are ready to try hard until the task is completed. A low commitment level, on the other hand, indicates that the person is not very interested in completing a task, finds it boring or repetitive, or is close to burning out. The other side of the coin is competence, which indicates the employee's ability to handle tasks by themselves. Low competence indicates that the person has no or low prior experience in the area, regarding the task they need to complete. A high competency level indicates that the employee has all the necessary knowledge and experience to complete the task. Situational leadership helps you keep motivation levels stable while ensuring that the employee gets all the necessary instructions so that their competence can grow without harming the task's resulting quality.

The following example shows how we can apply the situational leadership technique by determining an employee's competence and commitment before delegating a task:

1. Imagine that you've got a new team member, Jane. She does not have much experience and is taking a junior position in your team. Her motivation is high, and she is eager to learn new things. Here, the commitment level is high and the competence level is low, so we must take a directive leadership style. Obviously, she cannot solve complex tasks alone. It is better to take something simple, split the task into as many subtasks as you can, thoroughly describe everything, and check the correctness of every step. Employees from this category will take up a lot of your time, so be aware of your own resources. A team of 10 high-commitment-low-competency people can easily siphon all of your time.

2. Over some time, Jane has gained some skills, but her motivation has started to fall recently. This is the perfect time to coach. At this stage, you want to loosen control a bit to allow your teammate to make commitments.

3. Jane's competency levels have grown further, and you can tell that she has somewhere between a moderate to a high level of technical skill compared to others in your team. It is important to catch this transition because Jane's motivation is at risk again. To keep it up, you will want to change your leadership style to one that's supportive and focuses less on particular assignments. You will also want to share decision-making tasks with her. Jane's performance will probably be inconsistent at this stage, so provide any support she needs and help her transition into the last stage.

4. At this stage, Jane is already a senior expert. She is highly skilled, can make good decisions, and can provide a consistent output of good quality. This is the stage when you can delegate tasks. Your main goals at this stage are to set high-level goals, monitor progress, and take part in high-level decision-making.

Defining tasks in a clear way

The situational leadership model is useful, but it does not tell you how to describe tasks so that your teammates will be in sync with your vision. First, you should be aware that your task descriptions should not be the same for every team member. Your descriptions will vary, depending on competence and motivation levels. At the direction stage, a task description can resemble a low-level and detailed **to-do list**, and at the delegation stage, a task description may be comprised of two sentences. However, no matter what stage you are at, your task description should be clear, time-bounded, and realistic. SMART criteria helps create such descriptions.

SMART states that any task should be as follows:

- **Specific**: Be concrete and target a specific area or goal
- **Measurable**: Have some indicator of progress
- **Assignable**: Have an assignee(s) who will do the task
- **Realistic**: State which results can be achieved when given a set of constraints and available resources
- **Time-related**: State a time constraint or a deadline

Try to memorize this. The SMART criteria is a convenient checklist that will help your team understand you better. Nonetheless, no matter how detailed your task description is, talk it through with the assignee. Our language can be very ambiguous, and our thoughts are often unclear, even to ourselves. Just go over to your colleague after composing a task description and ask: *How did you understand this? Can we talk this through for 1-2 minutes?* Or talk through each task at your iteration planning meetings if you are using agile methodologies. These conversations are an essential part of a task's assignment. Even a subtle difference in understanding can give you unexpected and completely incorrect results.

Spending several minutes discussing the task at hand will help you make sure of the following:

- Your understanding of tasks and that their goals are correct and realistic
- Your task description is sufficient
- You and the assignee are in sync regarding what needs to be done
- The assignee understands what the result should look like
- The deadlines are realistic

Developing empathy

Basic concepts such as leadership by example, situational leadership, and the SMART criteria will help you structure and measure your work as a team leader. However, there is another crucial component, without which your team can fall apart, even with the perfect execution of formal leadership functions. This component is empathy. Being empathetic means to understand your emotions, as well as other people's emotions. Our reactions are mostly irrational, and we often confuse our own feelings and emotions. For example, it is easy to confuse anger for fear; we can act angrily when in reality we are just afraid. Understanding your own emotions and learning to recognize others will help you understand people and see subtleties and motives behind their actions. Empathy helps us find the logic behind irrational actions so that we can react properly. It may be easy to answer with anger in regard to aggressive behavior unless you can understand the motives behind those actions. If you can see those motives, acting angrily may seem foolish in the end. Empathy is the ultimate conflict-resolution tool; it helps build trust and coherency in the team. It also takes an important part in negotiations, which we will talk about later.

Being empathetic is not an innate ability. Of course, some people are naturally more empathetic than others, but this does not mean that empathy can't be acquired. It is a skill, and like any other skill, it can be mastered if you work on it. To increase your empathy, start with yourself. Be aware of your own emotions throughout the day. If you encounter a complex situation, think through your actions and emotions. Try to understand which of your responses were adequate and which were not to see what caused them and what you felt at that moment. Sometimes, you will find mismatches between your feelings and your actions. Learn from them. Over time, you will start to understand emotions better and better. First, learn to understand yourself, and then you will be able to read others' emotions much better than before.

Another important tool that will help you build empathy and understand others is active listening. We listen to others each day, but do we extract all the available information from their speech? In fact, we leave most of it behind. When listening, we are often distracted by our own thoughts. We do not pay attention to the speaker and are eager to talk.

You may have heard that you can achieve a lot more by letting others speak. Imagine yourself in a conflict situation. Your beloved teammate comes to the office at 3 P.M. without notice for the third day in a row. When you ask them what's wrong, they harshly ask you to go away. You may immediately want to react in the same aggressive way. However, in this situation, it is much better to understand the reason behind such behavior. Unknown factors can clarify such seemingly illogical behavior and show your teammate's situation in a different light.

Simply staring and hoping that the information will flow into you is optimistic. If the person in front of you is not in the mood to talk, this may make the situation worse. To get around this, you should listen actively. Active listening involves a set of techniques that will help others speak more openly.

To listen actively, do the following:

- **Pay full attention to the speaker**: We often drift into our own thoughts when others speak for long periods of time. The speaker will immediately notice that you are in the clouds, and it will negatively affect their urge to share information with you.
- **Show that you are paying attention**: Give feedback using *uh-huhs*, saying *yes*, by nodding, and by smiling. The other person shouldn't feel like they are talking to a concrete wall.
- **Paraphrase and mirror**: This is when you repeat the last two or three words of the last phrase. When you paraphrase, you repeat or sum up the last phrase in different words; for example, *I hear that you want to….* This may seem awkward at first, but believe me, mirroring works. This is the most important tool for active listening. It cultivates the flow of information between the speaker and the listener. After learning about paraphrasing and mirroring, I noticed that good speakers use them constantly, and they do not do this consciously. There is no reason for you not to employ this tool.
- **Do not judge, ever**: Openly judging others will trigger their defense mechanism and break the flow of information.
- **Verbalize emotions to understand what others feel**: Empathy is a hard skill to master, but often you can take a handy shortcut: verbalize the other person's feelings. *I feel that you are upset, am I right?* If you are right, the other person will confirm that, and if you are wrong, you will get a clue.

Active listening is simple on paper but may be tricky in the real world. As with any skill, you can practice it to perfection. Follow this simple advice in your daily conversations and you will notice the effects.

Facilitating a growth mindset

The last key component of team building we will cover is a growth mindset. The constant growth of your team is necessary if you do not want it to fall apart. Without growth, there will be no motivation, no new goals, and no progress. We can distill team growth into two components: the global growth of a team as a whole and the local growth of each individual team member.

Growing the expertise of your team as a whole

Global growth happens when your team gets through challenges, develops projects, and is given new opportunities. Global team growth happens alongside the expansion of your company. But the contrary is not true: if your company's business grows, it does not mean that your team will automatically get better and see new opportunities. Learning lessons as a team is a crucial part of the formula. It just so happens that you'll have more opportunities to learn when your company does not stagnate. Each time something good happens, you and your team should learn from it. When bad things arise, learn from them too. When something significant happens, make sure that the information propagates through your team and back to you again.

A great tool for learning is making retrospectives and internal meetups. Retrospectives are project team meetings where everyone on the team answers three simple questions:

- What have we done right?
- What have we done wrong?
- What should we do to improve?

Retrospectives allow you and your team members to get feedback and improve on it. They are also an effective project management tool that will improve your team's output. On a larger scale, everyone on the team should have a chance to share an experience with others, and to get useful feedback not only from their manager but from others in the team too.

Applying continuous learning for personal growth

While global team growth through learning from daily experience can be achieved by following a process, personal growth is not that easy. One important question I often ask myself is: *How do I get people motivated to learn?* It is extremely hard to grow as a professional from just day-to-day work experience in data science, which is the same for every other tech field. To grow individually, and as part of your team, your colleagues have to learn. Getting new knowledge is hard for some people, especially those who stopped actively learning right after graduating. Learning is a habit, and everyone can develop an urge to get new knowledge. The key idea behind a growth mindset is that we should not stop expanding our knowledge once we have graduated. Knowledge is limitless and, nowadays, anything you want to learn is at your fingertips; you just need to put some effort into it. The ability to learn continuously without pauses and interruptions through your life is a true treasure that allows unlimited self-development. If you think about it, almost any goal is achievable with enough knowledge and persistence.

The key to personal or local growth is learning continuously. If you want to motivate your team members to learn and grow, you must give them the following:

- The concept of continuous learning is a tool that will help your teammates make learning into a habit.
- Not everyone has personal time to learn, and even if they have, not everyone is eager to spend it on learning right from the start. Learning and research activities at work may be a good way to develop a habit.
- A personal learning plan will help everyone structure and track their goals.
- The project, learning, and other goals of a performance review process will help you with the feedback flow in the team.

We will now look at each point separately, starting with continuous learning. The main idea behind it is that it does not matter whether you read a whole book in one day or a single informative tweet: all learning counts. You should aim to learn something new each day—even a small amount. In the end, you will not only move a bit closer to the goal of learning something but also develop a set of habits that will allow you to gain more and more knowledge without even noticing it. After a while, continuous learning will be a part of your life, developing a natural hunger for new, useful information, like a scheduler that optimizes your free time in the background and squeezes spare minutes you spend commuting and waiting in long store lines to help you progress toward something that really matters to you.

The trick of continuous learning is to educate yourself to achieve your learning goals in small batches. If you are in the mood, you are likely to continue and do more work. If not, you will still have learned something new and moved on.

At first, this can be a way of achieving a singular goal. Then, after achieving the first accomplishments, you'll realize that this way of thinking allows you to learn more: apply it to a new area of expertise, skill, or topic of interest. A few months later, it will become a part of your life, helping you get better at it every day.

Giving more opportunities for learning

Starting a habit is not an easy process. To really stick, a habit should be repeated many times. You should provide as many learning opportunities for your team as possible. If you want your team to grow by itself and constantly develop, make sure you have the following:

- A learning plan template
- Planned time for research and education
- Compensation options for paid courses and books

Make sure that the learning plan template is easily reachable; place it on your company wiki or any other online source. The learning plan template should contain all the skills, books, and online courses that you and your team consider useful for gaining new competencies. This page should be frequently updated with links to new material that your team finds. Split all the material into categories.

In particular, for a data science learning plan template, you can consider the following categories:

- Mathematics:
    - Mathematical analysis and optimization
    - Linear algebra
    - Mathematical statistics
- Data science:
    - Machine learning
    - Deep learning
- Data engineering:
    - Relational databases
    - Data warehousing
    - Big data
    - Business intelligence
- Software engineering:
    - Software architecture and patterns
    - Code quality

All of those topics should contain links to books, online courses, and blog posts with commentaries about why this material is good and what the most useful parts of it are. It is even better to split each topic further into levels; for example, beginner, intermediate, and advanced. That way, you and anyone on your team can track which level of competency they are approximately at. This learning plan template can be used in a performance review to create and adjust personal learning plans. We will discuss this topic in more detail later in this chapter.

After creating the learning plan template, you can talk with everyone on your team to discover their professional goals. Ask them which areas they want to grow in and understand what interests them personally. Ask them to go through your learning plan template and write their approximate competency level in each topic and help them if they can't do this alone. With this information, you will understand where each team member is now and where they want to go. You can then create a personal learning plan. I find simple task-tracking systems such as Trello to be a good tool for tracking learning goals—create shared boards for your teammates and create cards in meetings. As with any task, a learning plan is better if it's defined in accordance with the SMART criteria. In particular, make sure it is realistic (reading 100 books a year may be a realistic goal for some people, but not for others) and time-bound. Each learning plan should have a deadline. At this deadline, you and your teammate should meet again and adjust the learning plan: decide on the next goal, create new cards, and delete obsolete goals. In your second meeting, you may discover that many learning plans have been unfinished. This means that you will need to adjust the amount of learning material for the next period. All that matters is that progress never stops, not how many learning cards have been completed.

Learning plans are worthless without planned time for research and education. Planned time can be personal, but you should not be confident that your team will educate itself only in their free time. Give them opportunities to learn in work hours too. It is common to have free gaps between projects or when waiting for someone to finish parts of the work you depend on. On rare occasions, some of your teammates could have several days of downtime, waiting for new tasks. Use this time wisely. You should communicate to your team that if they do not have any assigned tasks, they should learn according to their personal plan after reporting to you. In some cases, company policy can be against learning in the workplace. Try to communicate that learning is a long-term investment that will allow your team to perform better.

Another important component of forming a learning habit is to have compensation options for paid courses and books. Learning materials and online courses may be expensive. Your teammates may have other plans for their income than paying for books that will make them better at work. If someone understands that investing in education will have much greater returns, that's great, but not everyone will understand this from the start. People need to experience this process by themselves. They need to see that learning helps them to improve, both in terms of income and skills. Having corporate plans for compensating successfully finished courses or books is not expensive, and it will kick-start learning habits for your team.

Helping employees to grow with performance reviews

The last but not the least component, is a performance review. The sole purpose of a performance review is to share bidirectional feedback and have a clear view of individual progress. The number of ways you can try to track performance is infinite. Many companies use some kind of **key performance indicator** (**KPI**) system. A KPI is a single number that should be an adequate measure of your success. The total amount of sales in $ is a frequent KPI in sales departments. It may seem to be a good KPI at first. Sales departments should sell, right? Tying the department's success to this number is akin to telling everyone: *All you should think of is selling more. Nothing else.* But this is a very short-term goal. The reality of sales departments is much more high-dimensional than a single number. If we transition to software development or data science departments, KPIs become even more cumbersome and complex. How will you measure a programmer's or a data scientist's performance? Maybe we can take a number of experiments, or a number of lines of code per day? All of these measures are utterly irrelevant to real success.

In all honesty, I haven't seen a successful implementation of an individual KPI yet. KPIs work best for business processes, while personal KPIs are very one-dimensional and unrealistic. If you tie an individual's success to a single number, they will either end up fighting with the system or exploiting it. A better but more time-consuming way to track performance and set goals is by using performance reviews. A performance review is typically carried out once or twice a year.

The process is comprised of several steps:

1. Ask your teammate to write everything that they have done since the last performance review, such as completed projects, major achievements at work, open source contributions, books, and so on. Let's assume that the teammate's name is Matt.

2. Send a description of this to the colleagues who worked together with Matt. You should include as many people as you can: project managers, product owners, and team members. Ask them to answer the following questions:
   - What have you liked about working with Matt?
   - What could be improved? What parts did you not like?

3. If you have worked with Matt as a manager on some projects, prepare answers to those questions yourself.

4. Anonymize all the reviews and prepare a single performance review report.

After the report is done, you should share it with Matt and set up a meeting. It is a good idea to share the report before the meeting so that Matt can ponder the feedback for a while and derive conclusions. In the meeting, discuss each point and make sure that you are both on the same page regarding the feedback. Decide on the most important parts that need to be improved. If Matt has achieved new heights that you set in the previous performance review, you should be considering a promotion or a bonus. It is important to give equal attention to both positive and negative feedback. Try to make performance reviews stand out. They should be memorable. We should try to create nice-looking review templates, with good typography and a healthy dose of memes. We should also print all the reviews on nice paper so that anyone can take them out. A performance review should create positive memories, especially if the feedback is more on the bad side. You should give your team the motivation to improve and do not forget to collect reviews for yourself. As a manager, you can make many mistakes without even knowing about them. Getting feedback from your team is as important for you as it is for them.

It is important to lead by example if you want to facilitate the growth mindset in your team. If you want anyone to inherit principles of continuous learning, learning plans, and educational goals, do this yourself. Demonstrate that this works. That way, you will kill two birds with one stone: you will vastly improve yourself, and you will show your team how the ideas you speak about really work.

Now, let's look at how to apply the advice that's been provided in this chapter by looking at a case study.

Case study—creating a data science department

A large manufacturing company has decided to open a new data science department. They hired Robert as an experienced team leader and asked him to build the new department.

The first thing Robert did was research the scenarios his department should handle. He discovered that the understanding of data science was still vague in the company, and while some managers expected the department to build machine learning models and seek new data science use cases in the company, others wanted him to build data dashboards and reports. To create a balanced team, Robert first documented two team goals and confirmed that his views correctly summed up what the company's management wanted from the new team:

- **Data stewardship:** Creating data marts, reports, and dashboards from the company's data warehouses based on incoming requests from management
- **Data science:** Searching for advanced analytics use cases, implementing prototypes, and defending project ideas

Next, Robert thought about team size limits and asked about the approximate volume of requests they would get every month for each goal. For the data stewardship part, management already had a big backlog formed, and they needed all the tasks to be completed as soon as possible. As for the data science part, management did not have any preexisting requests, but they wanted the team to find and suggest new data science use cases in the next three months. Management noticed that they were ready to invest in the data science goal by creating a team of no more than four experts.

From this information, Robert derived the following team roles:

- **Data team leader**: To supervise two data teams and coordinate projects at a higher level. The workload in this role is not expected to be high during the first year of the team's existence.
- **Data stewardship team**:
    - **Team leader/project manager**: The goal definition clearly required someone to manage incoming requests and plan the work.
    - **Systems analyst**: Someone to document visualization and reporting requirements that come from the stakeholders.
    - **Data analyst**: To implement data reports and dashboards based on the requirements defined by the systems analyst.
- **Data science team**:
    - **Team leader/project manager**: Should be able to manage R&D processes in a business environment.
    - **Business analyst**: To interview company management and search for potential data science use cases.
    - **Systems analyst**: To search for data and provide requirements for the use cases provided by the business analyst.

- **Data scientist**: To implement prototypes based on the task definitions provided by the business analyst and systems analyst.
- **Backend software engineer**: To integrate prototypes with external systems and implement software based on the requirements.
- **User interface software engineer**: To implement interactive UIs and visualizations for prototype presentation.

Next, Robert thought about team size constraints and created the following positions from the preceding roles:

- **Data team leader**:
    - **Employees needed**: 1. This position will be handled by Robert.
- **Data stewardship team**:
    - **Team leader**: Employees needed: 1. Robert had no prior experience leading data analysis teams, so he decided to hire an experienced manager who will work under his supervision.
    - **Systems analyst**: Employees needed: 1.
    - **Data analyst**: Employees needed: 2.
- **Data science team**:
    - **Team leader**: Employees needed: 1. During the first year, this position will be handled by Robert, as the volume of projects won't be so high that this work will interfere with the data team leader role. As he will be acting as the best expert in the team, Robert has carefully thought about how to delegate tasks using situational leadership so that the data scientists on his team will be motivated and will have room to grow and take on more complex tasks along the way.
    - **Business analyst**: Employees needed: 1.
    - **Systems analyst**: Employees needed: 0. Robert has decided that there is no need for keeping system and business analysis separate since the system analysis could be performed cross-functionally by the whole team at the R&D stage.
    - **Data scientist and backend software engineer**: Employees needed: 2. Robert decided to combine data scientists and backend software engineers into a single position since the software engineering requirements for the prototype projects were easy enough to be handled by data scientists. He decided to hire two experts so that he could work on several ideas simultaneously.

Next, Robert defined a workflow for each position to create accurate job descriptions and interview scenarios, as described in Chapter 5, *Conducting a Data Science Interview*. To facilitate the growth mindset, he defined learning plan templates for each team role based on his experience. He focused on roles instead of positions because some combined positions may split when the team grows, and role-based growth tracks will allow those splits to occur naturally. Robert also created a quick team leader guide where he stated the standards for task delegation based on situational leadership and the SMART criteria and set up a performance review schedule for each team.

Summary

In this chapter, we explored the complex topic of building and sustaining a team. First, we dived into the concept of team balance and looked at why it is crucial for a team's survival in the long term. Then, we learned about several leadership styles, including the situational leadership model and leadership by example. We then saw how we can create good task descriptions using the SMART criteria. We also mentioned empathy and active listening as the most important soft skills of a leader. We also explored the concepts of continuous learning and a growth mindset. Finally, we saw how a performance review process can help learning habits develop in your team.

This chapter concludes the *Building and Sustaining a Team* section of this book; congratulations on finishing it! The next section of this book will cover the topic of managing data science projects.

Section 3: Managing Various Data Science Projects

Once you and your team start to build the project, you may realize that it requires effective management strategies. Can you use traditional software development methodologies for data science projects? What caveats do you have to look for? What processes should you use to manage development iterations? How can you sustain a balance between research and implementation? How should you deal with situations of extreme uncertainty?

This section contains the following chapters:

- Chapter 7, *Managing Innovation*
- Chapter 8, *Managing Data Science Projects*
- Chapter 9, *Common Pitfalls of Data Science Projects*
- Chapter 10, *Creating Products and Improving Reusability*

Managing Innovation 7

In the *Building and Sustaining a Team* section of this book, we looked at how we can create a balanced team that can deliver data science solutions. Now, we will look at how we can find projects and problems that have real value. In this section of the book, we will look at data science management at a greater scale. We are moving on from team leadership to the area of data science project management. We will develop specific strategies and approaches so that we can find, manage, and deliver projects that are valuable for the business.

For most companies, data science and machine learning belong in the area of innovation. Unlike software development, these disciplines are **terra incognita** (unknown territory) for your customers and business stakeholders. If you approach data science projects like any other project, you will face many unexpected problems. The domain of data science needs to be handled differently. When we step into the area of innovations, the definitions of best and good change.

In this chapter, we will explore innovation management and present answers to the following questions:

- Understanding innovations
- Why do big organizations fail so often?
- Exploring innovation management
- Balancing sales, marketing, team leadership, and technology
- Managing innovations in a big company
- Managing innovations in a start-up company
- Finding project ideas

Understanding innovations

Before we discuss failures in innovations, we need to understand what innovation is. The dictionary definition of innovation states that it is something new or something that's introduced in a different manner; an introduction of new things or methods. Every innovation is temporary. Edison's light bulb was once innovatory, as were cars. Successful innovations invade our daily lives like a tempest, change them forever, and then become mundane. Failed innovations fade and become forgotten.

If we look at history, the creation of technology does not guarantee success. Automobiles first appeared in 1886, but cars only really started changing our lives 27 years later, when the Ford Motor Company built the first moving assembly line in 1913. If you define innovation in terms of an inventor's success, the invention of the first car may be a huge breakthrough. But from a business perspective, we may only consider an innovation successful if it creates a new market with a stable income flow. Technical innovation advances the field, while business innovation creates some new, previously unavailable value. This value helps new markets emerge and new businesses rise.

Why do big organizations fail so often?

Big companies often see innovations as a gold mine. Many entrepreneurs think, *Have you heard about this new artificial intelligence start-up? Just imagine what we can achieve in this field. Our resources are vast compared to other companies.* However, history dictates otherwise, since emerging innovative technologies are often born inside small start-ups rather than in big, stable businesses. This is counterintuitive. Large companies have more resources, people, time, and risk immunity, while start-ups have almost none. Then why do big corporations fail at innovation? *The Innovator's Dilemma*, by Clayton Christensen (https://www.amazon.com/Innovators-Dilemma-Revolutionary-Change-Business/dp/0062060244), and *Crossing the Chasm*, by Geoffrey Moore (https://www.amazon.com/Crossing-Chasm-3rd-Disruptive-Mainstream/dp/0062292986), tell a convincing story that is supported by data. Innovations generate little to no revenue in the first stages of development. In large companies, innovative products will often compete with the best offers of the company. If you look at this from this angle, innovation seems legitimate in a start-up company, while being incompatible with the existing revenue channels of a big company. Small companies strive to get income, and competing with large corporations in developed markets is not an option. Small start-ups won't have enough resources to deliver competitive products that the market needs. Thus, the natural way for start-up survival is innovation.

New technologies are raw and unpolished, so they seem unattractive to new markets. Professor Clayton Christensen uses small **hard disk drives** (**HDDs**) as an example of this. In the era of large HDDs, everyone used them as an industry standard. Smaller models were fun in theory but unusable in practice since, at the time, the hardware was only supported on larger HDD models. Larger HDDs also had more capacity, speed, and reliability. When the market of personal computers emerged, small HDDs instantly became more attractive. Power consumption and size were the parameters that PC owners cared for. New revenue streams helped the development of small HDDs. After some time, smaller models surpassed their larger counterparts in terms of capacity, speed, and reliability. It was already too late for the old generation of HDDs. Large companies who seemed stable 5 years ago lost their market to new, superior technology.

Starting innovative projects in large companies is easy, but finishing them is troublesome. Innovations appear as nonsense according to a company's short to mid-term goals since they bring in no revenue and require large investments. However, bringing innovations to large organizations is not impossible. We will explore how we can grow ideas into the businesses of small and large organizations later in this chapter.

Game of markets

Data science is still a young field with great potential. Many experts state that even if we were to suspend new research, if we were to integrate new technologies that have emerged in the last 10 years, we will still be two to three decades ahead of the game. However, there is a large gap between research projects and widely applicable technologies. Like HDDs, a research project needs to grow its features in order to outrun its current competitors.

Data science uses research in machine learning, deep learning, and statistics to deliver software products that solve real-world problems. To become usable and widely applicable, software needs large time investments. The time of software engineers, data scientists, and other technical experts costs money. To earn money from your software, you need to solve people's problems. Your products need to bring something valuable to people. When this value is large enough to sustain a constant demand, you create a new market. This market is ruled by the laws of supply and demand: people and companies will exchange money for your products and services.

In their infancy, big organizations created their own markets or took part in existing ones. Markets can age and die like we do, giving new markets somewhere to live. If companies in a dying market do not transition to an emerging market, they cease to exist.

Creating new markets

Creating new markets is complex and risky. If you take too long and use too many resources to test your idea, you will fail. The risks are high, so testing ideas should be quick and easy. This testing allows you to convert mistakes into knowledge and improve your product, iteration after iteration. Failing fast and constantly learning by testing ideas are the key points behind the lean start-up methodology. The formula is simple: probe as many ideas as you can, iteratively pivot your product to match the market, and increase the demand for your services. The key characteristic of this process is speed.

Big companies rarely operate quickly. Long operational cycles and heavyweight organizational processes come up naturally with the company's scale. Without those crucial instruments, the company may fail to operate. Nonetheless, innovations do not tolerate long cycles. The cost of failure increases with the time span of an experiment, which makes innovations extremely costly for large businesses.

For organizations, data science is still an innovation, and most market niches haven't been developed or discovered yet. While innovations are hard, they are not impossible. In the upcoming sections of this chapter, we will look at how we can take control of new technologies by using innovation management in large and small companies.

Exploring innovation management

Innovations are very chaotic in nature. Innovators call for experimentation, but they cannot predict the end results and struggle to define deadlines. These qualities of innovations make them hard to implement in a business environment, where clearly defined goals, strict deadlines, and finite budgets are the norm. Innovation management provides a set of techniques that bring order into a chaotic realm of innovations. The word *management* is associated with direct control, but this is not the case for innovations. Freedom is critical for every innovation. You won't get any positive results by trying to micromanage. Innovation management is about providing support and integrating innovations into existing businesses so that they deliver helpful results.

To understand the main ideas behind innovation management, we should understand the different types of innovations, namely, sustaining and disruptive innovations:

- **Disruptive innovations** are what most people understand by the word innovation. This type of innovation brings drastic changes to the market. It introduces something that's new and technologically mature enough to create a new market. The iPod, iPhone, IBM PC, and electric light bulb were all disruptive innovations.
- **Sustaining innovations** feel more **organic** and **incremental**. A new version of your favorite operating system, the UI changes of social networks, and iPhone upgrades are all sustaining innovations. The goal of sustaining innovation is to keep up with competitors by introducing new features that will keep your customers from buying into a more attractive offer from a rival company.

Each sustaining innovation increases the gap between competitors slightly, while disruptive innovations change the way we live and work, thus creating new markets and making old ones obsolete. From a layman observer's perspective, disruptive innovations may appear all of a sudden, but in reality, they are not a flash of insight. *The Innovator's Dilemma* contains many examples of disruptive innovations that grew in small markets, where features of innovative products were more appealing for very specific use cases. A stable source of income allows innovative technology to grow to its potential, while companies that provide old-generation products do not see the direct competition on their market. When the new product disrupts the market, it is already too late.

Data science is not disruptive, nor does it sustain innovation by itself. It is a set of tools that we can use to create both kinds of innovations. In particular, self-driving cars are a good candidate for disruptive technology, while more accurate recommendation engines belong to the sustaining innovation side of innovation management.

In terms of risks, creating a disruptive innovation is a perilous and long-term investment, while creating a sustaining innovation should be a stable and well-researched process in any successful business.

We can view both types through the following life cycle:

1. **Search**: In this phase, the company searches for an idea to experiment with.
2. **Build**: Here, the company builds prototypes, conducts experiments, and measures results.
3. **Scale**: At this stage, the build phase gives us a promising direction to work on, so the company scales out. Prototypes are transformed into market-ready products and start to generate income.

4. **Expand**: Every innovation saturates its market. At this stage, the company expands its product to new markets to keep the growth rate intact.

5. **Sustain**: At this stage, the innovation becomes a stable business. Some companies can live for decades in the sustain stage. However, this comes with risks. Your current position in the market is not a constant irreducible resource of income. It can quickly saturate without long-term investments. Each minute of inactivity opens up new opportunities for your competitors to create disruptive innovations that can throw you out of the business. The sustain phase is a flag, signaling that the company needs to resume the **Search** stage.

Another important aspect of every disruptive innovation is the chasm. In *Crossing The Chasm*, Geoffrey Moore presents the famous market adoption curve:

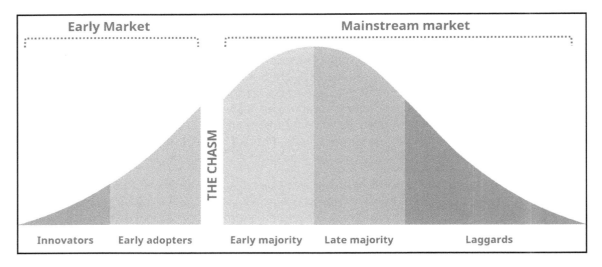

New technology can quickly find a seemingly stable source of income in the early market that comprises companies who are willing to pay money for risky, untested, experimental, but promising solutions. Many organizations think that the transition from the early market to the mainstream market will be smooth; the early market will produce enough income so that it can create new features that will be valuable to the mainstream market. However, this is not the case in practice. The gap between early and mainstream markets is much larger than it seems. When the early market saturates, the company enters the chasm. Its offering is not mature and developed enough for the mainstream market, where customers are used to feature-rich and stable products. So, the company is forced to live with a diminished income stream, while its product requires large investments so that it can create the features that have been requested by the mainstream market.

To find a way out of the chasm, the company must focus its efforts on a very specific area of application where its product's best features are more important than its current flaws. The goal is to find a tiny but reliable niche and concentrate on perfecting it. This creates a small market that will allow you to grow momentum through success stories, functionality, customer references, and new income streams. Consistent success in a small market will give you the resources and time that's necessary so that you can scale out to more mature markets.

In the next section, we will look at a case study of a fictional company called MedVision.

Case study – following the innovation cycle at MedVision

As an example, we will look at MedVision—a fictional AI start-up that brings computer vision technology to medical equipment and hospitals. During their search stage, they conducted applied research regarding deep learning applications in medicine.

The MedVision experts have also done market research and identified four potential ideas to work on, as follows:

- Detecting lung cancer using X-ray images.
- Analyzing data from wearable devices to detect heart attacks and other dangerous health conditions.
- Using a patient's medical history to create diagnostic assistants that will help therapists identify and classify illnesses while considering the patient's data.
- Analyzing pupil movement, EEG scans, and brain scans to identify and classify mental illnesses.

All of these ideas look promising from a commercial perspective and have a clear market base, that is, doctors and patients who wish to provide/get more accurate and less expensive medical diagnostics.

During the build phase, the MedVision team created several prototypes and showed them to potential buyers. They have also deepened their knowledge and researched the domain of every idea. The build phase identified unforeseen problems that the team could not identify during the search phase, as follows:

- Cancer detection suffers from bad data quality. Many datasets contain biased images that need manual cleaning. During the prototyping stage, the MedVision models got 0.97 F1 classification scores on a holdout test set but failed tests on newly gained data. The dataset that MedVision had used for model training contained bias: X-ray images with cancer rates were made using a scanner that left marks on the scans. The models learned to classify cancer using the simplest strategy: recognize markings. This led to a large model bias. Another source of bias was hidden in the timestamp, which was present in all X-rays. It turned out that patients with cancer are more likely to get scans on Tuesdays and Fridays because of the scheduling policy in the hospital. The MedVision team is now prepared to handle those issues when solving cancer classification problems for a real customer. The team decided that the issue of bias is solvable and shouldn't be a deal-breaker for this idea.

- Data from wearable devices has shown to be a good predictor of heart attacks and injuries from falling. Regardless, there were big problems with data availability. Only 1 out of 10 hospitals in MedVision's network reported that they had wearable device data, and only two planned to offer wearable devices to their patients in the next 5 years. MedVision decided to take this idea off the list because of the bad adoption of wearable devices in medicine.

- Using a patient's medical history to diagnose illness turned out to be a very challenging task because of the difficulties with data collection. Researching the data of three hospitals revealed that 30% of a patients' medical history was in paper-only format. Forms were standardized, but mostly filled in by hand. To test their idea, MedVision's team needed to build some reliable handwriting recognition technology, and then structure and error-correct large amounts of textual information. This process required large time investments and two additional experts in handwriting recognition and **natural language processing** (**NLP**). News about the failure of a big company working in this direction appeared during the data research process. MedVision has decided not to make further investments in this direction. They agreed that the risks were too high to continue with the prototype building phase.

- Mental illness classification fascinated several MedVision deep learning experts. The idea was new, unexplored, and promising. Further research showed that current diagnostic methodologies in psychiatry relied on patients' descriptions and external conditions, rather than on medical device measurements. Although researchers had already made significant achievements in this direction, psychiatry diagnostic manuals have not adopted the research. It turns out that to solve this task, MedVision also needed to advance the state-of-the-art in two disciplines: psychiatry and data science. This idea was looking more like a research project rather than a product implementation. They would need to attract long-term investments, professionals, and specialists in psychiatry and psychotherapy. This idea is transformational: MedVision will need to transition from a business to a research organization in order to implement this. All the team members decided that they wouldn't be able to handle this project without changing the company's goals and investors. They documented their choices and decided to return to this idea later if the scale of the company provides enough resources for long-term research projects.

MedVision's team decided to proceed with their cancer detection prototype. They have identified two hospitals that are interested in their solution: Oakland Hospital and Cancer Prevention Center. They have also found a medical research organization that may provide additional funding if their first tests with real patients succeed.

After 1 year, MedVision's system was successfully functioning at Oakland Hospital. The second project was canceled midway through because the Cancer Prevention Center wanted exclusive ownership of the developed product, which significantly limited MedVision's ability to scale and sell their product.

The first working deployment of the cancer detection system allowed MedVision and Oakland Hospital to publish their success story to major news sources. This allowed MedVision's team to start its expansion. They have extended their sales department and started to attract new customers for system trials. A myriad of new feature requests started to bombard MedVision's team, so they hired a product manager to research the market as well as catalog, prioritize, and manage the delivery of new features. Several other competitors entered the market to follow MedVision's success, so the team switched to delivering sustaining innovations to keep their leadership in the market.

Funds were growing, so after several years of successful operation, MedVision's team developed a new product for their customer base. They have started making transformative changes to their company by searching for new ideas, hoping to find some suitable ground so that they can start the second disruptive innovation cycle.

Next, we will look at the possible ways of integrating innovations into existing businesses.

Integrating innovations

Innovations require experimentation. New approaches fail often, but failure does not signify the end of the line. Failure just means that you have to distill the experience, learn from your mistakes, and try again as fast as you can. If you try to do this in a developed company, their processes and best practices may make you look like you are insane and that your actions may appear destructive and contradicting the company's values and goals. This happens because most businesses are oriented toward sustaining innovations. Existing values, goals, and KPIs react to disruptive innovations like an immune system would react to a virus—with defensive actions. This is the reason why most **research and development** (**R&D**) departments live a hard corporate life. They pursue goals that are incompatible with the values of the company they work for. To ease the integration of disruptive innovations into a large company, you may try to introduce another isolated business entity inside the company.

There are different ways to do this:

- **Acquisition**: Buy companies that have already managed to cross the chasm. The main challenge of this approach is to integrate the acquired company. Both technological and organizational integration needs to be done carefully so that it does not badly influence newly acquired products and teams.
- **Separate entity**: Create a branch company that will receive financing from the head company. The main challenges of this approach are large costs, risk management, and resisting the urge to have complete control. Honestly evaluate your company's potential in order to create and organize a new business with a set of goals that are aimed at the long-term development of disruptive technology.
- **Separate department**: This is the hardest way to create the innovations team. The main challenge here is creating a new set of goals and values for the existing company.

Thinking about data science projects from the perspective of innovations is helpful in many ways. Machine learning and deep learning can create sustaining and disruptive innovations. Innovation management will give you a broader context and let your main strategy succeed in the market. Organizations that do not integrate innovations will be outrun by their competitors. It is easy to blame technology for not being mature enough, or experts for not being as good as the competitor's rockstars. While doing this, many companies forget to consider the validity of their strategy for forming markets around new technologies. Data science solutions need a stable organizational foundation and a plan of action for income generation. Innovation management helps us take care of both components.

As you have seen, managing innovations involves dealing with lots of failures. Failures are not one-dimensional, and to avoid them, you will need to find a balance between different areas of expertise. The next section of this chapter will explore three main ways of thinking that will help you manage risks in data science projects.

Balancing sales, marketing, team leadership, and technology

To thrive in data science management, you need to find a balance between different specialties. The data science manager switches between the tasks of sales, marketing, and optimization every day. But aren't they supposed to care about data science the most? Since we do our jobs collectively, we tend to communicate a lot. Ask any technical expert working in a business environment about how much time they spend doing actual work. On average, a software engineer will tell you that they spend 2 to 3 hours coding. During the other 6 hours, they attend meetings, write or read documentation, create tickets, and discuss technical designs. Data scientists spend a lot of time talking about data definitions, metric choices, and the business impact of the model they are building.

The number of areas a data scientist can spend their time on is bewildering:

- Developing complex parts of your solution
- Code reviews
- Work planning, ticket management, and task definition
- Technology stack and tooling
- Employees
- Applied R&D
- Performance reviews
- Coaching
- Supporting the growth mindset and working on self-development plans for your employees
- Pivoting technology for a better market fit
- Working on presentations
- Practicing talks
- Creating written material
- Expanding your network and checking your connections for potential B2B applications for your technology

- Exploring the current offerings of your competitors
- Discovering possible pivots for your technology
- Seeking new use cases and refining the current ones

We can simplify this list by moving each activity into one of four common areas:

- **Technical leadership**: Everything related to data science, programming, and development process organization goes under this topic:
  - Developing complex parts of your solution
  - Code reviews
  - Work planning, ticket management, and task definition
  - Technology stack and tooling employees
  - Applied R&D

- **Team building**: This topic includes activities associated with your team:
  - Performance reviews
  - Coaching
  - Supporting the growth mindset and working on self-development plans for your employees

- **Sales**: Every item that helps you sell more of your product or services goes under this topic:
  - Working on presentations
  - Practicing talks
  - Creating written material
  - Expanding your network and checking your connections for potential B2B applications for your technology

- **Marketing**: Every item that is related to markets and pivoting goes here:
  - Exploring the current offerings of your competitors
  - Discovering possible pivots for your technology
  - Seeking new use cases and refining the current ones

In established teams, a dedicated expert will handle each management area. In an organization where data science has already made an impact, you will find cross-functional product teams where experts have one or two roles assigned to them. The picture is different for organizations that are just getting started with data science or who are working to establish a business using advanced data analytics and predictive modeling. In those teams, a data science manager is more likely to hold the majority, if not all, of the essential management areas.

Managing in different contexts during your workday is not only useful for emerging data science teams. Changing the setting can open up new perspectives and give you ideas about how you can proceed with the development of your technology, team, and business. We will briefly cover four key areas of management and relate them to the specifics of data science.

Technical leadership, along with team building, is a key activity for any data science manager. You need to make sure that your projects are implemented with the right tools and that they have been designed to achieve your customer's goals. On the other hand, you need to care about your team's motivation and long-term improvement. Advocating a growth mindset and building a balanced team will serve as a strong backbone when it comes to building better technology.

Your team will need a constant flow of tasks to work on. Even if your company has a dedicated sales department, you'll need to sell your ideas to them first. If data science is relatively new in your company, salespeople will be familiar with the existing offerings of the company, but they won't know how to sell data science solutions to customers. Either you need to know how to do it yourself, or you need to speak the language of sales to coach the sales department on how to approach data science solutions. Another case where you will need these skills is internal sales. For example, this skill set is necessary when the data science department is optimizing internal business processes. This is a frequent case in banking and internet companies. In this situation, a data science manager will need to find ideas, make them attractive and clear so that they can be understood, identify stakeholders, and close an internal sale to attract budgets for your project. Without sales, even the best teams and the most disruptive technology will find themselves without any work to do. Looking at your duty from the salesman perspective will open up a surprising number of opportunities, so don't miss them.

If the sales part of your job works as intended, you will start to see many opportunities, and each will need significant time investments from your team. Some opportunities will be realistic and match technology and expertise of your team, while others will be much less attractive. It's time to put on your marketing hat so that you can navigate through this sea of opportunities. Thinking about your work in terms of markets, demands, and products will allow you to choose the best direction to work toward. With each finished project, your team's skills and your technology will be drawn closer to one set of opportunities and further from the others. Marketing is all about searching in the most promising way and growing in the direction where your technology will meet the market's demands, thus creating new value.

Looking at your work from different perspectives is both illuminating and beneficial to your career and company. We do not live in a one-dimensional world, so it is important to look further than our main set of responsibilities. From now on, try to see the four hats of team management, technical leadership, sales, and marketing lying at your desk. Remember to change them from time to time so that you and your team have all the necessary ingredients for finding, growing, and delivering innovations.

Managing innovations in a big company

Most companies already know about the transformative power of data science. No one wants to fall out of competition, so companies create internal data science and R&D departments. Working in this environment is challenging because you are seen as the driving force of innovation by some and as a disturbing annoyance by others. Innovations often lead to significant changes in the existing business processes of the company, and many will not want to see these changes implemented.

Bringing disruptive innovations to existing businesses is a tricky process; to increase your chances of success, make sure you have the following:

- **Organizational power**: You will need direct or indirect organizational power to implement changes.
- **A migration plan**: You will need to have a complete vision of as-is (before integration) and to-be (after integration) business processes. You will also need a migration plan that guides you from as-is to to-be processes.
- **Success criteria and an integration strategy**: Making an abrupt change to the entire business process and quickly integrating innovations is a risky strategy. You should have measurable success criteria for your project and a risk management strategy that allows you to take control of losses in the worst-case scenario.
- **Open processes and clear explanations**: Everybody that's affected by the migration will need a crystal clear understanding of what is happening and how it will affect their workflow.
- **Involvement in integration**: You will need help in describing as-is processes and help with the migration plans. No one will be better at this than the people who already execute the as-is business process. Find people who are involved in the day-to-day execution of the existing process and make sure that they participate in the processes mentioned in points 3 and 4.

Next, we will look at a case study regarding the innovation management process in a retail business.

Case study – bringing data science to a retail business

In this case study, we will look at a data science manager, Carl, who is working in a fictional retail company. He and his team have prototyped a solution that will improve the availability of on-shelf goods. This solution will monitor goods across all the stores and notify the shop staff so that they can bring in new goods if the shelves are empty. The company's management has asked Carl to grow the prototype into a complete solution and integrate it into the existing on-shelf availability process.

In the current process, each store has two to five goods availability managers who manually monitor each shelf in the store using an app on their smartphones. The app showed up to date goods locations on each shelf, but the manager needs to manually check whether the goods are present. After the check, the manager can take note of all the missing products and go to the store's warehouse to get the goods and place them on the shelves.

First, Carl has asked the company's management to introduce him to the person who's responsible for the current on-shelf availability across all stores. It turns out that one of the executive directors, who manages logistics, delivery, and the on-shelf availability of goods, owns this process. Carl has prepared a detailed presentation that describes the results of the pilot project. He told the company that he needs the director's help in preparing the requirements for the system so that it can be integrated into the existing business process since the director has this organizational capability. The current business process was well-documented, and each step was assigned to a specific business role. To create a migration plan, they interviewed experts who executed the target process. Carl showed the current prototype to the experts and documented their ideas on how to improve the technology so that could be smoothly integrated into the workflow. Each new feature formed the backlog for the upcoming implementation project. Along with new features and ideas, changes regarding the business process came up naturally. Some of them were conflicting and poorly defined, so Carl assigned a business analyst to the project to formalize the migration plan into a coherent document.

After this, Carl presented the results to the director. The integration of the new system significantly changed the existing process. Previously, the store managers who monitored the on-shelf availability of goods were manually going through the store to monitor the availability of the goods, but now, this task can be fully automated using portable cameras near each shelf. A manager will receive task notifications through the mobile application and each task will contain precise information about the good's storage location, quantity, and shelf location. The application will batch tasks together and create optimal routes through the store's storage. Since all the store's availability managers already have smartphones, the integration will be simple: the users will need to update the app on their phone and familiarize themselves with the new features.

The key idea behind the integration strategy that was proposed by Carl was to test the system in a single store first. The test would be considered successful if the store could handle its current workload using only half of the availability management personnel. This way, the project would have measurable success criteria. If the first test succeeds, then the system will undergo tests on a larger number of stores. This process will be repeated and migrated to all the stores so that it's the to-be version of the process.

It's clear that each store will need fewer availability managers after the system integration process. To have open processes and clear explanations, the director has designed a special training program for personnel that won't be needed for this job after the system is online. Other departments are working hard to find new people, so redistributing the workforce is a very appealing option. Carl's team also created an in-depth on-site training course and in-app tutorials that describe how the users can work with the new app.

The innovation life cycle is much faster than the general project life cycle in large organizations. It also costs more in the short term because of the fast experimentation rates and increased risks of failure. This makes innovations tricky to work with in a large company. Existing short-to-mid term values and goals will reject innovations, just like an immune system would reject a virus. It is important to provide organizational and financial support to the R&D and innovation departments in established businesses. Innovation teams work best when they are deployed as a company inside a company. While the main business may be working efficiently with the organizational structures with many hierarchical departments and management chains, innovations work best when the organizational ladder is very high and there are one or two steps from an employee to a top manager.

In the next section, we will look at how we can manage innovations in a start-up company.

Managing innovations in a start-up company

If you work in a start-up, innovations will feel more natural and easier to implement than in a large, slowly moving business. However, there is a significant difference between a start-up and an established company. Start-ups cannot afford to make a lot of mistakes. Stable income streams allow large companies to test many ideas simultaneously, whereas start-ups are often limited to evolving in one simultaneous direction.

The concept of the chasm is important for start-ups. The main goal of a start-up is to find a new market where it can grow upon itself and provide value that doesn't exist. Matching your idea and your technology to market demands involves a lot of quantifiable experimentation. It is important to use a measurable approach that is advocated in *The Lean Startup* and *Crossing the Chasm* methods.

The Lean Startup method recommends that you test every idea and every feature on the market early. Conducting experiments and getting feedback is crucial for start-ups because each choice you make limits your future development. The sooner your product receives market feedback, the sooner you can change its course before it's too late. A company with good R&D practices and big budgets can test ideas in computer vision, NLP, and reinforcement learning for long-term payoffs. They can even create entire branch organizations so that they can test ideas. On the other hand, a computer vision start-up will have a much harder time pivoting to NLP because of the shorter profit expectations.

Start-ups need to be lean, fast, and agile to survive. Looking at your idea through the marketing lens is a crucial skill for a small aspiring company. Even the best idea won't survive long enough without proper economic development. Because of the large gap between the expectations of early adopters and the early majority, a start-up needs to have a narrow focus, seeking to satisfy the needs of a niche customer base. In this chapter's example, MedVision (see the *Case study – following the innovation cycle at MedVision* section) has implemented a lung cancer classifier. They have measured the market demand for several alternatives and identified cancer classification as the most promising and realistic use case. In the short term, they plan to have several successful deployments to attract income and new customers. In the long term, they plan to collect market feedback to expand their system's functionality to more medical equipment types and expand their disease identification list. The key idea is to direct your product toward market satisfaction by conducting experiments and collecting measurable feedback.

In the next section, we will explore different approaches to finding ideas that can fuel data science projects.

Finding project ideas

Before implementing your first prototype, you will need to find promising ideas to work on. To create ideas, you can work from one of two starting points: business or data.

Finding ideas in business processes

If you are working with an already established business, the first and the most obvious way to find ideas is to ask management about their needs. Merging data science expertise with deep domain knowledge will allow you to find a match between their requests and your team's capabilities. However, your customers will rarely have a problem they know about. The most likely response you will get while using this strategy is, *We know of this problem, and we are already working on the solution.*

On rare occasions, a problem may be presented to you on a silver platter. If that's not the case, you will need to dive deeper into the company's business. Start with their key revenue-generating processes. Educate yourself about how they work. Then, mark all the steps as manual, partially automated, or fully automated. Two key areas for the improvement of an existing business process are the automation of manual steps and the improvement of automated steps.

For manual steps, research why they are still performed that way. Manual labor can generate lots of digitalized data that you can use to train your models. Form validation, form filling, and customer support are frequent cases where you can replace repetitive manual labor with a data science solution.

For automated and partially automated steps, research the IT systems that implement those steps. Look at the data sources: databases, data warehouses, and file storage. Then, look at where you can deploy a machine learning model that can make this step better. Scoring, risk management, and algorithmic marketing algorithms are examples of this.

The best course of action when analyzing existing business processes is to find a step that is as follows:

- **Generates data**: This or any previous step of the process should constantly generate digital data that can be used by a model.
- **Is business-critical**: The improvement should provide direct business value to your customer. Increasing the value is always a strong selling point.
- **Has potential applications for data science**: You can use data to build an algorithm that provides insights or automates decision-making processes.

Using existing business processes to find promising ideas for data science projects is a solid approach when you are working in a B2B environment. It allows you to deepen your domain expertise and find the most valuable improvements.

Now, let's look at how we can source ideas from data.

Finding ideas in data

Another way to create project ideas is to look directly into the data:

1. First, you should create a data source map of the company you are working with. Sometimes, this information will be readily available for you to use. If it isn't, then your team should do some research and recover the data architecture of an organization. Using this data map, you can identify the largest and most complete data sources.
2. Then, sort all the data sources by the amount of data and data quality and look over possible data merges between different databases. The goal is to create several starting points for further research.
3. Finally, look deeper into the data sources you have selected. Seek datasets that can be used to build supervised or unsupervised models. At this stage, you should not build any models; just write down all your ideas—the more the better. After jotting them down, see if any of your ideas can create new business value.

This way of finding ideas is risky, time-consuming, and very creative. The chances of you succeeding are lower than in the previous approach, but if you are able to find a working idea that works bottom-up from the data, you are much more likely to stumble upon a unique data science use case that gives you a competitive advantage and provides new business value. The first approach is much more suited toward finding sustainable innovations, while the second approach can be used to mine for disruptive ideas, that is, transformative ideas.

Once in a while, some people come up with truly unique ideas. There may not be any data, nor a business—just a captivating idea. Transformative ideas that disrupt the industry often fuse several disciplines that have no close relationship at first glance:

- Medicine + computer vision and machine learning = automated disease risk analysis for patients
- Automobiles + computer vision = self-driving cars
- Call centers + deep neural networks = fully automated dialogue systems with speech recognition and generation

If there was a reliable formula for creating such ideas, they wouldn't be rare and surprising anymore. The only way to increase your chances of discovering new ideas is to acquire lots of knowledge and experience in different areas.

If you think that you have come up with a promising concept, do not rush it. Write down your idea and start researching it:

- Look for similar products that are already on the market. Chances are, you will find several at least vaguely similar products.
- Collect and classify a competitor's product features.
- Write down the core business model behind each product.
- Rank all the collected features into several categories:
    - **Best feature**: No one does this better; it's a distinctive feature of the product. This feature is often the defining purchase factor.
    - **Core feature**: The majority of competitors have this feature implemented fairly well.
    - **Basic feature**: This is implemented in a basic way. Lots of other competitors have a more complete implementation of this feature.
    - **Lacking feature**: The product lacks a feature.
- Start fleshing out your idea by describing the product's features. Create a profile for your product and think of the feature that distinguishes it from others.
- Think about your product's business model. How would it relate to other products on the market?

If you can't find any competitors on the market, or you can see that your product could easily throw competitors out of the market, then you have a chance of creating a disruptive technology. Remember that pushing disruptive innovations into the market requires careful planning, focus, and a strategy for crossing the chasm.

Next, we will look at a case study that's all about finding ideas and managing a data science project in an insurance company.

Case study – finding data science project ideas in an insurance company

In this case study, we will look at the fictional Insur Inc. company, where Rick was recently promoted and now works as the head of data science. Data science is a new field for the company. They have tried to create several prototypes, but none have made it to production. The first major task for Rick is to find a data science use case that will be beneficial and profitable for the company.

Rick already knew that the main income stream for the company was selling insurance policies, and the main losses were in insurance claims. Insur Inc. provides health, real estate, and automobile insurance programs. The company's largest product is its automobile insurance, which contributes to 75% of its overall revenue. Rick took a closer look at the processes in the automobile insurance department.

First, he looked at the process for new insurance policies, which are shown in the following diagram:

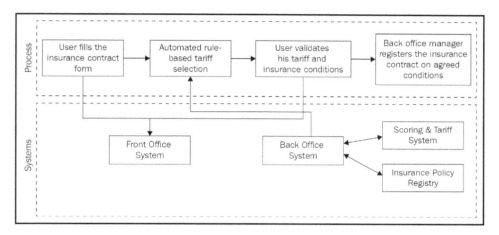

This process was backed by four IT systems:

- **Front Office System**: This is an insurance consultant UI that's used at all Insur Inc. offices. This system does not store much data and acts as a lightweight UI with limited functionality compared to the **Back Office System.**
- **Back Office System**: This manages all the data related to insurance contracts. Back office workers use this system to validate and process new contracts.
- **Scoring & Tariff System**: This is an auxiliary module for the **Back Office System** that takes insurance contract data and applies a set of rules to find the best matching tariff for this client.
- **Insurance Policy Registry**: This is a central data warehouse that stores all the data related to insurance contracts.

Rick wanted to research the profit loss cycle, but this process only included the profit part of the cycle. The losses are managed by another process, that is, insurance claim management:

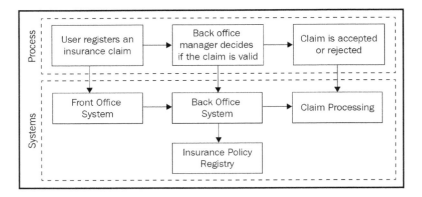

The IT systems that are involved in this process are almost the same, just like the insurance contracts, except for the **Claim Processing** system. Dedicated managers use this software to validate claims and assign on-site investigations regarding damaged vehicles. This system also identifies fraudulent claims. The fraud detection process is mostly manual; however, some simple rule-based detectors are also implemented in the system.

Rick decided to improve the **Scoring & Tariff System**. Predicting potential claims depending on a customer's data would improve risk identification and contract pricing. More risky customers would receive more expensive tariffs. Rick has assembled a team and has started prototyping the new scoring algorithm using data from the **Insurance Policy Registry**, **Back Office System**, and **Scoring & Tariff System**. The company was planning to implement a binary classifier that would estimate the probability of a valid claim for each new client. The business people at the car insurance department were already familiar with the concept of false-positive and false-negative errors, so they have used confusion tables to compare the performance of current and new scoring algorithms. The business department has refused to use more complex metrics such as an F1 score and suggested calculating the increase of profits directly from the confusion tables.

After three weeks of prototyping, Rick's team created a classifier that was superior to the current rule-based algorithm of the **Scoring & Tariff System**. They sent their predictions to the business department for evaluation. After 30 minutes, the business department asked for explanations for each score. It turned out that the current scoring system generated a detailed quarterly report and sent it to a regulatory organization that checked the validity of the scoring model that was used at the company. The model should be fully interpretable and understandable by humans. Rick's team used a black-box model with a large number of parameters to achieve high accuracy, so their model failed this requirement. Interpretable models such as logistic regression are more suitable here, but their performance was subpar for the current system, making them unsuitable for deployment.

Rick realized that he and his team lost three weeks of project time. This was bad news for his boss, and he was asked to not make the same mistake twice.

This time, Rick researched and documented all the conflicting requirements. He deepened his domain expertise by asking his colleagues from the car insurance department about every detail of the business process and documented it for clarity. While researching, he validated that the fraud detection process was far more suitable for migration to a machine learning model:

- No government regulations and special reporting requirements were present.
- The claim processing department struggled with fraud detection because it was one of their primary sources of loss. The decision process was time-consuming and every claim needs to be checked, so the overall quality of fraud detection was decreasing.
- There was a significant amount of data being collected in the **Claim Processing** database.

The main problem was that the clients needed more detailed reasoning behind claim rejection than, *Our model thought that your insurance claim is fraudulent, so we rejected it*. So, Rick has suggested that the company only uses an algorithm for fraud detection. The idea was to create a machine learning-based filter that would assess the probability of a claim being fraudulent. If this probability is high enough, it triggers the current fraud investigation process. Only 0.5% of all claims were fraudulent, so if the model is accurate, it should decrease the number of checks significantly.

Rick has prepared a solution architecture that shows how the new fraud detection system will be implemented and how it will be integrated into the existing process. He met with all the business stakeholders to validate his idea. Everyone agreed with the approach. The evaluation strategy they agreed on was the same as the scoring model. After that, the next prototyping stage began. The model was proven to be successful, and Rick was asked to implement the full fraud detection module that would be integrated into the existing business process.

Summary

In this chapter, we have explored innovations and learned about how to manage them. Good innovation management requires us to carefully plan our own activity and use different viewpoints such as sales, marketing, and technical leadership to match our ideas with market requirements.

First, we described how each viewpoint contributes to effective innovation management. Next, looked at the complexities of integrating innovations into big organizations and start-ups. Data science is an innovative activity for most organizations, and we have defined several strategies that we can use to find project ideas and make them work.

We have also looked at three case studies, each related to different topic related to innovation management. The first one, *following the innovation cycle at MedVision*, showed us how an innovation cycle can be applied in a real-world scenario. The second one was about *bringing data science to a retail business*, where we explored innovation management in large organizations. The last one, *finding data science project ideas in an insurance company*, demonstrated the importance of using a structured approach for finding data science project ideas.

In the next chapter, we will explore the data science project life cycle, which allows you to structure and plan tasks for your team.

8
Managing Data Science Projects

In the previous chapter, we looked at innovation management. We developed recipes that can help find ideas for data science projects and matched them with their market demand. In this chapter, we will cover the non-technical side of data science project management by looking at how data science projects stand out from general software development projects. We'll look at common reasons for their failure and develop an approach that will lower the risks of data science projects. We will conclude this chapter by diving into the art and science of project estimates.

In this chapter, we will look at how we can manage projects from start to end by covering the following topics:

- Understanding data science project failure
- Exploring the data science project life cycle
- Choosing a project management methodology
- Choosing a methodology that suits your project
- Estimating data science projects
- Discovering the goals of the estimation process

Understanding data science project failure

Every data science project ends up being a software system that generates scheduled reports or operates online. The world of software engineering already provides us with a multitude of software project management methodologies, so why do we need to reinvent a special approach for data science projects? The answer is that data science projects require much more experimentation and have to tolerate far more failures than software engineering projects.

To see the difference between a traditional software system and a system with predictive algorithms, let's look at the common causes of failure for data science projects:

- **Dependence on data**: A robust **customer relationship management** (**CRM**) system that organizes the sales process will work well in many organizations, independent of their business. A system that predicts the outcome of a sales process may work well in one organization, but will require a partial rewrite for another organization and may not work at all in another. The reason for this is that machine learning algorithms depend on data, and every organization will have its own data model of its customers and its own sales process.
- **Changing requirements**: While software development projects often suffer from changing requirements, the changes mostly flow from the customer to the implementation team. In data science projects, new insights and research results from the implementation team can create a feedback loop. Project stakeholders can generate new requirements and change the course of the project based on the new information that's discovered by data scientists.
- **Changing data**: In software development projects, the data model is mostly fixed or can be changed in a controlled manner. Data science projects often need to be integrated with new data sources for research purposes. Data is always changing and transforming, creating multiple intermediate representations inside the system. People and software components use these representations for reporting, data processing, and modeling. Software engineering projects use fixed or slowly changing data models, while data science projects use constantly evolving data pipelines.
- **Experimentation and research**: Data science projects involve completing many experiments. Typically, the number ranges from hundreds to thousands. Software engineering projects limit research by designing a system architecture and evolving it in a controlled manner. In data science projects, the next experiment may turn the project in a new direction, and you never know when this will happen.

Understanding data science management approaches

The traditional management approach to software engineering projects was not built with these problems in mind. The key problem that most modern software project management methodologies need to solve is the issue of changing requirements. Agile methodologies focus on planning and executing fast iterations. Each iteration aims to deliver functionality to the client as fast as possible. External feedback is the primary source of changes in the project.

In data science projects, changes come from every direction. They spread internally from the project's team and externally from the business' customers. Metrics should always confirm progress. Getting one step closer to your goal may take tens or even hundreds of failed experiments, which makes fast iterations a must.

The typical iteration length of an Agile project can stretch from 2 weeks to 1 month. The project team fixes the iteration scope for this duration and delivers it under a strict timeline. In a data science project, an experiment's result in the middle of the sprint can affect the sprint's goals and make working on other planned tasks less important due to the new discovery.

Management must provide a safety net for common issues and problems. Methodologies that come from the software engineering domain can give you a solid foundation here, but they do not provide any tools that we can use to manage research and govern data.

If you develop systems that use machine learning under the hood, it is necessary to take care of the following:

- **Requirements for validation and alignment**: You need to detect and manage requirement changes from external (customers) and internal (research team) sources.
- **Data governance**: Your project will need data governance standards, which should be rigorously applied to each piece of code that works with data. Ideally, each row of data going through your pipeline should be tracked back to its data source. All incoming and outgoing datasets, including intermediate reports, should be tracked and documented.

- **Research processes**: Each data science project will need to be researched extensively. Without control, research can quickly eat away at your budget without project completion being in sight. The essential components for managing a research project include the following:
    - **Research planning**: The project team should plan and prioritize all of their research.
    - **Experimentation methodology**: Each experiment should conform to a set of standards such as tracking, documentation, and reproducibility.
    - **Fail fast and recover early**: Experiments often fail. Your management approach should make experiments fast so that your team can iterate and learn as quickly as possible.
- **Software engineering processes**: Much of your work will be in creating software. Software project management already offers great tools for this, but they need to be tightly integrated with all the other components of the management methodology.

Next, we will look at common stages that arise in data science projects. We will tie those stages into a process that's comprised of the project life cycle so that we can see the whole picture behind data science projects.

Exploring the data science project life cycle

Each data science project has several distinct states. We can structure projects in different domains and different technologies into stages that comprise the data science project life cycle, as shown in the following diagram:

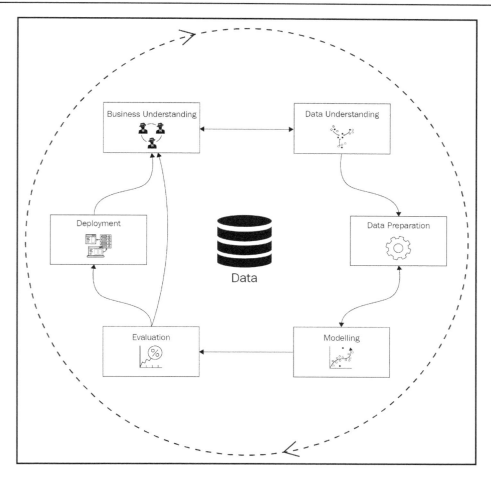

Let's explore each stage of the life cycle in more detail.

Business understanding

During this stage, you apply your domain expertise and research the business side of the project. You define the business requirements and confirm that their implementation would make the lives of your customers better. You should also define and document all the relevant business metrics that will allow you to measure and report on results in a way that is understandable by the business side. The output of this stage should be a business requirements specification that has been viewed, redacted, and agreed upon by the project stakeholders.

Data understanding

During this stage, you research the data architecture of the organization you are working with. You document data sources, their owners, and the technologies they use. You should not document every available data source unless you want to mine project ideas from data (see `Chapter 7`, *Managing Innovation*). Focus on data that's useful for the project.

After finding this data, perform an **exploratory data analysis** (**EDA**) and research the data thoroughly. Look at any anomalies and unusual artifacts in the data. Study the reasons behind their occurrence and document ways to handle them. For example, if the dataset has a lot of empty values, you should have a plan for how to deal with them, and your actions should not distort the data in an undesirable way.

You should also look at ideas regarding feature engineering during the EDA stage. Perform statistical analysis on the data and try to find causal relationships that will help to solve the task at hand.

The data understanding stage should have the following outputs:

- **Data source dictionary**: This document briefly describes all the data sources that are relevant to your project.
- **An EDA report that shows the conclusions of your data analysis**: This document should describe the approach that you will use to solve the task at hand and the strategies for handling errors that you have found in the data. You should include facts that may interest your customer.

Data preparation

This stage is where we start working with data. The data preparation stage involves taking raw data and changing it into a useful format. You read data from its sources and prepare it so that you can use the data to reach the project's goal. If you are solving a task based on structured data and plan to use machine learning, you will need to perform feature engineering. The previous stage should give you insights into the quirks of the data that you can fix during the data preparation stage. This stage's output is one or more reproducible data preparation jobs and a dataset that you can use to build and test models.

Optimizing data preparation

Data preparation and data understanding are surprisingly time-consuming. These stages can take up to 80% of the project's time, so don't forget to plan in advance. Since this stage is time-consuming, optimizing the team's performance is important. Open source tools for automated EDA and feature engineering can save you a lot of time at the start of the project, so don't hesitate to use them. In the *Creating the Development Infrastructure* section of this book, we will look at several libraries that you can use to speed up the data preparation and data understanding stages.

To make this process less error-prone and easier to monitor, you should care about data provenance and versioning. Every dataset should be able to be traced back to its source. Take care to save all the data files, regardless of whether they're intermediate and raw. Log the inputs and outputs of every data transformation job in your code. Data processing bugs are notoriously hard to spot unless you have complete control of your data streams.

Another important point to make is reusability. Code your data processing jobs well. It is tempting to create a large pile of tangled code lines in a single file and let them do their job. Doing this will increase your technical debt. The code will work for a while, and then it will fail without notice. Over time, you may also want to add additional features to the code. If it is badly written, you will spend an unexpectedly large amount of time making fixes and debugging.

To ensure that you have robust data processing code, use the following checklist during the code review:

- All the repeated code is encapsulated into functions
- The logically connected functions are encapsulated in classes and modules
- Your code has extensive logging
- All the configuration parameters can be changed via the config file or command-line arguments
- The inputs and outputs of your data job are saved somewhere
- The code is reproducible and has documentation

Modeling

This topic was covered in the *What is Data Science?* section of this book. In this stage, we apply our knowledge of data science, machine learning, and deep learning to solve the task at hand. This is done in the following stages:

1. First, we determine the task type, that is, supervised (classification and regression), unsupervised (clustering and document topic modeling), or reinforcement learning.
2. Then, prepare a list of algorithms that are suitable for solving the task.
3. Next, come up with a model validation and testing approach.
4. Finally, optimize the parameters of the model and select the best model.

Evaluation

While not being separate from the modeling and deployment steps, this stage deserves to stand on its own. You must test technical and business metrics, as well as checking the individual predictions of the model at this stage. Look at the biggest errors the model made on the test set and think about the changes that you can make to your data, features, or models that can fix those errors. This is also a good way to spot data processing bugs.

Your project should have two evaluation strategies: online and offline. Online evaluation takes care of tracking all the metrics for the already deployed model, while offline evaluation is used to decide which model will make it to the deployment stage.

Typical data science projects contain hundreds of experiments with different models, data, and parameters. Each experiment generates new data in the form of metrics, code parameters, and notes. Use a specialized experiment tracking tool to decide on the success or failure of a particular experiment. These tools can automatically collect all the logs, metrics, and artifacts of the experiment to ensure their reproducibility and to ease searching the experiment results. If you don't want to or can't use a special tool, a spreadsheet can be a good substitute, although you will need to spend more time working on it. Having a complete log of all the experiments and decisions you've made regarding modeling and data preprocessing will help you compare different experiments and make conclusions about their results.

If you need to know about the technical details of model testing, please refer to `Chapter 2`, *Testing Your Models*.

The modeling and evaluation stages are closely related and are often repeated several times in successive iterations before the final stage is reached.

Deployment

At the deployment stage, you publish your best model for your end users and examine the results. At this stage, complexities are often overlooked. Production code has a separate set of strict requirements and **service level agreements** (**SLAs**) that your model needs to meet. We can separate those requirements into two categories: functional and nonfunctional. Functional requirements define your service's features, while nonfunctional requirements define your SLAs.

Some examples of the functional requirements for your model service are as follows:

- Request/response format
- Capability for model versioning
- A UI for tracking deployments and request statistics

Nonfunctional requirements define the quality of service and availability of your service, and some of them are as follows:

- Desired request throughput (1,000 requests per second)
- Availability schedule (24/7 and 5/8)
- Secure communication
- Elastic scalability so that the system will stay available when the user load peaks

The requirements for model deployment are similar for different projects, so this part of the process is subject to reusability. Instead of repeating the same work for each project, you can develop your own model-serving framework or use an existing one.

Another important point to remember at the deployment stage is evaluation. This does not end at the previous stage; you should evaluate all of the model's metrics online. Your system may trigger alerts or compensative actions such as model retraining if the online metrics drop below a certain threshold. A/B testing and multi-armed bandits are also a part of the deployment process and can be supported as features of your model server.

Now, you should be familiar with the common stages of each data science project. Let's see how we can execute each stage with a proper management approach.

Choosing a project management methodology

Project management methodologies provide a set of rules and processes that can distinguish chaotic projects from coherent ones. They provide a framework where everyone can act toward a greater goal. Laws do the same for our society. However, laws are not perfect and they often fail. There is no silver bullet in the world of software management either. Some management practices are better suited to one type of project and will let you down in another. In the following sections, we will explore the most popular ways of managing software projects and learn how to adapt them to a data science environment so that we can draw conclusions and choose the one that suits our project the best.

Waterfall

The most intuitive way to manage a project is to approach it like you're building a house. The steps for this are as follows:

1. Prepare the building site
2. Lay a foundation
3. Create a framework
4. Build a roof
5. Build walls
6. Connect the electricity and water
7. Finish the exterior and interior

To build a software system, you do the following:

1. Prepare the development environment
2. Analyze and document the requirements
3. Analyze and document the architecture and software specification
4. Build the system
5. Test that everything is working according to the requirements
6. Finish the project

This management methodology is called a **waterfall**. It is logical on paper, but real-world applications rarely end up being very successful. The reason behind this is that all the steps are laid out sequentially and are only repeated once. If you make a single mistake, the project plan will fall apart. A single undocumented requirement, such as the one at *step 2*, can result in a disaster at *step 6*. Clients do not have a complete view of the end result and they can make mistakes too. Requirements can change after customers see the actual implementation of their requests.

Software project managers know that a single waterfall won't solve their issues, so they compose many smaller waterfalls into sequential iterations. This stage of evolution is called iterative and incremental software development. The iterative project is comprised of several phases that are managed in a waterfall fashion. The length of a single iteration is measured in months. At the end of each phase, the development team shows intermediate results to the end user for the purpose of collecting feedback. This feedback is used to jumpstart the next iteration. With each cycle, the understanding of the desired result evolves until it satisfies the customer's needs.

Agile

The iterative approach is still too heavy for most software projects. They suffer from changes that pile up in a mountain of technical requirements. In 2001, some of the brightest heads of the software development world created an Agile manifesto (`https://agilemanifesto.org`), which described a new management approach in four simple points:

- Individuals and interactions take precedence over processes and tools
- Working software takes precedence over comprehensive documentation
- Customer collaboration takes precedence over contract negotiation
- Responding to change takes precedence over following a plan

That is, while there is value in the latter of each point, we value the former of each point more.

Today, we associate agile with Kanban and Scrum. These methodologies take somewhere between 50 and 500 pages to explain. Nonetheless, at its core, Agile is simple. Any project can go astray with the agile manifesto, and many did. If you leave out the last sentence in the manifesto, you may end up creating a project without a plan or specification, which will inevitably end in an uncontrollable mess. People needed a more direct guide when it comes to managing software projects. This is why Kanban and Scrum were invented.

Kanban

First, let's cover Kanban. The best metaphor for explaining Kanban is a conveyor belt. Imagine that all of your tasks go through a fixed number of stages before they're finished. The concrete definition of those stages is up to you.

In software projects, you may want to use the following process:

1. Backlog (a buffer where all incoming tasks are collected before they're processed)
2. Requirements specification
3. Development
4. Code review
5. Testing
6. Deployment

Kanban visualizes each task on a board, as shown in the following diagram:

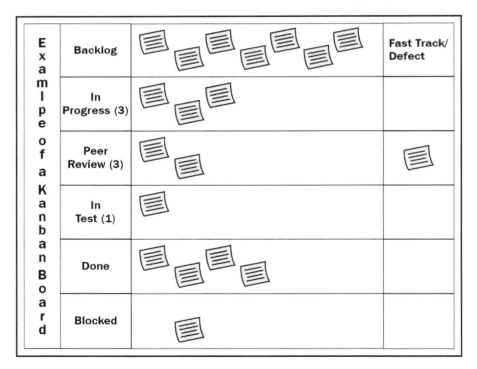

Each stage should have a limit regarding the tasks that can be done in parallel. Kanban purposefully limits the number of simultaneous tasks to increase throughput. If the team becomes blocked because there are too many tasks sitting in the deployment stage, then all the team members who are capable of making shipments of the end product to production should stop doing their tasks and switch to getting rid of the bottleneck. Once the problem has been resolved, the team may decide to work on other tasks according to their priority. Because of this, Kanban favors cross-functional teams where everyone can help push tasks through each stage. Kanban does not remove the concept of roles, but it states that no matter the role, each team member should be able to help in dealing with a bottleneck.

Kanban focuses on completing a single task from start to finish as fast as possible. The main metrics that we can use to measure the effectiveness of Kanban projects are as follows:

- **Lead time**: The time it takes for a task to move from the backlog to being completed on average.
- **Cycle tile**: The time it takes for a task to move from the starting stage to being completed on average. In our example, the cycle time would be between the requirements specification and deployment.
- **Throughput**: The average number of tasks you can get done during a time interval, that is, a day, a week, or a month.

In general, you don't create a fixed project plan with fixed deadlines when using Kanban. Also, you don't have to estimate each task individually since the metrics will take care of that. Measure your team's throughput for several weeks so that you have an idea of how much you will be able to deliver in the near future.

Kanban's powers are also its limitations, some of which are as follows:

- Kanban works best when the amount of work in each of your tasks is the same. If some tasks are taking significantly longer than the others, your metrics will stop being useful.
- If you don't want to work as a cross-functional team, your throughput will suffer from bottlenecks, which makes using Kanban worthless.
- Kanban does not give you the tools you need to manage deadlines, project scope, and budgets. The single thing it takes care of is optimizing throughput.

Kanban is a great software management approach for projects with repetitive tasks. It can also be partially applied to parts of your project where it makes sense to use it. Here are some examples of projects where using Kanban is a good idea:

- In a software support project, where you should take care of deployment and fixing frequent issues.
- If your data science project has a dedicated team that performs experiments with machine learning models, using Kanban will help increase their throughput.
- Projects where you need to create lots of similar things, such as hundreds of web forms, data mappings, or identical machine learning models.

 The surprising thing about カンバン (Kanban) is that it was originally developed to make the car manufacturing process more efficient. Toyota invented Kanban in 1959 and integrated it into their production environment in 1962. You can see that all of Kanban's pros and cons make sense in terms of a manufacturing environment, where car parts go through different stages on a conveyor belt.

Scrum

Another popular management methodology from the agile family is Scrum. The main idea behind Scrum is the sprint. The sprint is a set of tasks with a fixed deadline and duration. Typical sprint durations are one week, two weeks, and one month. Explaining the entirety of Scrum would take another book, so we will only present the basics here.

The Scrum process includes the following steps:

1. Backlog grooming
2. Sprint planning
3. Sprint execution
4. Retrospective

Akin to other agile methodologies, all the tasks go into the project backlog. The project backlog needs periodic grooming: all of the obsolete tasks should be deleted; the rest of the tasks need to be ordered by priority.

The main component of Scrum is the sprint. A sprint is an iteration with a fixed deadline and a defined goal. The typical length of a sprint is 2 weeks. It always starts with a sprint planning meeting, where team members observe the project backlog and take tasks into a sprint. Each task is estimated in abstract story points. The goal of estimating in story points rather than hours is to make estimations relative rather than absolute. For example, we can consider a task with one story point trivial and a task with two story points as being slightly harder but still easy to complete. Four to six story points would indicate a normal task. Another system of story point estimates suggests using powers of 2 to 128 as task estimates. On the first sprint, the estimations are fairly approximate. On the second sprint, you compare the new tasks with the previous ones and see how many story points the task is worth. After four sprints, you can see how many story points your team can complete on average. You can also calculate an approximate hour equivalent of a single story point, although this should only be used as a reference and not as a substitute for story points during the sprint planning process.

During planning, each team member estimates the task on their own, and then their estimations are compared. This helps ensure everyone understands the task definition in the same way. Differences in estimates signify that the task needs a clearer explanation and evaluation in terms of the SMART criteria.

The sprint starts after the planning phase. When you start working on the sprint, it will be locked. You cannot change the scope you defined during the planning phase. The primary focus of the team is to complete all the tasks in the sprint before it ends. This strategy allows you to achieve your planned goals while being robust to changes. The main strength of Scrum is also its main weakness. If your customer comes into work in the middle of the week with an *extremely important task that needs to be done ASAP*, you should do your best to convince them that the team will deliver this during the next sprint. Scope locking is an essential mechanism that makes sprints work. If you depart from this rule often, Scrum will become an obstacle rather than a beneficial and effective management approach.

In practice, scope locking can cause problems, especially if you are working in a B2B environment. For situations where you have no options and are forced to change sprint scope, you have two options:

- **Trade tasks**: You can remove a task from the sprint and add a new one.
- **Start a new sprint**: You can stop the current sprint and plan a new one.

Using these options frequently makes Scrum ineffective. Try to negotiate a fixed sprint scope with your customers and show them that it brings benefits such as planned delivery while leaving space for requirement changes.

A good strategy you can use to avoid unexpected scope changes is to ask your customers to take part in backlog grooming and sprint planning. Scrum experts suggest that you should assign a special product owner role for this task. The product owner should decide on task priorities, sprint goals, and negotiate all the conflicting requirements with project stakeholders.

Scrum came directly from the software development world, so it has fewer limitations than Kanban. The price lies in its complexity: Scrum is not an easy methodology, and it will create management overhead. Each team member should understand Scrum if you want it to work. In complex projects, you may need to give someone the dedicated role of Scrum master. This is someone who will take care of applying the methodology to one or several of your projects.

In the next section, we will look at choosing a methodology according to the needs of your project.

Choosing a methodology that suits your project

Choosing a project management methodology can become a captivating and complex task. You can spend a lot of time thinking about how one approach will support your processes better than another, and what limitations it will have. Try not to spend much of your time on methodological considerations. It is much more important to choose something and stick with it unless it is clearly harming your project. To simplify this process, we will explore some simple guidelines when it comes to choosing a management approach.

Creating disruptive innovation

If you create a solution that should disrupt the market, the only thing that matters is the efficiency of your methodology. You won't have many customers at the start of the project, so you should be able to collect feedback and perform focused work to iterate on the next version of your product. Scrum works best in such situations. You can implement new features regarding the sprint and collect feedback at the end of each sprint to start a new iteration. Kanban will work too, but it will provide fewer benefits in terms of disruptive innovation.

Providing a tested solution

If you implement a system that resembles some of your past projects, it will presumably require much less research than in previous iterations. This is also the case for system integration projects, where you provide services that can integrate your product into the customer's IT environment. In those projects, you can define many customer-focused tasks that can be divided into three to five groups depending on the total amount of work that needs to be done. In this setting, Kanban will provide the most benefit. Using Kanban will allow you to focus on delivering more results to the customer in less time.

Developing a custom project for a customer

Using Agile methodologies can be extremely tricky when you're working on a project for a customer. Your clients will want to have the best of both worlds: fixed deadlines with constantly changing requirements. Your job is to decide on the best approach for this project and explain its pros and cons. Many teams settle for something between Scrum and waterfall: you develop the initial scope of the project, estimate it, and show it to the client. Next, you implement the project scope piece by piece using sprints. The requirements will inevitably change during the implementation stage, so it is important that you manage these changes and keep the customer involved in sprint planning.

Choosing a project methodology goes hand in hand with estimating data science projects. In the next section, we will define the goals of the estimation process and learn how to make estimates.

Estimating data science projects

If you need to explain the basic principles of forecasting to someone, ask them if they have ever worked on a software project. If so, they already know the basics of forecasting: everyone who has worked on one has estimated tasks. Everyone needs estimates. Your customers need them to plan and control when they will start to use the results of your project. The project manager needs estimates to understand the scope, amount of work, and approximate costs for individual tasks or an entire project.

Estimation is beneficial in several areas, such as the following:

- **Understanding work structure**: Break down a task into multiple subtasks to view the main steps that you need to complete.
- **Understanding complexity**: While it is hard to estimate a complex task by itself, estimating each individual part of the work structure is simpler. It allows you to get an idea of how complex the task is and how long it will take to finish it.
- **Understanding costs**: In most businesses, you won't be able to start working on a project if you don't explain and defend its costs and required resources first.

The largest problem with estimations is that they fail. Our plans are inaccurate, incomplete, and often irrelevant to how the real work will be done. Even experienced software developers struggle to estimate the total amount of hours that it will take to do a single task unless they have done it multiple times already.

Research shows that humans are bad at absolute estimates. Our brains are simply not suited to making accurate mental models of complex multilayered projects. For example, if we were to ask a bunch of strangers about the height of the nearest building, the majority would fail to give you the correct answer. However, if you told them the height of several buildings, their estimates would be much more accurate. This is true not only for building height estimates but for all kinds of estimation.

To use relative estimates in data science projects, you need two things: relevant samples and a good estimation process. We can think of relevant estimates as simple statistical estimators that average the length of all previous relevant tasks. To create such an estimator, we first need to collect a dataset. If you follow a waterfall process, then to get one new data point in your estimation dataset, you need to complete a whole project from start to end. You may need to fail estimates in many projects before you get good at estimating one particular type of project.

The trick is to get down to the individual task levels. Scrum suggests that you use relative story points instead of absolute hours for this reason. First, your estimates become relative at the task level, then at the sprint level, and finally at the project level. If you have no prior experience that will help you to make relative estimates, the only absolute estimate you should make is one for the first sprint of the project. From here, you should use the previous tasks as a basis for making new estimations.

You don't have to use Scrum to benefit from relative estimations. Scrum provides one way to make them work, but it may not be ideal for your circumstances. If that is the case, you can adapt any management methodology for relative estimation.

Differentiating between business and implementation estimates:

We can look at estimates from two perspectives. The first one will be familiar to project managers and team leaders who are mostly concerned with project delivery: the implementation perspective. The main goal of estimates in this example is to provide correct expectations regarding how much time and money will be required to build the solution.

 Another perspective is closely related to the business goals of the project and is often unseen by the implementation team. Every project is generally backed up by a business model that fixes expectations on revenue increases, customer satisfaction, reduced costs, and so on.

This business model should always be considered when you're creating implementation estimates. In data science projects, business estimations can be included in the project by deriving budget constraints from a business model and creating a set of business metrics that will evaluate the project's performance.

Learning to make time and cost estimates

Using relative estimates is an effective strategy, but it becomes useless if someone asks you, *When exactly will you be able to finish this?* Scrum and Kanban do not give you project estimation tools. In fact, both methodologies argue that making such estimates is unnecessary. This line of thought is true if your goal is to efficiently complete a project with known deadlines and known budget constraints. However, there are situations where you may need to set budgeting and time constraints yourself.

Let's take a consulting environment as an example. We need to build a custom analytics system for a client. The main task is to estimate the probability of buying a certain product based on the user's profile. This customer needs an entirely new solution that will meet the requirements of various stakeholders from several departments. They also ask you to integrate the solution with various IT systems. They have invited several companies to compete for the project. The first thing they ask each candidate company is, *How much will this cost and how fast will you be able to build it? How can we approach this if we know the limitations of absolute estimations?*

Let's start with the outline. The outline is a hierarchical list of high-level tasks that you will need to complete. The simplest outline for a waterfall project may look like this:

1. Collect the requirements
2. Implement the requirements
3. Test the system
4. Deploy the system

Using a waterfall project is risky, so we will split the system into several stages, with each going through several successive steps. Depending on the complexity of the stage, you will need to make one or several iterations of the same stage to complete it. In theory, you could try to create an outline for every two-week sprint, but this is unrealistic because of the ever-changing nature of data science projects.

For example, let's look at the outline for requirements collection:

1. Collect the requirements:
    - Software architecture:
        - Nonfunctional requirements specification
        - Nonfunctional requirements implementation strategy
        - Component diagram
        - Integration diagram
    - Functional requirements specification:
        - UI:
            - UI requirements
            - UI mockups
        - Backend services
        - Data analysis and modeling:
            - EDA
            - Creating an experimentation backlog

You should start by defining the rough steps and then detail them. If you have created similar projects before, you can look at their outlines so that you know where to start. Collecting and using data from other projects can serve as a primary source of relative estimates, so do not underestimate your prior experience.

You will have difficulty decomposing some tasks. Being unsure about an approach to a task is a red flag signaling that you need to communicate with your customers and figure this out. If you do not how many systems you will need to integrate with, you will have a hard time decomposing all the stages and tasks related to integration. In this case, we need to call the customer and quickly discover the necessary information. However, you may have hundreds of such questions during the estimation process, and tracking new information will quickly become ineffective. It is a good idea to prepare a numbered list of questions first. Answers can change during the estimation process, so each question should be assigned a date. Ideally, those questions should be shared in a format that makes collaboration easy.

When your outline is detailed enough, it is time to design a software architecture proposal. This is a crucial step because matching outlines with customer requirements is not always economically viable or even possible from a technological standpoint. You should have at least a rough idea of what technologies you will use, how they will integrate with the rest of the customer's system, and how your solution should be deployed. If there are any crucial nonfunctional requirements, such as 24/7 availability, the software architect should also think about how to implement them in terms of technology and system design. Drafting a high-level architecture vision will help explain this outline. Do not hesitate to change the outline if you think that's necessary. Software design is a complex task an experienced engineer should do, so if you do not have deep expertise in designing software solutions, ask for help from someone on your team, or even better, make software design a collaborative effort.

After you've completed the outline and have a software architecture vision, you can start estimating the project. I recommend using simple statistical estimation procedures such as the **program evaluation and review technique** (PERT).

In PERT, you give each task a three-point estimate:

- **Optimistic estimate**: The time you plan to spend on the task if everything goes well; minor technical problems and requirements issues may arise.
- **Most likely estimate**: The most realistic estimate you can give for the task.
- **Pessimistic estimate**: The time that's required to finish the task if problems arise. This includes additional risks for dealing with experiments that have gone wrong, complex debugging sessions, and having long debates with the customer.

Then, you can calculate a simple weighted average to get the final estimate:

$$PERT\ Estimate = \frac{Optimistic\ estimate + 4 \times Most\ likely\ estimate + Pessimistic\ estimate}{6}$$

Calculating the standard deviation is also useful when it comes to making confidence intervals:

$$PERT\ Standard\ Deviation = \frac{Pessimistic\ estimate - Optimistic\ estimate}{6}$$

Pert Estimate $\pm 3 \times PERT\ Standard\ Deviation$ will give you a 99.7% confidence interval, meaning that the task will end up somewhere between these numbers with a 99.7% probability. If this range is too wide for you, you can use $2 \times PERT\ Standard\ Deviation$, which will give you a 95.5% confidence interval.

Use data from any finished projects as a base for relative estimation. The more external resources you use for estimation, the more accurate and risk-averse your estimates will become.

Since we are ineluctably bad at estimation, all of the estimates are only a rough idea of your current view of the project implementation plan. Project outlines and estimates should constantly change and be adapted to the current situation. You should periodically check whether the original plan should be changed and updated. If so, convey this to the customer and work through the necessity of the changes. It may be that the customer added several new features to your backlog, thinking that they were present in the original scope. If this is not the case, negotiate a scope expansion, followed by a budget and deadline extension. If these features are not critical enough, advise the customer to remove them from the backlog. With each completed task on a particular type of project, your experience will grow. As a result, you will be able to anticipate more of the customer's needs and include them in the base plan, which will make estimates more accurate. Store all of the versions of the project estimations so that you can track all scope changes effortlessly.

Project architecture vision should also be robust in terms of changes. The more customized your solution is, the less likely it is that it will create an ideal architecture vision that will survive all scope changes. Plan ahead and include several variation points in the parts of your solution that are the most likely to change. A vacation point is a software component (or a set of software components) that was going to change from the start. A plugin architecture and microservices with fixed contracts are examples of variation points that allow for easy extension or substitution.

Discovering the goals of the estimation process

It is important to keep the end goal in mind while making estimations. You can build a data science system without making a grand plan. Creating estimates and keeping them up to date requires a lot of effort and time. Data science projects are complex and unpredictable, so the more you and your customers believe in your estimates, the more likely they're going to fail. Estimates become more uncertain if your team has no prior experience in building solutions for a new business domain or if you are trying to apply new types of algorithms or use new technologies.

Having a fine-grained view of how to achieve the end goal is useful. In contrast, relying on the exact calculations of how long it will take you, or using extremely detailed outlines, is not. Use estimates wisely; they will help you align your implementation plans with customer demands.

Summary

In this chapter, we looked at how to manage data science projects. We explored how analytical projects differ from software engineering projects and studied the data science project life cycle. We looked at how we can choose a project management methodology that suits our needs and uncovered practical guidelines for estimating data science projects, and also discussed the limitations of long-term plans. No matter how good your plans and estimates are, data science projects have many inherent risks that can become the failing points of your projects.

In the next chapter, we will look at common pitfalls of data science projects.

9
Common Pitfalls of Data Science Projects

In this chapter, we will explore the common pitfalls of data science projects, as well as the mistakes that increase the risks your projects may encounter and that are easy to commit. It's important that you know how to deal with them for the success of your projects. Different types of data science solutions have many tempting ways of executing the project that can lead to undesired difficulties in the later stages of the project. We will pick and mitigate those issues one by one while following the data science project life cycle.

In this chapter, we will cover the following topics:

- Avoiding the common risks of data science projects
- Approaching research projects
- Dealing with prototypes and **minimum viable product** (MVP) projects
- Mitigating risks in production-oriented data science systems

Avoiding the common risks of data science projects

The first and most important risk of any data science project is the goal definition. The correct goal definition plays a major part in the success formula. It is often tempting to jump into the implementation stage of the project right after you have the task definition, regardless of whether it is vague or unclear. By doing this, you risk solving the task in an entirely different way from what the business actually needs. It is important that you define a concrete and measurable goal that will give your team a tool that they can use to distinguish between right and wrong solutions.

To make sure that the project goal is defined correctly, you may use the following checklist:

- You have a quantifiable business metric that can be calculated from the input data and the algorithm's output.
- The business understands the most important technical metrics that you use.
- The task is defined in data science terminology. You know if you are solving classification, regression, or another kind of task and have an idea of how to approach it technically.
- You understand the details of the (business) process and domain of the problem.
- All of the data sources that are required for the start of the project exist and can be accessed by the implementation team.

Another important issue is the documentation. In data science projects, experiment results can often change the course of the project. It is important to log all the experiments, along with the decisions and conclusions that you make. Fixing any incoming changes when it comes to data and requirements is also necessary. When you have this information, you will be able to see the whole line of thought that makes your solution work as it does.

Being aware of the common risks of data science projects will help you recover from major mistakes, but the devil is in the detail. In the next section, we will cover the different management approaches to research projects, prototypes, and end-to-end production systems and cover their specifics.

Approaching research projects

A research project is any project that gives you solutions to new, not well-known problems. Research projects aren't always about advancing science. If your team deals with a new kind of business domain, or a new type of machine learning library, these are also considered to be research projects. Discovering ways to apply data science to new business domains is also research. Almost every data science project includes a research subproject that takes care of the modeling process.

The first pitfall of research projects is the absence of scope. Every research project must have a clear scope, otherwise it won't be possible to finish it. It is also important to fix any external constraints for a research project. Your research budgets will grow as the scope's size increases, so limited budgets may also affect the depth and length of research that you will be able to do.

When you have an idea of your research capacity, you can start filling in the experiment backlog with your team. Each entry in a backlog should contain an idea that may advance your model's quality or help you reach your desired functionality. Each experiment should be defined in accordance with the SMART criteria.

For example, an initial experiment backlog for a binary classification problem may look like this:

1. Perform **exploratory data analysis** (**EDA**) and familiarize yourself with the data.
2. Create a baseline model using gradient boosting and basic preprocessing.
3. Test the encoding for categorical variables: Hash encoding.
4. Test the encoding for categorical variables: Target encoding.
5. Feature engineering: Measure the effect of date features.
6. Feature engineering: Aggregate the features day windows.

To be SMART-compliant, each entry should also contain deadlines, links to datasets, computation resources, and metric recommendations. We have omitted those details for brevity.

You should always prioritize experiments by expected returns. Some experiments may take a lot of time to complete in full, but less time for initial tests. If you and your team are unsure about priority, it is better to go wide rather than deep. Perform quick initial quality checks for all of the experiments in your current research iteration to determine the approximate time investment for each experiment.

It is also important to keep track of everything in an experiment, such as the following:

- Input data
- Date and time of the experiment
- Exact code version that produced the experiment's results
- Output files
- Model parameters and model type
- Metrics

You can use a simple shared document for this purpose or invest in integrating a specialized experiment tracking framework with a **user interface** (**UI**) into your project. Experiment tracking frameworks pay for themselves in projects that have lots of experimentation.

Finally, care about making each experiment reproducible and document the conclusions you drew from the results. To check for reproducibility, use the following criteria for each individual experiment:

- Input data is easily accessible and can be discovered by anyone on the team.
- The experiment code can be run on input data without errors.
- You don't need to enter undocumented configuration parameters to run the experiment. All of the configuration variables are fixed in an experiment configuration.
- The experiment code contains documentation and is easily readable.
- The experiment output is consistent.
- The experiment output contains metrics that you can use for comparison with other experiments.
- Conclusions from experiment results are present in the documentation, comments, or output files.

To avoid pitfalls in research projects, make sure you do the following:

- Define a clear goal
- Define the success criteria
- Define constraints, including the time and budget limitations
- Fill in the experiment backlog
- Prioritize by expectations
- Track all the experiments and their data
- Make the code reproducible
- Document your findings

Successful research projects can help you find an answer to a complex question or push the boundaries of scientific fields and practical disciplines. Research projects are often confused with prototypes, though prototypes pursue different goals in general. In the next section, we will look at the properties of prototyping projects, along with specific management strategies for these types of projects.

Dealing with prototypes and MVP projects

If you are dealing with data science, I bet you will find yourself doing a lot of prototyping. Prototypes often have very strict time and money limitations. The first lesson of prototyping is to approach every prototype as an MVP. The key idea behind MVP is to have just enough core features to show a working solution. Bells and whistles can be implemented later, as long as you are able to demonstrate the main idea behind your prototype.

Focusing on core features does not mean that your prototype should not have a pretty UI or stunning data visualizations. If those are the main strengths of your future product, by no means include them. To identify the core features of your product, you should think in terms of markets and processes.

Ask yourself the following questions to check whether a particular feature should be included in the MVP:

- Who are your users?
- What (business) processes are your solutions targeting?
- What problem do you want to solve?

Then, look at what features are crucial for reaching the desired goal, what is complementary, and what is unrelated to the goal. After that, look at your competitors and think about what will distinguish your MVP from them. If you have no distinguishing features or you don't solve a different problem, you will have a hard time competing with an already developed and possibly highly adopted competitive product.

It is beneficial to decompose your competitor's products into feature lists and perform the same analysis on them to see what supplementary features you should implement to be on par with the market. Doing a detailed feature analysis of competitor products is more about product development than creating an MVP, so we won't go any further into this topic.

With the information you will have acquired from feature analysis, you should be able to rank all the features and select a few core ones for your MVP. Keep in mind that you may change the priority of some features if you know that they are extremely important for success.

Another important aspect of delivering MVPs is to cut corners. If you have a lot of prototypes, having project templates, internal rapid prototyping tools, and document templates will save you a great deal of time and money. If you feel that your team spends more time creating MVPs using particular types of algorithms or technologies, think about creating tools that will automate most of the work. It is crucial to remember that MVP should be only good enough for your customers and users to see the benefits. As Voltaire said, *The best is the enemy of the good.*

For a more complete review of creating prototypes that can be transformed into real projects, please go to `Chapter 7`, *Managing Innovation.*

In the next section, we will have a brief overview of how we can manage an MVP in a consulting company environment.

Case study – creating an MVP in a consulting company

Our friend Mark works at a consulting company. His team has created a defect detection system prototype for a large manufacturing company. The system should analyze the video stream of products on a conveyor belt and detect products that are defective. Mark has answered the initial MVP question list:

- Who are your users?
  The manufacturing plant product quality department.

- What (business) processes are your solutions targeting?
  We target the core product quality control process.

- What problem do you want to solve?
  We want to decrease the total amount of defected products that are left undetected by the current quality control process.

Using these answers, Mark has created the core feature list for the MVP:

- Defect detection model
- Integration by monitoring cameras over the conveyor belt

Mark knows that the manufacturing plan director, Anthony, who is the key decision-maker, appreciates systems with a slick and intuitive UI. Also, Mark is sure that preparing a model quality report is essential for comparing the efficiency of as-is and to-be quality control processes.

These two insights added some more deliverables to the MVP:

- A UI for monitoring defects in real time
- A model quality report that provides an efficiency comparison between the old process and the improved process, along with an automated quality control step

After the customer approved the scope, Mark decided to use Scrum as a management methodology and focused on delivering the first working version as fast as possible. To get up to speed, Mark's team, who were already experienced in applying computer vision algorithms, used internal software libraries that they can develop for rapid prototyping. The report template meant that they didn't have to spend a lot of time writing documents, which meant they could focus on MVP development.

This example concludes our overview of prototypes. Now, we are ready to dive into the topic of assessing and mitigating risks in data science projects.

Mitigating risks in production-oriented data science systems

End-to-end data science projects encompass one or several full iterations of the data science project life cycle. End-to-end data science projects comprise of all the risks of research projects and MVPs, along with a new set of risks related to change management and production deployment.

The first major risk is the inability to sustain a constant change stream. Data science projects involve scope changes, and you should be able to work with them without making the project fall apart. Scrum gives you the basic tools you need for change management by freezing the development scope over the course of the week. However, for any tool to work, your customer should understand and follow the required processes, along with your team.

Another issue is that the implementation of a given change may cause a lot of unexpected bugs. Data science projects often lack automated testing procedures. The absence of constantly testing existing functionality may cause ripple effects when one simple change causes several bugs. Without tests, a lot more bugs also go unnoticed and get passed into production. It is also important to implement online testing modules since quality assurance does not end in the development phase. Models can degrade in performance over time, and your system should monitor abrupt changes in business and technical metrics.

If your team has not planned for production in advance, you will face many complex engineering issues related to nonfunctional requirements such as the availability, scalability, and reliability of your system. To avoid this, care about system design and software architecture from the start of the project.

Even if everything has gone well technically, the final result may bewilder your customers. If key stakeholders do not see the benefit of your system, you must look for any mistakes that were in your goal definitions. It is often the case that project goals change midterm, along with the customer's views of what's best for their business. To avoid this major risk, you should constantly check that the task you are working on is important and that the solution method is correct.

In the following table, we have enumerated the common risks and their solutions to sum up this chapter:

Risk group	Risk	Solution
Common	Vague goal definition.	Make sure that the goal's definition is complete and includes all the items from the checklist in this chapter.
Common	The project goal is not quantifiable.	Define quantifiable business metrics that can be understood by the customer. Define one or several technical metrics that correlate with your business metrics.
Common	Decision-making without keeping track of the record.	Document every major decision and conclusion you make throughout the project. Fix data and code versions in order to reproduce the results that lead to your decisions.
Research	The team can't reproduce the experiment's results.	Track the experiment's results and data, along with the code.

Research	The research has no scope and plan of action.	Plan ahead using the research backlog. Prioritize entries in the research backlog and periodically check whether there are any obsolete entries that should be removed. Assess your expectations of each experiment by performing quick tests, if possible.
MVP	The prototype does not show how to solve the user's problem.	Think about every prototype as an MVP that solves your customers' problems. Define your scope by taking the minimum amount of functionality required to solve your customers' problems into account.
MVP	The MVP includes too many unnecessary features that take time to develop.	Use feature analysis to define the MVP scope.
MVP	The MVP takes a lot of time to develop.	If your team makes a lot of MVPs, think about creating rapid prototyping frameworks and project templates to speed up the development process.
Project development	The customer is constantly pushing the team to make urgent scope changes.	Advocate for the use of Agile development methodology for your project. Track project scope changes to show how they affect project deadlines.
Project development	The customer does not see how the system solves their problem.	Constantly review your project goals and make sure that your way of solving the problem has been confirmed by the customer.
Project development	New changes introduce a lot of bugs.	Write automated tests.
Production deployment	The model's quality is degraded in production and the system has no tools to solve this problem.	Develop an online testing module to track metrics in production. Validate incoming data. Periodically retrain your models on new data.

Production deployment	The system is not suitable for production usage.	Fix functional and nonfunctional requirements for your system. Prepare an architecture vision that provides a production-ready system design.

Let's move on to the next case study that will demonstrate how you can detect and control these common risks.

Case study – bringing a sales forecasting system into production

Jane works as a senior manager in a start-up company that provides sales forecasting solutions to various logistic companies all over the world. During a major tech conference, a logistics company representative called Max asked if Jane's company could benefit from using an AI. Jane mentioned that tools alone won't make the company better, and that AI is a tool too, such as their ERP software, only more flexible. She started by creating a more concrete task definition in order to close off risks from the **common** group in the risk table:

Jane: What about forming a more defined goal? I know it can be hard without knowing about the technical details of AI and machine learning, so let me help you. Our company provides sales forecasting solutions for logistics companies like yours. The typical use case is to integrate our system into your ERP so that your personnel won't waste time making forecasts by hand. Does this sound interesting to you?

Max: Sure, can you tell me more?

Jane: OK. Our system makes demand forecasts for each item in your warehouse. We can estimate the expected number of items that you will need to ship by a given date in the future. To do this, we need access to your ERP database. I bet your employees already do this, but the process generally takes a lot of time and the results are not as accurate as they could be, especially if your product catalog contains hundreds or thousands of items.

Max: Yes, the process takes a lot of time indeed. We even struggle to add new items to the catalog since this will require us to hire twice as many people in the future.

Jane: If what I've offered sounds interesting to you, I'd be happy to assist you in making a small MVP project that will show you how beneficial our system will be to your business. However, we'll need a bit of assistance from your side. To show you the positive effect of using the system, we'll need to make sure that the goal is stated in numbers that can be understood by the company's management. Let's set up a meeting so I can show you how we can quantify the project results and what support we'll need from your IT specialists.

Max: Sure, thanks!

After this discussion, Jane had a meeting with Max, where she showed him a common approach to evaluating the project's performance from the business side. She documented all the decisions in a small business requirements document and confirmed that the results of the discussion were correct by showing it to Max. Jane also discussed the success criteria for the MVP. Max agreed that the production deployment is not necessary at this stage of the project and that they can make a decision about production integration by looking at the offline testing results, which Jane's team will present at a meeting. This way, she covered all three major risks in the **common** group.

Since this is an MVP project, she also considered risks in the MVP group. Jane asked Max how they could present the system to end users and company management so that they can understand the benefits of such a system. They settled on integrating the system directly into the company's ERP solution as this was the most cost-efficient way for both sides. Max had lots of ideas regarding what useful features they could include in the MVP, along with visualization dashboards and system administration tools. Jane noticed that those features did not add to the core value of the system and would be better for the implementation stage to implement.

After creating a clear goal definition and shaping the MVP constraints, Jane's team proceeded to the implementation stage. To close the risks in the project development group, Jane coordinated with the customer about project management methodology. Based on her previous experience, Jane decided to use Scrum for this MVP. She explained the importance of fixed scope iterations to the customer and made sure that everyone agreed on how changes will be incorporated into sprints during the planning phase. She also shared the project's backlog with Max using a software project management system so that he could add new tasks and prioritize them with the team, acting as the product owner. Jane made sure that Max will have the time to participate in the spring planning meetings so that the project won't go astray. The general software development practices in Jane's start-up have already closed risks related to code quality, delivery pipeline automation, and automated testing, so she doesn't need to care about them.

Summary

In this chapter, we have explored the common pitfalls of data science projects, as well as how to manage research projects with tools such as experiment backlog and experiment tracking. We have also seen how prototypes differ from research projects and looked at how to manage prototype development from the standpoint of an MVP. Those techniques were then summarized in a case study that concerned MVP development in a consulting company. Finally, we enumerated and systematized the major risks and their solutions for research, prototype, and production systems.

In the next chapter, we will look at how to grow data science products and improve internal team performance by using reusable technology.

10
Creating Products and Improving Reusability

In this chapter, we will conclude the *Managing Data Science Projects* section by looking at how we can help products grow and improve reusability. This chapter focuses on teams who work to deliver custom solutions for customers. You will find the content in this chapter helpful if your team helps internal business stakeholders at the company or external customers who want to buy expertise, services, and software solutions. The benefits of product thinking and reusability are underappreciated when it comes to the consultation stage, whereas they become more obvious if your team is developing a product that is focused on a market niche.

In this chapter, we will cover the following topics:

- Thinking of projects as products
- Determining the stage of your project
- Improving reusability
- Seeking and building products

Thinking of projects as products

To benefit from the ideas in this chapter, you must think about your work as product development. While many companies deliver software products to the market, you deliver services. We can perceive services as a product; they also obey the laws of supply and demand, and there are markets for different types of services.

Like software products, you can decompose your activity into service features. Some of the aspects of your service that your team is good at will separate your department or company from your competitors, but you will likely find some of these aspects lagging behind other organizations that focus on this particular type of service. For example, a data science consulting company may shine in creating custom models. However, their **user interfaces (UIs)** will be worse than that of a specialized UI development company. These tradeoffs are justified by market demands: companies who want to buy services on a custom model development rarely need the same team to deliver a high-end UI.

Thinking about services as products opens up new possibilities for improvement. You can analyze your best service feature and think about the improvements that you can introduce to make your service better and more profitable, thereby opening up new possibilities for continuous service quality improvement.

In most cases, the best team delivers more functionality in less time and at a lower cost while being more customizable and better in quality than products that are optimized toward a broader market. As a service provider, you can do one thing that no product is capable of: creating solutions that are highly specialized for solving a specific problem for your customer. The question is, how can we make custom solutions easier to implement while not losing the key benefit of providing a custom solution to a customer's problem?

The first step of thinking about projects in terms of products is to consider the project's stage. In the next section, we will consider the concept of reusability in relation to different project types and stages.

Determining the stage of your project

To develop the action plan of service improvement, you need to determine the type and stage of the project you are working on. We can divide projects into two major categories:

- Products
- Custom solutions

While products are reusable by nature, often, custom solutions aren't. However, custom solutions can be built from reusable components while not losing the qualities of made-to-order software. To grow these internal components and improve reusability, you should care about them through each stage of the project:

- **Minimum viable product** (**MVP**): Think about the results of your previous projects that you can reuse while having a minimal investment of time. Even if it looks like building this functionality from scratch will be easier, creating a reusable component can save you a lot more time over a longer time span.
- **Development**: Think about what reusable components you can include in the system that you are building. Decide if any new functionality that you are building can be transformed into a reusable component.
- **Production**: Stabilize and integrate any existing technology.

The next big step in improving reusability is managing research. The question that arises is: how do we decide when a project needs a research phase? First, let's look at what kinds of research we can do in data science projects:

- **Data**: Improving your understanding of customer's data by performing **exploratory data analysis** (**EDA**) and searching for insights in data.
- **Models and algorithms**: Improving your models and searching for new approaches to solving a problem.
- **Technology**: Researching new technologies to improve your solution. Technology can be directly applicable to your project or supplement the development process by improving operations, requirement management, code or data versioning, and so on.

Research is hard to plan and estimate, but it is necessary for finishing data science projects successfully. It opens up new opportunities, provides insights, and changes processes. Finding the right balance between research and implementation is crucial for the project's success. To manage research efficiently, you can split your project into two logical subprojects: research and solution development.

You can integrate research phases into the solution development project in several ways, as follows:

- **In parallel with solution development**: This approach requires a separate research team working full time. It is useful because the research process provides results in the background of the main project. Items from the research backlog that yielded good results are converted into research integration tasks in the main project backlog. This way of managing research is useful for data and model research because those activities can take a long time to finish and are straightforward to integrate into the main code base most of the time.
- **Before or after each development iteration**: This approach requires your team to switch focus from solution development to research and is most effective when the results of the research can influence the long-term method of building the system. Technology research is the best candidate for this form of integration. You can tie technology research into software design stages so that your team can integrate new technologies into a project in a controlled manner.

To conclude, let's look at a way in which we can integrate research with implementation.

Case study – building a service desk routing system

Lucas works as a data science team leader in a large retail company. He was asked to build a system that will help bring down the load on the support department, thereby solving the issues of 10,000 retail stores on a daily basis. The issue creation process in the department support portal is as follows:

1. Choose an issue category.
2. Fill in the template form.
3. Wait for the solution or information inquiry.
4. If you do not know the issue category, select **No category** in the form and describe the issue in the free-form text box.

The team has noticed that **No category** issues are the most difficult and time-consuming for the support team to fix. This is because the free-form description often lacked the information that was requested by the templates, and so the support engineer needed to ask for a lot of additional information to determine the issue category and fill in the template form by himself. The idea was to use historical data to classify the incoming **No category** issues and ask the user to fill in the information that's required by the template before sending the issue to the support department.

The project had two major challenges:

- Building a text classifier that was capable of handling an extensive list of issue categories (more than 1,000)
- Creating an issue classification system that would reliably operate on a 24/7 schedule and integrate this system with the company's support portal

Lucas thought that the project actually consisted of two subprojects: research and system implementation. The research project had an unbounded time span and required the data scientists on the team to build various text classifiers and assess their quality. The main goal of the system implementation project was to build a highly available model server and change the company's support portal code so that they could integrate the model into the issue creation workflow.

Lucas has created two project teams for each project and created separate task backlogs for them:

- **The research team**: The text classification task was not standard and did not have a direct solution because most pre-built text classification models can only handle a very limited number of classes and this project required the model to be stable with 1,000 classes. The research team had a team leader who managed and prioritized the research backlog so that the team would focus only on the most cost-effective and promising ideas. Everyone understood that this research could not have clear deadlines, so the team decided to use the artificial constraint of the general project deadline. The goal was to train the best possible text classifier, given the time constraints and the company's data.
- **The implementation team**: They were focused on building a software solution. It consisted of a machine learning engineer, backend software developer, UI software developer, a system analyst, and a team leader. Lucas decided that it would be best to use Scrum for this part of the project. The team discussed the deadlines, set up a fixed number of sprints, and made sure that they will be able to complete all the work during the time frame. The task was clear from a technical standpoint and didn't require extensive research or prototyping. The team had previously built model servers, so they decided to reuse their existing technology and add a few missing features.

The last question that remained was how they could integrate new research results into the system without breaking the system. This integration could easily become the project's bottleneck because the research team constantly switched data preprocessing methods and machine learning frameworks in search of the best result for the project. Lucas decided that the research team will need to provide their models as a software library with a fixed interface that's been designed and documented with the implementation team. This interface will establish the communications contract between the research and implementation teams so that new model versions can be changed by simply updating the research team's library version.

After you have decided on the best approach for integrating research, along with the solution development process, and thought about which reusable components you can benefit from, you can move on and see how your team can gradually improve the reusability of the technology that you deliver.

Improving reusability

Improving reusability is a custom project development setting where you develop and reuse internal components to build better solutions faster. Look at what parts of your work are repeated in all of your projects. For many companies, it's the model deployment and serving. For others, it is building the dashboards on top of the model.

Use open source projects as a starting point. In many fields, the best tools are provided by commercial companies. Thankfully, the data science community is a very open-minded group, and the best tools you can find are open source. Of course, there are great commercial products too, but you can build production-grade systems with state-of-the-art models using open solutions. They will give you a very solid foundation to build upon.

See if you can use those tools to decrease the total amount of time your team spends on similar repetitive activities over different projects. If you find that no open source solution solves your problem, then you have two options: build a reusable software component from scratch or buy a product. But how can you choose between buying a rebuilt solution versus building one for yourself? Prebuilt products are best suited for solving the common problems of data science teams. On the contrary, building custom internal reusable solutions should be left for the parts of the process that are unique to your team and company. To find a solution to your problem, you should look to open source solutions first, then to the product market, and lastly consider building a new technology internally.

Keep in mind that reusable components require special care. As your toolchain grows, your team will need to spend more time supporting it. Reusable tools necessitate designing APIs and workflows that will stand the test of time. Maintaining reusable tools that are used in multiple projects is not an easy task, but it will allow your team to build upon itself, making each successive project more efficient than its predecessor.

To build or to buy?

Often, your team will have this dilemma. You can build something yourself, use an open source solution, or buy a commercial product. This decision is never easy and has lasting consequences. Building something by yourself from scratch will require significant investment. You can cut corners by using an open source solution, but you may easily run into constraints or bugs that will force your team to dive into the development of this open source component. Trying to fix bugs or add features to large amounts of existing code that's been written by people from all around the world will require significant engineering efforts and will make switching to a different technology harder. Commercial products are the least customizable of the three, so your team must devote time to deciding which product matches your needs best.

Things will be easier if you approach this decision analytically. Define success criteria and think about the strategic importance of the component or technology that you are planning to build, use, or buy. Define, document, and weigh all the pros and cons of having a complete picture. Finally, discuss the matter with as many stakeholders as you can, including your team members and management.

Reusable components can make your team a lot more efficient, without making your solutions generic, so that each client will have a customized service. Sometimes, you will spot an opportunity that will allow your team to make a jump into a totally different business model by turning the highly demanded custom solution into a product. In the next section, we will see how we can seek and build products.

Seeking and building products

Over time, it is natural to have teams that are dedicated to the development of the most complex and popular parts of your reusable toolchain. If you have a reusable component that has stood the test of time in multiple projects and is backed up by an experienced team, it is worth considering turning it into a product.

Another sign that you should make products out of your projects is a high demand for some type of custom solution that you built. If every client asks you to build a customer support chatbot and you have already built tens of them, why not make a product to make everyone's lives easier?

If your company has no prior experience of delivering new products to the market, take this task seriously and be ready to transition into a new world. If you want to avoid mistakes, take the time to read the literature related to product management and consider hiring or consulting product managers that have the relevant experience. Product development differs from making a custom solution. In fact, it is an entirely different business, with processes and values that may seem bizarre to a consulting project manager.

Finally, remember that building products is risky and expensive. The product team will need to spend a substantial amount of effort converting any internal code base into a market-ready product. It the idea has no real market demand, this job will be a wasted effort.

Good product ideas are very attractive from a business perspective. However, if you provide services for different customers, you should always think about privacy before turning your projects into products for wide markets.

Privacy concerns

Privacy is of paramount importance for every data science team, especially for teams that are trusted by other businesses. When you're considering building a new product based on your internal code base or data, always check that everything you plan to use can be sold to other customers. If this is not the case, you may end up building the product from scratch, which will greatly increase the development costs. Ask your company's legal team if all the related NDAs and contracts allow for planned use cases.

You also need to consider licensing your internal reusable components so that you can legally reuse them across different projects. This book is not a legal consultant, so do not hesitate to consult with one if you plan to reuse software components and build products.

Summary

In this chapter, we have looked at the benefits of product thinking in a custom project development environment. We studied why reusability matters and how we can build and integrate reusable software components at each stage of the data science project. We also went over the topic of finding the right balance between research and implementation. Finally, we looked at strategies for improving the reusability of our projects and explored the conditions that allow us to build standalone products based on our experience.

In the next section of this book, we will look at how we can build a development infrastructure and choose a technology stack that will ease the development and delivery of data science projects. We will start by looking at ModelOps, which is a set of practices for automating model delivery pipelines.

Section 4: Creating a Development Infrastructure

In the final section, we aim to create a product that helps real people. Often, this means creating a stable piece of software that operates in production under a heavy load. Any data science product is also a software product. Teams can use existing best practices from software development to circumvent numerous caveats. This part of the book offers an overview of the must-have practices and tools required to build and deploy data science solutions.

This section contains the following chapters:

- Chapter 11, *Implementing ModelOps*
- Chapter 12, *Building Your Technology Stack*
- Chapter 13, *Conclusion*

11
Implementing ModelOps

In this chapter, we will look at ModelOps and its closest cousin—DevOps. We will explore how to build development pipelines for data science and make projects reliable, experiments reproducible, and deployments fast. To do this, we will familiarize ourselves with the general model training pipeline, and see how data science projects differ from software projects from the development infrastructure perspective. We will see what tools can help to version data, track experiments, automate testing, and manage Python environments. Using these tools, you will be able to create a complete ModelOps pipeline, which will automate the delivery of new model versions, while taking care of reproducibility and code quality.

In this chapter, we will cover the following topics:

- Understanding ModelOps
- Looking into DevOps
- Managing code versions and quality
- Storing data along with code
- Managing environments
- Tracking experiments
- The importance of automated testing
- Continuous model training
- A power pack for your projects

Understanding ModelOps

ModelOps is a set of practices for automating a common set of operations that arise in data science projects, which include the following:

- Model training pipeline
- Data management

- Version control
- Experiment tracking
- Testing
- Deployment

Without ModelOps, teams are forced to waste time on those repetitive tasks. Each task in itself is fairly easy to handle, but a project can suffer from mistakes in those steps. ModelOps helps us to create project delivery pipelines that work like a precise conveyor belt with automated testing procedures that try to catch coding errors.

Let's start by discussing ModelOps' closest cousin—DevOps.

Looking into DevOps

DevOps stands for **development operations**. Software development processes include many repetitive and error-prone tasks that should be performed each time software makes a journey from the source code to a working product.

Let's examine a set of activities that comprise the software development pipeline:

1. Performing checks for errors, typos, bad coding habits, and formatting mistakes.
2. Building the code for one or several target platforms. Many applications should work on different operating systems.
3. Running a set of tests that check that the code works as intended, according to the requirements.
4. Packaging the code.
5. Deploying packaged software.

Continuous integration and continuous deployment (CI/CD) states that all of those steps can and should be automated and run as frequently as possible. Smaller updates that are thoroughly tested are more reliable. And if everything goes wrong, it is much easier to revert such an update. Before CI/CD, the throughput of software engineers who manually executed software delivery pipelines limited the deployment cycle speed.

Now, highly customizable CI/CD servers rid us of manual labor, and completely automate all necessary activities. They run on top of a source code version control system, and monitor for new code changes. Once a new code change is present, a CI/CD server can launch the delivery pipeline. To implement DevOps, you need to spend time writing automated tests and defining software pipelines, but after that, the pipeline just works, every time you need it.

DevOps took the software development world by storm, producing many technologies that make software engineers more productive. Like any technology ecosystem, an expert needs to devote time to learning and integrating all tools together. Over time, CI/CD servers became more complicated and feature-rich, and many companies felt the need to have a full-time expert capable of managing delivery pipelines for their projects. Thus, they came up with the role of DevOps engineer.

Many tools from the DevOps world are becoming much easier to use, requiring only a couple of clicks in a user interface. Some CI/CD solutions such as GitLab aid you in creating simple CI/CD pipelines automatically.

Many benefits of CI/CD infrastructure apply to data science projects; however, many areas remain uncovered. In the next sections of this chapter, we will look at how data science projects can use CI/CD infrastructure, and what tools you can use to make the automation of data science project delivery more complete.

Exploring the special needs of data science project infrastructure

A modern software project will likely use the following infrastructure to implement CI/CD:

- Version control—Git
- Code collaboration platform—GitHub, GitLab
- Automated testing framework—dependent on the implementation language
- CI/CD server—Jenkins, Travis CI, Circle CI, or GitLab CI

All of these technologies miss several core features that are critical for data science projects:

- Data management—tools for solving the issue of storing and versioning large amounts of data files
- Experiment tracking—tools for tracking experiment results
- Automated testing—tools and methods for testing data-heavy applications

Before covering solutions to the preceding issues, we will familiarize ourselves with the data science delivery pipeline.

The data science delivery pipeline

Data science projects consist of multiple data processing pipelines that are dependent on each other. The following diagram displays the general pipeline of a data science project:

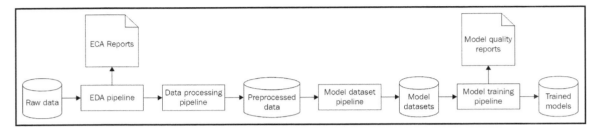

Let's quickly sum up all of the stages in the preceding diagram:

1. Each model pipeline starts with the **Raw data**, which is stored in some kind of data source.
2. Then, data scientists perform **exploratory data analysis** (**EDA**) and create **EDA Reports** to deepen the understanding of the dataset and discover possible issues with the data.
3. The **Data processing pipeline** transforms raw data into an intermediate format that is more suitable for creating datasets for training, validating, and testing models.
4. The **Model dataset pipeline** creates ready-to-use datasets for training and testing models.
5. The **Model training pipeline** uses prepared datasets to train models, assess their quality by performing offline testing, and generate **Model quality reports** that contain detailed information about model testing results.
6. At the end of the pipeline, you get the final artifact—a **Trained model** that is saved on a hard disk or a database.

Now, we are ready to discuss implementation strategies and example tools for ModelOps.

Managing code versions and quality

Data science projects deal with a lot of code, so data scientists need to use **source version control** (**SVC**) systems such as Git as a mandatory component. The most obvious way of using Git is to employ a code collaboration platform such as GitLab or GitHub. Those platforms provide ready-to-use Git servers, along with useful collaboration tools for code reviews and issue management, making working on shared projects easier. Such platforms also offer integrations with CI/CD solutions, creating a complete and easily configurable software delivery pipeline. GitHub and GitLab are free to use, and GitLab is available for on-premises installations, so there is no excuse for your team to miss the benefits of using one of those platforms.

Many teams synonymize Git with one of the popular platform offerings, but it is sometimes useful to know that it is not the only option you have. Sometimes, you have no internet access or the ability to install additional software on server machines but still want the benefits of storing code in a shared repository. You can still use Git in those restricted environments. Git has a useful feature called **file remotes** that allow you to push your code basically everywhere.

For example, you can use a USB stick or a shared folder as a remote repository:

```
git clone --bare /project/location/my-code /remote-location/my-code #copy
your code history from a local git repo
git remote add usb file:///remote/location/my-code
# add your remote as a file location
git remote add usb file:///remote/location/my-code
# add your remote as a file location
git push usb master
# push the code


# Done! Other developers can set up your remote and pull updates:
git remote add usb file:///remote/location/my-code # add your remote as a
file location
git pull usb mater # pull the code
```

By changing the `file:///` path to the `ssh:///` path, you can also push code to the remote SSH machines on your local network.

Most data science projects are written in Python, where static code analysis and code build systems are not as widespread as in other programming languages. Those tools allow you to groom code automatically and check it for critical errors and possible bugs each time you try to build a project. Python has such tools too—look at pre-commit (`https://pre-commit.com`).

The following screenshot demonstrates the running of pre-commit on a Python code repository:

```
$ pre-commit run --all-files
[INFO] Initializing environment for https://github.com/pre-commit/pre-commit-hooks.
[INFO] Initializing environment for https://github.com/psf/black.
[INFO] Installing environment for https://github.com/pre-commit/pre-commit-hooks.
[INFO] Once installed this environment will be reused.
[INFO] This may take a few minutes...
[INFO] Installing environment for https://github.com/psf/black.
[INFO] Once installed this environment will be reused.
[INFO] This may take a few minutes...
Check Yaml...............................................Passed
Fix End of Files.........................................Passed
Trim Trailing Whitespace.................................Failed
hookid: trailing-whitespace

Files were modified by this hook. Additional output:

Fixing sample.py

black....................................................Passed
```

Having covered the main recommendations for handling code, let's now see how we can achieve the same results for data, which is an integral part of any data science project.

Storing data along with the code

As you have seen previously, we can structure code in data science projects into a set of pipelines that produce various artifacts: reports, models, and data. Different versions of code produce changing outputs, and data scientists often need to reproduce results or use artifacts from past versions of pipelines.

This distinguishes data science projects from software projects and creates a need for managing data versions along with the code: **Data Version Control** (**DVC**). In general, different software versions can be reconstructed by using the source code alone, but for data science projects this is not sufficient. Let's see what problems arise when you try to track datasets using Git.

Tracking and versioning data

To train and switch between every version of your data science pipeline, you should track data changes along with the code. Sometimes, a full project pipeline can take days to calculate. You should store and document not only incoming but also intermediate datasets for your project to save time. It is handy to create several model training pipelines from a single dataset without waiting for the dataset pipeline to finish each time you need it.

Structuring pipelines and intermediate results is an interesting topic that deserves special attention. The pipeline structure of your project determines what intermediate results are available for use. Each intermediate result creates a branching point, from where several other pipelines can start. This creates the flexibility of reusing intermediate results, but at the cost of storage and time. Projects with lots of intermediate steps can consume a lot of disk space and will take more time to calculate, as disk input/output takes a lot of time.

Be aware that model training pipelines and production pipelines should be different. A model training pipeline might have a lot of intermediate steps for research flexibility, but a production pipeline should be highly optimized for performance and reliability. Only intermediate steps that are strictly necessary to execute the finalized production pipeline need to be executed.

Storing data files is necessary for reproducing results but is not sufficient for understanding them. You can save yourself a lot of time by documenting data descriptions, along with all reports that contain summaries and conclusions that your team draws from data. If you can, store those documents in a simple textual format so that they can be easily tracked in your version control system along with the corresponding code.

You can use the following folder structure to store the data in your projects:

- Project root:
    - Data:
        - Raw—raw data from your customer
        - Interim—intermediate data generated by the processing pipeline
        - Preprocessed—model datasets or output files
    - Reports—project reports for EDA, model quality, and so on
    - References—data dictionaries and data source documentation

Storing data in practice

We have explored why it is important to store and manage data artifacts along with the code but did not look at how we can do it in practice. Code version control systems such as Git are ill-suited for this use case. Git was developed specifically for storing source code changes. Internally, each change in Git is stored as a `diff` file that represents changed lines of a source code file.

You can see a simple example of a `diff` file in the following screenshot:

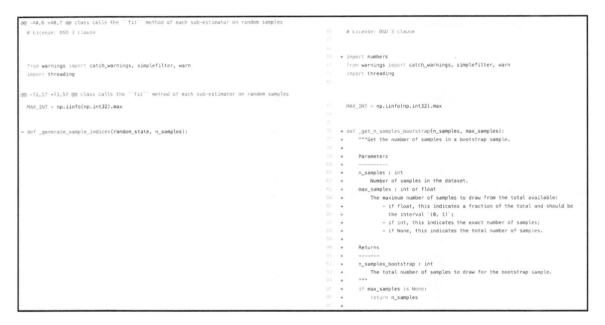

The highlighted lines marked with + represent added lines, while highlighted lines marked with – stand for deleted lines. Adding large binary or text files in Git is considered bad practice because it results in massive redundant `diff` computations, which makes repositories slow to work with and large in size.

`diff` files serve a very specific problem: they allow developers to browse, discuss, and switch between sets of changes. `diff` is a line-based format that is targeted at text files. On the contrary, small changes in binary data files will result in a completely different data file. In such cases, Git will generate a massive `diff` for each small data modification.

In general, you needn't browse or discuss changes to a data file in a line-based format, so calculating and storing `diff` files for each new data version is unnecessary: it is much simpler to store the entire data file each time it changes.

A growing desire for data versioning systems produced several technical solutions to the problem, the most popular being GitLFS and DVC. GitLFS allows you to store large files in Git without generating large diffs, while DVC goes further and allows you to store data at various remote locations, such as Amazon S3 storage or a remote SSH server. DVC goes beyond just implementing data version control and allows you to create automated reproducible pipelines by capturing code along with its input data, output files, and metrics. DVC also handles pipeline dependency graphs, so that it can automatically find and execute any previous steps of the pipeline to generate files that you need as input for your code.

Now that we are equipped with the tools to handle data storage and versioning, let's look at how to manage Python environments so that your team won't waste time with package conflicts on a server.

Managing environments

Data science projects depend on a lot of open source libraries and tools for doing data analysis. Many of those tools are constantly updated with new features, which sometimes break APIs. It is important to fix all dependencies in a shareable format that allows every team member to use the same versions and build libraries.

The Python ecosystem has multiple environment management tools that take care of different problems. Tools overlap in their use cases and are often confusing to choose from, so we will cover each briefly:

- **pyenv** (https://github.com/pyenv/pyenv) is a tool for managing Python distributions on a single machine. Different projects may use different Python versions, and pyenv allows you to switch between different Python versions between projects.
- **virtualenv** (https://virtualenv.pypa.io) is a tool for creating virtual environments that contain different sets of Python packages. Virtual environments are useful for switching contexts between different projects, as they may require the use of conflicting versions of Python packages.

- **pipenv** (`https://pipenv-searchable.readthedocs.io`) is a step above virtualenv. Pipenv cares about automatically creating a sharable virtual environment for a project that other developers may easily use.
- **Conda** (`https://www.anaconda.com/distribution/`) is another environment manager like pipenv. Conda is popular in the data science community for several reasons:
  - It allows sharing environments with other developers via the `environment.yml` file.
  - It provides the Anaconda Python distribution, which contains gigabytes of pre-installed popular data science packages.
  - It provides highly optimized builds of popular data analysis and machine learning libraries. Scientific Python packages often require building dependencies from the source code.
  - Conda can install the CUDA framework along with your favorite deep learning framework. CUDA is a specialized computation library that is required for optimizing deep neural networks on a GPU.

Consider using conda for managing data science project environments if you are not doing so already. It will not only solve your environment management problems but also save time by speeding up the computation. The following plot shows the performance difference between using the TensorFlow libraries installed by **pip** and **conda** (you can find the original article by following this link: `https://www.anaconda.com/tensorflow-in-anaconda/`):

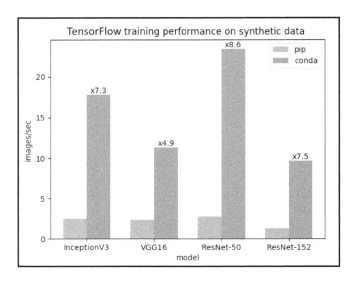

Next, we will cover the topic of experiment tracking. Experiments are a natural part of every data science project. A single project might contain the results of hundreds or even thousands of experiments. It is important to keep a record so that you can make correct conclusions about experiment results.

Tracking experiments

Experimentation lies at the core of data science. Data scientists perform many experiments to find the best approach to solving the task at hand. In general, experiments exist in sets that are tied to data processing pipeline steps.

For example, your project may comprise the following experiment sets:

- Feature engendering experiments
- Experiments with different machine learning algorithms
- Hyperparameter optimization experiments

Each experiment can affect the results of other experiments, so it is crucial to be able to reproduce each experiment in isolation. It is also important to track all results so your team can compare pipeline variants and choose the best one for your project according to the metric values.

A simple spreadsheet file with links to data files and code versions can be used to track all experiments, but reproducing experiments will require lots of manual work and is not guaranteed to work as expected. Although tracking experiments in a file requires manual work, the approach has its benefits: it is very easy to start and pleasant to version. For example, you can store the experiment results in a simple CSV file, which is versioned in Git along with your code.

A recommended minimum set of columns for a metric tracking file is as follows:

- Experiment date
- Code version (Git commit hash)
- Model name
- Model parameters
- Training dataset size
- Training dataset link
- Validation dataset size (fold number for cross-validation)
- Validation dataset link (none for cross-validation)
- Test dataset size

- Test dataset link
- Metric results (one column per metric; one column per dataset)
- Output file links
- Experiment description

Files are easy to work with if you have a moderate amount of experiments, but if your project uses multiple models, and each requires a large amount of experimentation, using files becomes cumbersome. If a team of data scientists performs simultaneous experiments, tracking files from each team member will require manual merges, and data scientists are better off spending time on carrying out more experiments rather than merging other teammates' results. Special frameworks for tracking experiment results exist for more complex research projects. These tools integrate into the model training pipeline and allow you to automatically track experiment results in a shared database so that each team member can focus on experimentation, while all bookkeeping happens automatically. Those tools present a rich user interface for searching experiment results, browsing metric plots, and even storing and downloading experiment artifacts. Another benefit of using experiment tracking tools is that they track a lot of technical information that might become handy but is too tedious to collect by hand: server resources, server hostnames, script paths, and even environment variables present on the experiment run.

The data science community uses three major open source solutions that allow the tracking of experiment results. These tools pack much more functionality than experiment tracking, and we will briefly cover each:

- **Sacred**: This is an advanced experiment tracking server with modular architecture. It has a Python framework for managing and tracking experiments that can be easily integrated into the existing code base. Sacred also has several UIs that your team can use to browse experiment results. Out of all the other solutions, only Sacred focuses fully on experiment tracking. It captures the widest set of information, including server information, metrics, artifacts, logs, and even experiment source code. Sacred presents the most complete experiment tracking experience, but is hard to manage, since it requires you to set up a separate tracking server that should always be online. Without access to the tracking server, your team won't be able to track experiment results.
- **MLflow**: This is an experimentation framework that allows tracking experiments, serving models, and managing data science projects. MLflow is easy to integrate and can be used both in a client-server setup or locally. Its tracking features lag a bit behind Sacred's powerhouse but will be sufficient for most data science projects. MLflow also provides tools for jumpstarting projects from templates and serving trained models as APIs, providing a quick way to publish experiment results as a production-ready service.

- **DVC**: This is a toolkit for data versioning and pipeline management. It also provides basic file-based experiment tracking functionality, but it is subpar in terms of usability compared to MLflow and Sacred. The power of DVC lies in experiment management: it allows you to create fully versioned and reproducible model training pipelines. With DVC, each team member is able to pull code, data, and pipelines from a server and reproduce results with a single command. DVC has a rather steep learning curve but is worth learning, as it solves many technical problems that arise in collaboration on data science projects. If your metric tracking requirements are simple, you can rely on DVC's built-in solution, but if you need something more rich and visual, combine DVC with MLflow or Sacred tracking—those tools are not mutually exclusive.

Now you should have a complete understanding of what tools can be used to track code, data, and experiments as a single entity in your project. Next, we will cover the topic of automated testing in data science projects.

The importance of automated testing

Automated testing is considered to be mandatory in software engineering projects. Slight changes in software code can introduce unintended bugs in other parts, so it is important to check that everything works as intended as frequently as possible. Automated tests that are written in a programming language allow testing the system as many times as you like. The principle of CI advises running tests each time a change in code is pushed to a version control system. A multitude of testing frameworks exists for all major programming languages. Using them, developers can create automated tests for the backend and frontend parts of their product. Large software projects can include thousands of automated tests that are run each time someone changes the code. Tests can consume significant resources and require a lot of time for completion. To solve this problem, CI servers can run tests in parallel on multiple machines.

In software engineering, we can divide all tests into a hierarchy:

1. End-to-end tests perform a full check of a major function of a system. In data science projects, end-to-end tests can train a model on a full dataset and check whether the metrics values suffice minimum model quality requirements.

2. Integration tests check that every component of the system works together as intended. In a data science system, an integration test might check that all of the steps of the model testing pipeline finish successfully and provide the desired result.

3. Unit tests check individual classes and functions. In a data science project, a unit test can check the correctness of a single method in a data processing pipeline step.

If the world of software testing is so technologically developed, can data science projects benefit from automated tests? The main difference between data science code and software testing code is the reliability of data. A fixed set of test data that is generated before a test run is sufficient for most software projects. In data science projects, the situation is different. For a complete test of the model training pipeline, you may need gigabytes of data. Some pipelines may run for hours or even days and require distributed computation clusters, so testing them becomes impractical. For this reason, many data science projects avoid automated testing. Thus, they suffer from unexpected bugs, ripple effects, and slow change integration cycles.

 A ripple effect is a common software engineering problem when a slight change in one part of the system can affect other components in an unexpected way, causing bugs. Automated tests are an efficient solution for detecting ripple effects before they cause any real damage.

Despite the difficulties, the benefits of automated testing are too great to ignore. Ignoring tests turns out to be much more costly than building them. This is true for data science projects and software projects. The benefits of automated testing grow with project size, complexity, and team size. If you lead a complex data science project, consider automating testing as a mandatory requirement for your project.

Let's look at how we can approach testing data science projects. End-to-end testing for model training pipelines might be impractical, but what about testing individual pipeline steps? Apart from the model training code, each data science project will have some business logic code and data processing code. Most of this code can be abstracted away from distributed computation frameworks in isolated classes and functions that are easy to test.

If you architect a project's code base with tests in mind from the start, it will be much easier to automate testing. Software architects and lead engineers on your team should take the testability of the code as one of the main acceptance criteria for code reviews. If the code is properly encapsulated and abstracted, testing becomes easier.

In particular, let's take the model training pipeline. If we separate it into a series of steps with clearly defined interfaces, we can then test data preprocessing code separately from model training code. And if data preprocessing takes a lot of time and requires expensive computation resources, you can at least test individual parts of the pipeline. Even basic function-level tests (unit tests) can save you a lot of time, and it is much easier to transition to full end-to-end tests from the basis of unit tests.

To benefit from automated testing in your projects, start from the following guidelines:

- Architect your code for better testability.
- Start small; write unit tests.
- Consider building integration and end-to-end tests.
- Keep at it. Remember that testing saves time—especially those nights when your team has to fix unexpected bugs in freshly deployed code.

We have seen how to manage, test, and maintain code quality in data science projects. Next, let's look at how we can package code for deployment.

Packaging code

When deploying Python code for data science projects, you have several options:

- **Regular Python scripts**: You just deploy a bunch of Python scripts to the server and run them. This is the simplest form of deployment, but it requires a lot of manual preparation: you need to install all required packages, fill in configuration files, and so on. While those actions can be automated by using tools such as Ansible (`https://www.ansible.com/`), it's not recommended to use this form of deployment for anything but the simplest projects with no long-term maintainability goals.

- **Python packages**: Creating a Python package using a `setup.py` file is a much more convenient way to package Python code. Tools such as PyScaffold provide ready-to-use templates for Python packages, so you won't need to spend much time structuring your project. In the case of Python packages, Ansible still remains a viable option for automating manual deployment actions.
- **Docker image**: Docker (`https://www.docker.com/`) is based on a technology called Linux containers. Docker allows packaging your code into an isolated portable environment that can be easily deployed and scaled on any Linux machine. It's like packaging, shipping, and running your application along with all dependencies, including a Python interpreter, data files, and an OS distribution without entering the world of heavyweight virtual machines. Docker works by building a **Docker image** from a set of commands specified in a **Dockerfile**. A running instance of a Docker image is called a **Docker container**.

Now, we are ready to integrate all tools for dealing with code, data, experiments, environments, testing, packaging, and deployment into a single coherent process for delivering machine learning models.

Continuous model training

The end goal of applying CI/CD to data science projects is to have a continuous learning pipeline that creates new model versions automatically. This level of automation will allow your team to examine new experiment results right after pushing the changed code. If everything works as expected, automated tests finish, and model quality reports show good results, the model can be deployed into an online testing environment.

Let's describe the steps of continuous model learning:

1. CI:
    1. Perform static code analysis.
    2. Launch automated tests.

2. Continuous model learning:
    1. Fetch new data.
    2. Generate EDA reports.
    3. Launch data quality tests.
    4. Perform data processing and create a training dataset.
    5. Train a new model.
    6. Test the model's quality.
    7. Fix experiment results in an experiment log.

3. CD:
    1. Package the new model version.
    2. Package the source code.
    3. Publish the model and code to the target server.
    4. Launch a new version of the system.

CI/CD servers can automate all parts of the preceding pipeline. CI/CD steps should be easy to handle, as they are what CI/CD servers were created for. Continuous model learning should not be hard either, as long as you structure your pipeline so that it can be launched automatically from the command line. Tools such as DVC can aid you in creating reproducible pipelines, which makes it an attractive solution for the continuous model learning pipeline.

Now, let's look at how we can build a ModelOps pipeline in a data science project.

Case study – building ModelOps for a predictive maintenance system

Oliver is a team leader of a data science project for a large manufacturing company called MannCo, whose plants can be found in multiple cities around the country. Oliver's team developed a predictive maintenance model that can help MannCo to forecast and prevent expensive equipment breakages, which result in costly repairs and long production line outages. The model takes measurements of multiple sensors as input and outputs a package probability that can be used to plan a diagnostics and repair session.

 This example contains some technical details. If you are unfamiliar with the technologies mentioned in this case study, you may want to follow links to get a better understanding of the details.

Each piece of this equipment is unique in its own way because it operates under different conditions on each one of MannCo's plants. This meant that Oliver's team would need to constantly adapt and retrain separate models for different plants. Let's look at how they solved this task by building a ModelOps pipeline.

There were several data scientists on the team, so they needed a tool for sharing the code with each other. The customer requested that, for security purposes, all code should be stored in local company servers, and not in the cloud. Oliver decided to use GitLab (`https://about.gitlab.com/`), as it was a general practice in the company. In terms of the overall code management process, Oliver suggested using GitFlow (`https://danielkummer.github.io/git-flow-cheatsheet/`). It provided a common set of rules for creating new features, releases, and hotfixes for every team member.

Oliver knew that a reliable project structure would help his team to properly organize code, notebooks, data, and documentation, so he advised his team to use PyScaffold (`https://pyscaffold.readthedocs.io/`) along with the plugin for data science projects (`https://github.com/pyscaffold/pyscaffoldext-dsproject`). PyScaffold allowed them to bootstrap a project template that ensured a uniform way to store and version data science projects. PyScaffold already provided the `environment.yml` file, which defined a template Anaconda (`https://www.anaconda.com/distribution/`) environment, so the team did not forget to lock the package dependencies in a versioned file from the start of the project. Oliver also decided to use DVC (`https://dvc.org/`) to version datasets using the company's internal SFTP server. They also used a `--gitlab` flag for the `pyscaffold` command so that they would have a ready-to-use GitLab CI/CD template when they needed it.

The project structure looked like this (taken from the `pyscaffold-dsproject` documentation):

```
├── AUTHORS.rst <- List of developers and maintainers.
├── CHANGELOG.rst <- Changelog to keep track of new features and fixes.
├── LICENSE.txt <- License as chosen on the command-line.
├── README.md <- The top-level README for developers.
├── configs <- Directory for configurations of model & application.
├── data
│   ├── external <- Data from third party sources.
│   ├── interim <- Intermediate data that has been transformed.
│   ├── processed <- The final, canonical data sets for modeling.
│   └── raw <- The original, immutable data dump.
├── docs <- Directory for Sphinx documentation in rst or md.
├── environment.yaml <- The conda environment file for reproducibility.
├── models <- Trained and serialized models, model predictions,
│   or model summaries.
├── notebooks <- Jupyter notebooks. Naming convention is a number (for
│   ordering), the creator's initials and a description,
│   e.g. `1.0-fw-initial-data-exploration`.
├── references <- Data dictionaries, manuals, and all other materials.
├── reports <- Generated analysis as HTML, PDF, LaTeX, etc.
│   └── figures <- Generated plots and figures for reports.
├── scripts <- Analysis and production scripts which import the
```

```
|   actual PYTHON_PKG, e.g. train_model.
├──── setup.cfg <- Declarative configuration of your project.
├──── setup.py <- Use `python setup.py develop` to install for development
or
|   or create a distribution with `python setup.py bdist_wheel`.
├──── src
|   └──── PYTHON_PKG <- Actual Python package where the main functionality
goes.
├──── tests <- Unit tests which can be run with `py.test`.
├──── .coveragerc <- Configuration for coverage reports of unit tests.
├──── .isort.cfg <- Configuration for git hook that sorts imports.
└──── .pre-commit-config.yaml <- Configuration of pre-commit git hooks.
```

The project team quickly discovered that they would need to perform and compare many experiments to build models for different manufacturing plants. They evaluated DVC's metric tracking capabilities. It allowed tracking all metrics using a simple versioned text file in Git. While the feature was convenient for simple projects, it would be hard to use it in a project with multiple datasets and models. In the end, they decided to use a more advanced metric tracker—MLflow (https://mlflow.org). It provided a convenient UI for browsing experiment results and allowed using a shared database so that every team member would be able to quickly share their results with the team. MLflow was installed and configured as a regular Python package, so it easily integrated into the existing technology stack of the project:

The team also decided to leverage DVC pipelines to make each experiment easily reproducible. The team liked to prototype models using Jupyter notebooks, so they decided to use papermill (https://papermill.readthedocs.io/en/latest/) to work with notebooks as they were a set of parametrized Python scripts. Papermill allows executing Jupyter notebooks from the command line without starting Jupyter's web interface. The team found the functionality very convenient to use along with the DVC pipelines, but the command line for running a single notebook started to be too long:

```
dvc run -d ../data/interim/ -o ../data/interim/01_generate_dataset -o
../reports/01_generate_dataset.ipynb papermill --progress-bar --log-output
--cwd ../notebooks ../notebooks/01_generate_dataset.ipynb
../reports/01_generate_dataset.ipynb
```

To solve this problem, they wrote a Bash script to integrate DVC with papermill so that the team members could create reproducible experiments with less typing in the terminal:

```bash
#!/bin/bash
set -eu

if [ $# -eq 0 ]; then
 echo "Use:"
 echo "./dvc-run-notebook [data subdirectory] [notebook name] -d [your DVC
dependencies]"
 echo "This script executes DVC on a notebook using papermill. Before
running create ../data/[data subdirectory] if it does not exist and do not
forget to specify your dependencies as multiple last arguments"
 echo "Example:"
 echo "./dvc-run-notebook interim ../notebooks/02_generate_dataset.ipynb -d
../data/interim/"
 exit 1
fi

NB_NAME=$(basename -- "$2")

CMD="dvc run ${*:3} -o ../data/$1 -o ../reports/$NB_NAME papermill --
progress-bar --log-output --cwd ../notebooks ../notebooks/$NB_NAME
../reports/$NB_NAME"

echo "Executing the following DVC command:"
echo $CMD
$CMD
```

When using several open source ModelOps tools in a single project, your team might need to spend some time integrating them together. Be prepared, and plan accordingly.

Over time, some parts of the code started to duplicate inside the notebooks. The PyScaffold template provides a way to solve this problem by encapsulating repeated code in the project's package directory—src. This way, the project team could quickly share code between notebooks. To install the project's package locally, they simply used the following command from the project's root directory:

```
pip install -e .
```

Closer to the project release date, all stable code bases migrated to the project's src and scripts directories. The scripts directory contained a single entry point script for training a new model version that was output into the models directory, which was tracked by DVC.

To be sure that new changes did not break anything important, the team wrote a set of automated tests using pytest (https://docs.pytest.org/) for the stable code base. The tests also checked model quality on a special test dataset created by the team. Oliver modified a GitLab CI/CD template that was generated by PyScaffold so that tests would be run with each new commit that was pushed in a Git repository.

The customer requested a simple model API, so the team decided to use an MLflow server (https://mlflow.org/docs/latest/models.html), as MLflow was already integrated into the project. To further automate the deployment and packaging process, the team decided to use Docker along with GitLab CI/CD. To do this, they followed GitLab's guide for building Docker images (https://docs.gitlab.com/ee/ci/docker/using_docker_build.html).

The overall ModelOps process for the project contained the following steps:

1. Create new changes in the code.
2. Run pre-commit tests for code quality and styling (provided by PyScaffold).
3. Run pytest tests in GitLab CI/CD.
4. Package code and trained models into a Docker image in GitLab CI/CD.
5. Push the Docker image into the Docker registry in GitLab CI/CD.
6. After manual confirmation in the GitLab UI, run the update command on the customer server. This command simply pushes the new version of the Docker image from the registry to the customer's server and runs it instead of the old version. If you're wondering how you can do this in GitLab CI/CD, take a look here: https://docs.gitlab.com/ee/ci/environments.html#configuring-manual-deployments.

Please note that, in real projects, you may want to split the deployment into several stages for at least two different environments: staging and production.

Creating an end-to-end ModelOps pipeline streamlined the deployment process and allowed the team to spot bugs before they went into production so that the team was able to focus on building models instead of carrying out repetitive actions to test and deploy new versions of a model.

As a conclusion to this chapter, we'll look at a list of tools that you can use to build ModelOps pipelines.

A power pack for your projects

The data science community has a great number of open source tools that can help you in building ModelOps pipelines. Sometimes, it is hard to navigate the never-ending list of products, tools, and libraries so I thought this list of tools would be helpful and beneficial for your projects.

For static code analysis for Python, see these:

- Flake8 (http://flake8.pycqa.org)—a style checker for Python code
- MyPy (http://www.mypy-lang.org)—static typing for Python
- wemake (https://github.com/wemake-services/wemake-python-styleguide)—a set of enhancements for Flake8

here are some useful Python tools:

- PyScaffold (https://pyscaffold.readthedocs.io/)—a project templating engine. PyScaffold can set up a project structure for you. The dsproject extension (https://github.com/pyscaffold/pyscaffoldext-dsproject) contains a good data science project template.
- pre-commit (https://pre-commit.com)—a tool that allows you to set up Git hooks that run each time you commit the code. Automatic formatting, style cakes, code formatting, and other tools can be integrated into your build pipeline even before you decide to use a CI/CD server.

- pytest (`https://docs.pytest.org/`)—a Python testing framework that allows you to structure your tests using reusable fixtures. It comes in handy when testing data science pipelines with many data dependencies.
- Hypothesis (`https://hypothesis.works`)—a fuzz testing framework for Python that creates automated tests based on metadata about your functions.

For CI/CD servers, see these:

- Jenkins (`https://jenkins.io`)—a popular, stable, and old CI/CD server solution. It packs lots of features but is a bit cumbersome to use compared to more modern tools.
- GitLab CI/CD (`https://docs.gitlab.com/ee/ci/`)—is a free CI/CD server with cloud and on-premises options. It is easy to set up and easy to use, but forces you to live in the GitLab ecosystem, which might not be a bad decision, since GitLab is one of the best collaboration platforms out there.
- Travis CI (`https://travis-ci.org`) and Circle CI (`https://circleci.com`)—cloud CI/CD solutions. Useful if you develop in cloud environments.

For experiment tracking tools, see these:

- MLflow (`https://mlflow.org`)—experiment tracking framework that can be used both locally and in a shared client-server setup
- Sacred (`https://github.com/IDSIA/sacred`)—a feature-packed experiment tracking framework
- DVC (`https://dvc.org/doc/get-started/metrics`)—file-based metric tracking solution that uses Git

For data version control, see these:

- DVC (`https://dvc.org/`)—data version control for data science projects
- GitLFS (`https://git-lfs.github.com`)—a general solution for storing large files in Git

For pipeline tools, see these:

- Reproducible pipelines for data science projects:
  - DVC (`https://dvc.org/doc/get-started/pipeline`)
  - MLflow Projects (`https://mlflow.org/docs/latest/projects.html`)

For code collaboration platforms, see these:

- GitHub (`https://github.com/`)—the world's largest open source repository, and one of the best code collaboration platforms
- GitLab (`https://about.gitlab.com`)—feature-packed code collaboration platforms with cloud and on-premises deployment options
- Atlassian Bitbucket (`https://bitbucket.org/`)—code collaboration solution from Atlassian, which integrates well with their other products, Jira issue tracker and Confluence wiki

For deploying your code, see these:

- Docker (`https://www.docker.com/`)—a tool for managing containers and packaging your code into an isolated portable environment that could be easily deployed and scaled on any Linux machine
- Kubernetes (`https://kubernetes.io/`)—a container orchestration platform that automates deployment, scaling, and the management of containerized applications
- Ansible (`https://www.ansible.com/`)—a configuration management and automation tool that's handy to use for deployment automation and configuration if you do not use containers in your deployment setup

Summary

In this chapter, we covered ModelOps – a set of practices for automating a common set of operations that arise in data science projects. We explored how ModelOps relates to DevOps and described major steps in the ModelOps pipeline. We looked at strategies for managing code, versioning data, and sharing project environments between team members. We also examined the importance of experiment tracking and automated testing for data science projects. As a conclusion, we outlined the full CI/CD pipeline with continuous model training and explored a set of tools that can be used to build such pipelines.

In the next chapter, we will look at how to build and manage a data science technology stack.

Building Your Technology Stack 12

Technology choices have lasting consequences. A project's technology stack determines the functional and nonfunctional capabilities of your system, so it is critical to make thoughtful choices. The bidirectional link between technologies and requirements opens up an analytical approach for choosing between different technologies by matching their features against the project's needs. In this chapter, we will see how we can use software design practices to form project-specific technology stacks and see what technologies should constitute the core technology stack that's shared among all of your projects. We will also explore an approach that compares different technologies so that you can make a rational choice between apparently similar options.

In this chapter, we will cover the following topics:

- Defining the elements of the technology stack
- Choosing between core- and project-specific technologies
- Comparing tools and products

Defining the elements of a technology stack

A technology stack is a set of tools that your team uses to deliver products and finish projects. When choosing technologies, you start by defining their goals and thoroughly documenting all the requirements. From there, you and your team can see what technologies will help you to reach the end goal.

Shaping a technology stack goes toe-to-toe with designing software architecture, so the engineers on your team should start by drafting a system design that will meet everyone's requirements. Software architecture is a wide and deeply technical topic, so we won't discuss it in depth in this chapter. Instead, we will present an overview of the necessary steps when it comes to choosing the best technologies for reaching specific goals. Let's get started:

1. Collect the requirements and define the goals clearly.
2. Choose a set of architecture views for your project. An architecture view contains visual and textual descriptions of some of the aspects of the system. The most prominent examples of architecture views are as follows:
   - **Infrastructure view**: Represents the physical parts of the system. Servers, storage arrays, and networks are documented inside this view.
   - **Component view**: Represents the logical components of the software system that you are going to build. The component view should define the isolated parts of the system and the interfaces that they communicate through.
   - **Deployment view**: Matches the logical representation of the component view with the physical reality of the infrastructure view. The deployment view should describe how the system components will be delivered to the corresponding hardware.
   - **Other views**: Different methodologies for designing software architecture define many useful views. For example, the ArchiMate 2.1 specification defines 18 architecture views that can be useful for different stakeholders. For the sake of brevity, we will cover only the main views that can affect the technology stack and omit the others.
3. Define a list of necessary functions for technologies that you will use for the development and operations of your system based on the requirements and software design that has been produced by your team. Don't forget to include cross-cutting technologies that will optimize the experimentation, development, delivery, and operations of your system. Cross-cutting technologies may not help you find any specific functional requirements but will be beneficial to the project in general. Experimental tracking frameworks, data version control systems, and **Continuous Integration/Continuous Deployment (CI/CD)** servers are all examples of cross-cutting technologies.

As an example, let's build a technology stack for a customer churn prediction system. Our customer has defined the following list of requirements for the churn prediction module. We'll omit the technical details so that we can focus on the overall process:

1. Process the data from the marketing database. This contains customer information. The size of the dataset is under 5 GB of raw data.
2. Train the churn prediction model on a weekly basis, every Monday. We should consider customers that have made no purchases for a month as churned.
3. Notify the team about the potential customer churn by using remote API calls. The service should be available on business days.

> Decomposition classifies every requirement into two categories: **functional requirement** (**FR**) and **nonfunctional requirement** (**NFR**). FRs includes all the requirements that are related to the functions of the system that affect core use cases and end users. NFRs includes all the requirements that apply to the system in general and define a set of constraints in which the system will work. Service-level agreements and availability requirements are good examples of NFRs.

The team has decomposed customer requirements into the following list:

1. **FR**:
   - **FR1**: The system must be integrated with the customer's marketing database.
   - **FR2**: The system must provide a customer churn prediction model. We can consider customers that have made no purchases for a month as churned.
   - **FR3**: The system must call a remote API to notify the marketing department about potential customer churn.
   - **FR4**: The model should be executed every Monday.

2. **NFR**:
   - **NFR1**: The system should handle processing 5 GB of data every week.
   - **NFR2**: The API should be available on business days.

Based on this requirements list, the team has come up with the following system design, which has been drawn in ArchiMate 2.1 notation using the Archi software (https://www.archimatetool.com/):

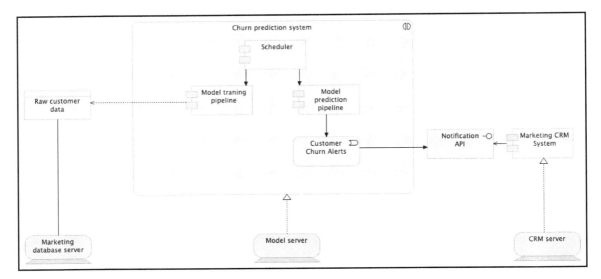

The preceding diagram consists of two levels: the infrastructure and software implementation.

The software level describes the relationships between different components and services:

- **Raw customer data:** Represents the raw data that's used by the churn prediction system.
- **Model training pipeline:** Represents a set of data processing and model training steps, grouped as a software component.
- **Model prediction pipeline:** Represents the component that's responsible for taking trained models to make churn predictions and generate customer churn alerts.
- **Scheduler:** Orchestrates the work of other components by running pipelines based on a schedule.
- **Customer churn alerts:** Notification events about potential customer churn.
- **Marketing CRM system:** The customer's CRM system, which has already been deployed and used in production.
- **Notification API:** A service that allows us to create notifications about customers inside the CRM system.

The infrastructure level, which describes the physical allocation of software to specific hardware resources, has three components:

- **Marketing database server**
- **Model server**
- **CRM server**

The preceding software architecture diagram omits many technical details for the sake of simplicity since our goal is to demonstrate how to make technology choices. The core idea of the following text is not to deepen your knowledge of the vast area of software architecture, but to give you a general feel for the process where requirements flow into sound technology choices. Understanding this process can help you guide your team of experts toward an efficient technology stack choice. The project did not seem very complicated to the team, and the task was fairly standard for them. The team has decided to use a general set of cross-cutting technologies that they use for every project as a corporate standard:

- Python as a programming language
- Git for source version control
- **Data version control** (**DVC**) for data version control
- GitLab CI/CD as a CI/CD server
- Jupyter Notebook for data analysis and visualization

To implement FR, they have decided to use the following technologies:

- **FR1**: The SQLAlchemy library for database access.
- **FR2**: scikit-learn as a machine learning library.
- **FR3**: Requests for API calls. The team has also decided to use a separate database to store prediction results and model execution logs.
- **FR4**: The team has decided to use cron (a popular Unix scheduler that can run commands based on a predefined scheduling table) as the main scheduling solution.

To implement NFR, they have decided to do the following:

- **NFR1**: Perform load tests and determine the minimum necessary server configuration for model training. From the team's previous experience, a virtual server with 8 CPU, 1 GB RAM, and 15 GB HDD should be sufficient, so they set this configuration as a baseline for tests.
- **NFR2**: The team has decided to request more detailed information on API usage and ask how many requests they can expect per day. It turns out that the API will be executed up to 10 times a day, so a single API server should suffice for this availability requirement.

In this section, we have explored how to develop a project-specific technology stack. However, there is another important dimension where technology choice matters: your team's expertise and skills. In the next section, we will look at the relationship between the team and project technology stacks.

Choosing between core- and project-specific technologies

Technology choices should help with project requirement realization, but it is also crucial to take your team's expertise and capabilities into account, as well as the constraints. For example, if your team consists entirely of Python developers, choosing Julia as a primary programming language may be a bad idea, even if the team sees it as a better fit for the project:

- All of the team members will spend time learning a new language, practically destroying all productivity gains from using the technology.
- The team's conclusions may be over-optimistic because of their lack of experience with the new technology.

Those two risks abate if your team pursues a growth mindset and gains new knowledge continuously, but they never vanish completely.

The core expertise in your team puts limits on what technologies you can use in projects. If you want more options, it is important to develop a team technology stack separately. Continuous internal research processes should keep your core technology step up to date. Project-specific technology stacks can be formed by adapting the core technology stack for your project's requirements.

We can view the internal technology research process as a separate long-running project, which is best managed by using Kanban:

1. Someone on the team spots a potentially useful technology.
2. The experienced team members do a quick review of this technology. If the technology looks promising, they put it into the internal research backlog.
3. Once the team manager decides that some time can be invested in internal research processes, they start a backlog grooming session. There, the team prioritizes tasks in the backlog and enriches their definitions according to the **specific measurable achievable relevant time-bound** (**SMART**) criteria.
4. The assignee takes a single task from the backlog and tries to finish it as quickly as possible. If they encounter a blocking problem, it should be instantly reported and solved, preferably with the help of other team members.
5. Once the research has been done, the assignee reports the results in the form of a document or a talk so that the team can decide on whether they will include the technology in the core technology stack.
6. If the decision is positive, it is crucial to create an educational program for wider internal technology adoption. The main result of this task is to prepare a workshop, guide, instruction booklet, or some other educational material that new and existing team members can use to familiarize themselves with the technology.

The core technology stack should not include overly specific technologies that are applicable to only a small set of projects. The sole purpose of this content is to help your team form a technological basis that solves the majority of requirements that arise in your projects. The more widely focused your team is, the more general the core technology stack should be. If the entire team is building a specific product, then project-specific and core technology stacks start to merge into a single entity.

The process of adapting the core technology stack into a new project is as follows:

1. Determine a set of project requirements.
2. See what requirements are satisfied by the core technology stack.
3. If some requirements are violated by the core technology stack, search for alternatives.
4. If some requirements are not met by the core technology stack, search for additions that can be integrated into the core technology stack.
5. At the end of the project, evaluate the new technologies that were added to the project and decide whether they are a good fit for the core technology stack.

Using these processes, you can turn often chaotic and desire-driven technology choices into a consistent and logical series of steps that lead to meaningful decisions. However, even the most deliberate requirement decompositions may leave your team wondering which technology to choose because there are many intersections and alternatives between different frameworks, libraries, and platforms. In the next section, we will explore how we can choose from a variety of technologies.

Comparing tools and products

Should we choose R or Python? What's better, TensorFlow or PyTorch? A list of endless quarrels about which is the best X for doing Y can be found all over the internet. Those discussions are ceaseless simply because there is no silver bullet in the technology world. Every team of professionals has their specific use cases, which makes a certain technology choice work for them. There is no technology that will equally satisfy everyone.

X versus Y disputes often happen inside project teams, which is the most unproductive activity engineers can spend their time on. If you try to transition from X versus Y debates to searching for technologies that fit your specific needs (which are clearly stated, classified, and documented), you will get far more useful results in less time. Choosing the most modern or fashionable technologies is the closest analogy for playing Russian roulette for data scientists and software engineers. Let's explore how we can make thoughtful decisions about technology stacks.

To make meaningful technology choices, you need to make the process more systematic. First, you need to derive a set of comparison criteria that will allow you to benchmark different technologies and provide a template for research activities. These criteria should test different dimensions or groups of requirements that make the technology useful in your specific case.

Let's examine the specifics of comparing different technologies by looking at a case study.

Case study – forecasting demand for a logistics company

Let's imagine that we need to choose a time series forecasting framework for our project. Our team works primarily in Python and has to provide a tool that will provide forecasts for time series data. The main goal of this system is to forecast demand on a set of given products that are shipped by the company. The team has discovered that there are many different forecasting frameworks.

To choose between these products, the team has created the following comparison criteria:

ID	Requirement definition	Substantiation	Score	Priority
		Ease of development		
D1	Compatible with Python	Python is the major programming language for the team.	3	Mandatory
D2	Compatible with scikit-learn interfaces	The team has good expertise in the `scikit-learn` library. It would be beneficial if the time-series forecasting library were compatible with `scikit-learn`.	2	Important
D3	Has good documentation		1	Supplementary
D4	Forecasting can be done in under 10 lines of code		1	Supplementary
D5	Can handle timeseries as a native data type	The framework should work with raw time series data so that the team doesn't spend additional time on dataset preparation and feature engineering.	2	Important
		Forecasting algorithm requirements		
F1	Does not require manual hyperparameter tuning	Since the library will be used with a large number of time series, manual model tuning is not practical. The tool should support automated hyperparameter tuning or be robust when it comes to which hyperparameter is chosen, thus providing good forecasts with the default settings.	3	Mandatory
F2	Provides several forecasting methods	The availability of several forecasting methods will allow us to evaluate several models and choose the one that fits the best for each specific time series.	1	Supplementary
F3	Works with seasonal time series	All the time series in the customer data have seasonal patterns.	3	Mandatory

F4	Provides confidence bounds, along with forecasts	Confidence intervals can be used to provide uncertainty bounds for each forecast, which the customer considers a useful feature.	2	Important
Performance and data requirements				
P1	Forecasts for time series with 100 data points can be done in under 15 seconds	A large number of time series limits the total amount of time we can spend on a single time series.	2	Important
P2	Can handle time series with a variable length and empty data	Data quality is not ideal and some gaps are present in the data. Some items have more historical data than others.	2	Important

The preceding comparison table consists of the following columns:

- **ID**: This can be used as a short identifier in the technology comparison table (provided next).
- **Requirement definition**: This should describe the capability of interest.
- **Substitution**: This should provide the motivation behind the requirement.
- **Score**: This shows the relative importance of the requirement and will be used to summarize each requirement category.
- **Priority**: This indicates the necessity of each requirement and will provide additional scores for each technology.

Next, the team has prepared a list of frameworks to compare, as follows:

- **Pmdarima** (https://www.alkaline-ml.com/pmdarima/)
- **statsmodels.tsa** (https://www.statsmodels.org/stable/tsa.html)
- **Prophet** (https://github.com/facebook/prophet)
- **LightGBM** (https://lightgbm.readthedocs.io/en/latest/) and **tsfresh** (https://tsfresh.readthedocs.io/en/latest/)

The team has also come up with the following comparison table:

Framework	D1 (M)	D2 (I)	D3 (S)	D4 (S)	D5 (I)	F1 (M)	F2 (S)	F3 (M)	F4 (I)	P1 (I)	P2 (I)
pmdarima	3	2	0	2	3	3	0	3	2	0	0
statsmodels.tsa	3	0	2	0	3	0	1	3	2	2	0
Prophet	3	0	2	2	3	3	0	3	2	0	2
LightGBM and tsfresh	3	2	2	0	0	0	0	3	0	2	0

This table can be further summarized to give you the following final results:

Framework	Ease of development score	Forecasting algorithm requirements score	Performance and data requirements score	Mandatory requirements satisfied	Important requirements satisfied	Supplementary requirements satisfied
pmdarima	10/12	8/9	0/4	3/3	3/5	1/3
statsmodels.tsa	8/12	6/9	2/4	2/3	3/5	2/3
Prophet	10/12	8/9	2/4	3/3	3/5	2/3
LightGBM and tsfresh	7/12	3/9	2/4	2/3	2/5	1/3

If you wish, you can use weighted averages to summarize each framework's score into a single number. However, remember that simplifying complex decisions into one number can lead to errors if this is done incorrectly.

These research results show that Prophet comes up as a better choice according to the initial requirements. However, the results do not mean that Prophet is the best choice for every application. Technology choices should be biased and opinionated since no technology can be the best fit for every project. For example, the ranking could be entirely different if the team took the desired average metric value into consideration. In this setting, other frameworks could have won because they provided more accurate models.

Summary

In this chapter, we have seen how we can choose a technology based on its requirements rather than the hype surrounding it. We also explored how to structure requirements and derive the main elements of a technology stack from software architecture. Finally, we discussed the difference between core and project-specific technology stacks and examined an analytical approach to comparing different technologies.

The next chapter will conclude this book; congratulations on finishing it!

13
Conclusion

First of all, thank you for reading this book! I hope that the material was helpful in presenting the overall management approach to data science projects. Data science management is a multidimensional topic that requires a manager to show technical, organizational, and strategic proficiency so that they can execute a data science strategy inside any organization.

First, the data science manager needs to understand what data science can do, as well as its technical limitations. Without an understanding of the basic concepts, it is extremely easy to misunderstand your colleagues or provide over-promising project results to the customer. The *What is Data Science* section of this book described the basics of machine learning and deep learning, including explanations behind the mathematical concepts that comprise machine learning algorithms. We explored the world of technology and business metrics, defined mathematical optimization, and looked into statistics and probability. These concepts helped us define how machines learn using maximum likelihood estimation. In particular, we can explain almost every machine learning algorithm using this mathematical framework. We have also seen that there is no silver bullet in the machine learning world thanks to the no free lunch theorem. This theorem states that no machine learning algorithm will be better than random choice if you measure its accuracy over all possible datasets and tasks.

After that, our journey continued toward the *Building and sustaining a team* section, where we learned about balancing long-term and short-term team building goals. We talked about the flaws of over-complicated technical interviews and how to avoid them. The main idea here was to look at what you need and then search for people with specific skill sets, rather than a rockstar data scientist who can do anything. We also discussed how to conduct data science interviews using real-world experience. Then, we explored the concept of team balance, which forms the long-term stability of teams that allows them to grow and develop. We also touched on the important topic of the growth mindset. By following this practice yourself, you become an example to your team.

In the *Managing data science projects* section, we focused on project management, starting from a bird's-eye strategic view on innovations and marketing. We drew connections between innovations and data science and provided high-level strategies for managing innovations in different kinds of organizations. We have looked at data science project management on a lower scale and examined processes that we can use to manage individual projects. Then, we defined the data science project life cycle based on CRISP-DM and looked over common mistakes that customers, managers, and implementation teams make when delivering data science solutions. We also touched on the topic of software component reusability and stated that creating reusable components will ease the development of your projects and increase your team's business potential.

In conclusion, the *Creating development infrastructure* section comprised discussions on engineering aspects of data science projects. We discussed how to create a technology stack based on customer requirements and your own core technological expertise. Finally, we saw how to create comparison matrices in order to choose between different technologies.

Advancing your knowledge

If you want to continue deepening your knowledge in the domain of data science management, here is a list of books to look at:

- **Machine learning:**
    - *An Introduction to Statistical Learning*, by Rob Tibshirani and Robert Hastie (`http://faculty.marshall.usc.edu/gareth-james/`), along with a MOOC (`https://lagunita.stanford.edu/courses/HumanitiesSciences/StatLearning/Winter2016/about`). The code in this book is in R, but it's not a bad idea to read it, even if you are only interested in coding in Python. The main benefit of this book is its presentation of theory, which is independent of your favorite programming language.
    - *Introduction to Machine Learning with Python*, by Andreas C. Müller (`https://www.amazon.com/Introduction-Machine-Learning-Python-Scientists/dp/1449369413`).
- **Deep learning:**
    - FastAI course, by Jeremy Howard (`http://fast.ai`)
    - *Deep Learning*, by Ian Goodfellow (`https://www.amazon.com/Deep-Learning-Adaptive-Computation-Machine/dp/0262035618/`)

- **Software architecture:**
    - *Designing Data-Intensive Applications*, by Martin Kleppmann (`https://www.amazon.com/Designing-Data-Intensive-Applications-Reliable-Maintainable/dp/1449373321`)
    - *Documenting Software Architectures: Views and Beyond*, by Paul Clements, Felix Bachmann, Len Bass, David Garlan, James Ivers, Reed Little, Paulo Merson, Robert Nord, Judith Stafford (`https://www.amazon.com/Documenting-Software-Architectures-Views-Beyond/dp/0321552687/`)

- **Software engineering:**
    - *Fluent Python*, by Luciano Ramalho (`https://www.amazon.com/Fluent-Python-Concise-Effective-Programming/dp/1491946008`)
    - *The Pragmatic Programmer*, by Andrew Hunt and David Thomas (`https://www.amazon.com/Pragmatic-Programmer-Journeyman-Master/dp/020161622X`)

- **Innovation management:**
    - *The Innovator's Dilemma*, by Clayton M. Christensen (`https://www.amazon.com/Innovators-Dilemma-Revolutionary-Change-Business/dp/0062060244`)
    - *Crossing the Chasm*, by Geoffrey Moore (`https://www.amazon.com/Crossing-Chasm-3rd-Disruptive-Mainstream/dp/0062292986/`)
    - *The Lean Startup*, by Eric Ries (`https://www.amazon.com/Lean-Startup-Entrepreneurs-Continuous-Innovation/dp/B005MM7HY8`)

- **Project management:**
    - *The Deadline*, by Tom DeMarco (`https://www.amazon.com/Deadline-Novel-About-Project-Management-ebook/dp/B006MN4RAS/`)
    - *Peopleware: Productive Projects and Teams*, by Tom DeMarco and Tim Lister (`https://www.amazon.com/gp/product/B00DY5A8X2/`)

- **Emotional intelligence:**
    - *Emotional Intelligence*, by Daniel Goleman (`https://www.amazon.com/Emotional-Intelligence-Matter-More-Than/dp/055338371X`)
    - *Never Split the Difference*, by Chris Voss (`https://www.amazon.com/Never-Split-Difference-Negotiating-Depended/dp/0062407805`)

Summary

Congratulations on finishing this book! I hope that it helped you deepen your knowledge of data science and systemize management techniques for data science projects. Please don't leave what you have read about the theory of data science behind. To master the concepts we have covered in this book, you should apply them to your daily work. I also strongly advise you to acquire a growth mindset, if you haven't already. You will be amazed by how far you can go by learning something new each day, even if it's the smallest bit of knowledge. No book can fully cover every aspect of data science management, but you can continue this journey by referring to one of the books mentioned in this chapter or discovering your own path while mastering data science.

Other Books You May Enjoy

If you enjoyed this book, you may be interested in these other books by Packt:

Python Data Science Essentials, Third edition

Alberto Boschetti, Luca Massaron

ISBN: 978-1-78953-786-4

- Set up your data science toolbox on Windows, Mac, and Linux
- Use the core machine learning methods offered by the scikit-learn library
- Manipulate, fix, and explore data to solve data science problems
- Learn advanced explorative and manipulative techniques to solve data operations
- Optimize your machine learning models for optimized performance
- Explore and cluster graphs, taking advantage of interconnections and links in your data

Hands-On Data Science with Anaconda

James Yan, Dr. Yuxing Yan
ISBN: 978-1-78883-119-2

- Perform cleaning, sorting, classification, clustering, regression, and dataset modeling using Anaconda
- Use the package manager conda and discover, install, and use functionally efficient and scalable packages
- Get comfortable with heterogeneous data exploration using multiple languages within a project
- Perform distributed computing and use Anaconda Accelerate to optimize computational powers
- Discover and share packages, notebooks, and environments, and use shared project drives on Anaconda Cloud
- Tackle advanced data prediction problems

Leave a review - let other readers know what you think

Please share your thoughts on this book with others by leaving a review on the site that you bought it from. If you purchased the book from Amazon, please leave us an honest review on this book's Amazon page. This is vital so that other potential readers can see and use your unbiased opinion to make purchasing decisions, we can understand what our customers think about our products, and our authors can see your feedback on the title that they have worked with Packt to create. It will only take a few minutes of your time, but is valuable to other potential customers, our authors, and Packt. Thank you!

Index

domain expertise 111
dsproject extension
  reference link 248

E

emotional intelligence
  references 265
empathy
  developing 142, 143
empirical probability distribution 69
ensemble models
  about 82
  tree-based ensembles 83, 84
environments
  managing 235, 236
epsilon 55
estimation process, goals
  discovering 201
experiments
  tracking 237, 239
exploratory data analysis (EDA) 127, 184, 205
extract transform load (ETL) 119

F

F1-score
  using 48
False Negatives (FN) 45
False Positive (FP) 46
file remotes 231
Flake8
  URL 248
frequentist probabilities 66
fully connected neural network (FCNN) 91
functional requirements (FR)
  about 253
  implementing 255

G

garbage in, garbage out principle 19
Gaussian distribution 69
Generative Adversarial Networks (GANs) 28
Git 231
GitHub
  URL 250
GitLab CI/CD

URL 249
GitLab
  URL 250
GitLFS
  URL 249
GPT-2 model
  reference link 25
gradient boosting algorithm 127
gradient boosting machine (GBM) 129
gradient descent 63, 64
growth mindset, facilitating
  about 143
  continuous learning, applying for personal growth 144, 145
  employees, helping to grow with performance reviews 148, 149
  opportunities, giving for learning 146, 147, 148
  team expertise, growing as whole 144

H

hard disk drives (HDDs) 157
Hypothesis
  URL 249

I

image classification 27
ImageNet 23
imbalanced classes 48, 49, 50, 51
implementation team 219
independent events 67
innovation management
  exploring 158, 160
  references 265
innovations
  about 156
  integrating 164
  managing, in big company 168
  managing, in startup company 171
instance segmentation
  about 27
  reference link 27
interview process
  purpose, discovering 121, 122
interviews
  ethics 123, 124

good interviews, designing 125
values 123, 124

J

Jenkins
  URL 249

K

K-means 85
k-nearest neighbors (kNNs) 119
Kanban 190, 191, 192
key performance indicator (KPI) 51, 148
Kubernetes
  URL 250

L

leadership by example 138
leadership
  about 137
  downside 138
leave-one-out cross-validation 43
LightGBM
  reference link 260
linear models 80
Linux containers 242
long short term memory networks (LSTMs) 100

M

machine learning engineer 104
machine learning model
  about 78
  building 77
  data 15, 16, 17
  decisions 14
  insights 14, 15
  stages 80
machine learning project cost estimator
  building 74
machine learning, in retail company
  case study 108, 109, 110
machine learning
  about 13, 14, 73, 107
  anatomy 18
  applying, to prevent fraud in banks 107, 108

exploring 79
  goals 80
  origins 17
  references 264
  tasks 18, 19, 20, 21, 22
markets
  creating 158
mathematical optimization 59, 61, 62, 63, 64
maximum likelihood estimation (MLE) 65
mean absolute error (MAE) 44
MedVision
  innovation cycle 161, 162, 163
MLflow Projects
  URL 249
MLflow
  about 238
  URL 249
model errors
  about 35, 36
  bias 37
  decomposing 36, 38, 39
  variance 38
ModelOps 227
ModelOps, building for predictive maintenance
    system
  case study 243, 245, 246, 247
Multi-Armed Bandits (MABs) 55
MVP projects
  dealing with 207
MVP
  creating, in consulting company 208, 209
MyPy
  URL 248

N

natural language processing (NLP) 24, 25, 95, 96,
    162
neural networks
  building 90, 91, 92
no free lunch theorem 18, 79
non-sensible absurd correlations, examples
  reference link 30
nonfunctional requirements (NFR)
  about 253
  implementing 256

null hypothesis 53

O

object detection 27
offline model testing 35
online data testing 56, 57
online model testing
  about 52, 53, 54, 55, 56
  alternative hypothesis 53
  null hypothesis 53
  risks 52
optimization 59
overfitting 39, 40, 41, 42, 43

P

people management 137
pipenv
  URL 236
pmdarima
  reference link 260
pre-commit
  URL 248
precision 48
probability distribution 69
production-oriented data science systems
  risks, mitigating 209, 210
products
  building 221
  privacy 222
  seeking 221
  versus tools 258
program evaluation and review technique (PERT)
  199
project ideas
  finding 172
  finding, in business processes 172
  finding, in data 173, 174
project management methodology
  Agile 189
  custom project, developing for customer 195
  disruptive innovation, creating 194
  Kanban 190, 191, 192
  Scrum 192, 193
  selecting 188, 194
  tested solution, providing 195

  waterfall 188, 189
project management
  references 265
project stakeholders 104
project users 104
project-specific technologies
  versus core technologies 256, 257
project
  as products 215, 216
  stage, determining 216, 217
Proof of Concepts (PoC) 104
Prophet
  reference link 260
prototypes
  dealing with 207
pyenv
  URL 235
PyScaffold
  about 242
  URL 248
pytest
  URL 249

R

random variable 70
recall 48
receiver operating characteristic curve (ROC AUC)
  about 50
  reference link 51
rectified linear unit (ReLU) 88
recurrent neural networks (RNNs) 99
Relational Database Management System
  (RDBMS) 113
research and development (R&D) 164
research phases
  integrating, into solution development project
  218
research projects
  approaching 204, 205
  pitfalls, avoiding 206
research team 219
reusability
  improving 220, 221
risks
  mitigating, in production-oriented data science

systems 209, 210
roles 135
root mean square error (RMSE) 44, 76

S

Sacred
  about 238
  URL 249
sales forecasting system
  bringing, into production 212, 213
sample variance 71
Scrum 192, 193, 194
service desk routing system
  building 218, 219, 220
service level agreements (SLAs) 187
situational leadership
  using 138, 140
social credit system 12
software architect 105
software architecture
  references 265
software engineering 111, 113
software requirements document (SRD) 104
software team 105, 106
source version control (SVC) 231
specific measurable achievable relevant time-
    bound (SMART) 126, 141, 257
sprint 193
statistical modeling 72, 73
statistics
  about 65
  calculating, from data samples 70, 71
statsmodels.tsa
  reference link 260
strong AI 10
supervised learning 19
support vector machines (SVM) 119
system analyst 104, 106

T

team Zen
  achieving 133, 135, 136

technical interviews
  flaws 118, 119, 120, 121
technical metrics
  using 44, 45, 46, 47, 48
technology stack
  about 251
  elements, defining 253, 254, 255
test assignments
  designing 125, 126, 127, 129
text summarization model
  reference link 24
time series forecasting framework
  for logistics company 258, 259, 260, 261
tools
  versus products 258
Travis CI
  URL 249
tree-based ensembles 83, 84
True Negatives (TN) 45
True Positive (TP) 46
tsfresh
  reference link 260

U

unbalanced teams
  about 134
  examples 134
user interface (UI) 205

V

variance 38
virtualenv
  URL 235

W

waterfall 188, 189
weak AI 10
weight 89
wemake
  URL 248
word optimization 60

CPSIA information can be obtained
at www.ICGtesting.com
Printed in the USA
BVHW010627291221
625023BV00004B/100